Craig Claiborne's Favorites from The New York Times

SERIES IV

Craig Claiborne's Favorites from The New York Times

SERIES IV

BONANZA BOOKS
NEW YORK

We are indebted to a number of photographers and artists whose work is reproduced in this book:

Bill Aller, pages 16, 17, 21, 23, 28, 36, 41, 46, 47, 48, 73, 74, 75, 93, 101, 111, 112, 113, 129, 130, 142, 144, 145, 146, 148, 153, 158, 162, 166, 188, 211, 217, 218, 219, 239, 271. Bettmann Archive Inc., pages 169, 173. Conrad, pages 296, 297. Culver Pictures Inc., pages 276, 286. Regine Esser, page 222. Foto Gioberti, page 180. James Hamilton, pages 107, 119, 120, 121, 122, 123, 236, 237. Frank Lodge, page 207. Gene Maggio, pages 83, 87, 126, 165, 171. Magnum/Erich Hartmann, page 103. Larry Morris, page 230. The New York Times Company/(Jacqueline Chwast), pages 8, 9, 11. The New York Times Company/(Robert Strimban), page 50. Mickey Pfleger, pages 247, 248, 251. Lithograph by Odilon Redon, courtesy of Museum of Modern Art, New York, page 142. Alfred Wegener, page 118. Randy Wood, page 257. Teresa Zabala, pages 198, 199, 200.

This 1984 edition is published by Bonanza Books, distributed by Crown Publishers, Inc. by arrangement with Times Books, The New York Times Book Company, Inc.

Manufactured in the United States of America.

Library of Congress Cataloging in Publication Data

Claiborne, Craig.
　Craig Claiborne's favorites from the New York Times.

　Vols. subtitled series III and series IV are reprints of vols. 3 and 4 of the edition published by New York Times Book Co., 1975-1978.
　Includes indexes.
　1. Cookery.　I. New York Times.　II. Title.　III. Title: Favorites from the New York Times.
[TX715.C5743　1984]　　641.5　　84-20412

ISBN: 0-517-459965

h g f e d c b a

Contents

October

November

December

Craig Claiborne's Favorites from The New York Times

SERIES IV

January

THERE ARE GULFS in the world of food as vast and diverse as the waters of the deep blue sea. To my mind, good food is good food. Period. But in the case of chili con carne, it is certainly one of the most controversial yet universally admired American inventions. It is served and eaten with gusto at church socials. It is food for the well-heeled and the down-at-the-heels alike. Adults make it and children make it; people with good taste make it and people with absolutely no taste or talent make it, and almost everybody loves it, including a few people with stomach ulcers. It has been associated with jailhouses (there seems to be some question in Texas as to whether the version in the Dallas jailhouse is better than that of the San Antonio jailhouse) and the White House.

In January, Pierre Franey and I also explored an area of unusual appeal to me—that is the field of what we chose to call nursery desserts. These are the foods—soft, creamy and utterly irresistible—we were fed as children. They are the same desserts that nourish us in mind, body and spirits now that we are a bit beyond the half-century mark. Speaking of spirits, we must confess we have added a few highly sophisticated spirits to those nursery desserts—things that were unfamiliar in childhood but bring joy to the palates of many adults.

The Great
Chili Controversy

That Americans love to argue about food, there can be no question. New Englanders can expound for hours on the virtues of a well-made clam chowder or pot of Boston baked beans. Arguments as to the merits of using lard, Crisco or butter as the proper fat for frying chicken are sufficient unto themselves to render asunder close ties in the South. In Pennsylvania Dutch country, one man's Schnitz un Gneppe may very well be anathema.

But these are regional arguments. On the national scene, there is one single dish that has, within the past decade, inspired more controversy than any other dish in America. It is chili con carne.

And what is to account for this national preoccupation with a dish whose origins are so obscure, a dish that varies from kitchen to kitchen, yet whose appeal is almost universal? What inspires such extraordinary enthusiasm for a dish so thoroughly basic, unsophisticated and down-to-earth? It is simply this. Chili is a dish that almost anyone, including a reasonably intelligent 6-year-old, can make with pride and pleasure and the thought that his or hers is the best darn chili in the land.

Instinctively, one knows that chili originated in the southwestern United States of Mexican inspiration and that it moved eastward to the southern states in the early part of this century.

Although American Indians used such chilies as could be found in various parts of America, chili con carne was not an Indian invention. Carolyn Niethammer, in her book *American Indian Food and Lore*, (Collier Books, 1974), states that the tiny round chili known as chillipiquin was known in New Mexico and Arizona, but the Indians did not know the large, domesticated chilies such as those used in chili con carne "until the Spaniards brought them [here] after passing through Mexico."

Frank X. Tolbert, a columnist for the *Dallas News* and perhaps the nation's leading historian on the subject of chili, indicates in his book *A Bowl of Red* (Doubleday, 1972) his assurance that chili originated in San Antonio. Incidentally, a bowl of red, for the enlightenment of non-chiliheads, is a Texas term for a bowl of chili. Mr. Tolbert advances the idea that chili con carne was the food of the poor families of Texas.

He quotes one J. C. Clopper, who wrote about his first visit to San Antonio in 1828: "When they have to pay for their meat in market, very little is made to suffice for a family; it is generally cut into a kind of hash with nearly as many peppers as there are pieces of meat—this is all stewed together."

Last year, according to a spokesman for the American Spice Trade Association, Americans consumed more than eight million pounds of dried chili peppers in one form or another, the vast majority of them converted into powder for the nation's chili kettles. Chilies, by the way, have a high and admirable concentration of vitamins A and C.

The initial, large-scale hoisting of chili con carne into the national consciousness came about through the efforts, no matter how unwittingly, of three men. First of these was H. Allen Smith, the humorist and author, best known for his book *Low Man on a Totem Pole*. Smith ignited the fires beneath the chili pot in 1966 with an article in *Holiday* magazine, "Nobody Knows More About Chili Than I Do."

The impact of that article was devastating. "No living man," he wrote, "can put together a pot of chili as ambrosial, as delicately and zestfully flavored as the chili I make. This is a fact so stern, so granitic that it belongs in the encyclopedias as well as in all the standard histories of civilization."

Although Mr. Smith was a native of Illinois, he had long since become a New Yorker when the article was published, and this bit of Yankee bombast was more than a couple of Texans—namely Frank Tolbert and one Wickford (Wick) Fowler, a newspaperman and celebrated, locally at least, as the grand Texas afficionado of chili-making—could tolerate.

Mr. Tolbert termed Mr. Smith's chili a "chili-flavored, low-torque, beef and vegetable soup." The recipe did call for tomatoes, onions, green pepper and—sacrilege of sacrileges—canned pinto beans. The addition of beans to a genuine Texas chili is grounds in some camps for a nice little Western auto-dafé.

With Mr. Tolbert's encouragement, Mr. Fowler pitted his talents against Mr. Smith's. The event took place in 1967 and attracted only a thousand spectators, but it made a few hundred headlines around the country. The contest ended in a draw, but Texas chili cook-offs subsequently became an annual event.

Chili-cooking contests are held annually in thirty-four states of the Union. In the interest of chili research, we recently accepted an invitation to act as a judge at the World Championship Chili Cook-Off at an old abandoned gold mine near Rosamond, California, about ninety miles north of Los Angeles. This contest is a spin-off of the Texas original, and it is generally conceded to be the principal chili event in the United States.

We did not regret our decision, for a national chili-cooking contest is a fascinating spectacle, a cunning bit of Americana, side show, carnival, rodeo and circus rolled into one. The judges, who roamed from one chili pot to another, included Chill Wills, Rory Calhoun, Maude Chasen, the owner of Chasen's Restaurant, and Joanne Dru. Various groups walked around carrying signs with slogans like "Bad Chili is Super," "Chili Today and Hot Tamale" and "Bullrun Chili Has Balls." Macho-type males wearing Stetsons and sombreros roamed the grounds and the cast was awash in a sea of leather boots and Levis.

When we arrived at the cook-off grounds around nine A.M., the chili pepper eating contest, one of the weirdest endurance contests ever conceived, was underway.

This year there were twenty-four contestants—three women and twenty-one men—chewing and swallowing chilies scaled from the relatively mild to the hideously ultimate, a small green chili known as Bahamian. At the end of fifty-five minutes, half the fire-eaters had withdrawn. The contest was eventually won by a never-say-die participant named Don Horner. He had consumed a total of twenty-six peppers. He was being loudly cheered as an ambulance arrived to cart away one of his colleagues on a stretcher.

C. V. Wood, the man who masterminds the California competition, has justly been labeled the P. T. Barnum of chilidom. He is a born showman with a long, colorful and successful history in promotional endeavors. He was, for example, a central figure in the planning and development of Disneyland in 1955. Professionally he is now president of the McCulloch Oil Corporation, which is involved in land development, particularly in the West.

The festival has drawn thirty thousand visitors two years in succession. The cost of admission is three dollars per adult. After all expenses are paid for staging the event, the net profits are turned over to the Children's Hospital of Los Angeles.

Each of the state finalists—thirty-four in all—were assigned cooking stations, each equipped with a Coleman stove. As the cooking progressed, the chili mixtures in the kettles varied widely on many counts. Some resembled soups and stews, some thick, some watery, some dark, some light, some with large chunks of meat, others with small chunks, others with ground meat.

There were dishes made with beef, chicken and pork, and the contestant from New York, R. S. (Red) Holmes, made what was basically an excellent creation. At the last moment, unfortunately, he threw in a pint or so of shucked raw oysters and heated them up. Inspiration at a chili cook-off knows no bounds.

The man from Tennessee, a fellow named Jack Powell, made his chili of freshly skinned raccoon, which, he assured us, is one animal whose flesh is particularly suited to the dish. Truth to tell, it was excellent. There are, in fact, no limits to the kinds of meat that may be used to make chili. The list includes armadillo, bear, buffalo, cayote, kangaroo and moose.

The published rules and regulations for the cook-off define "true" chili as any kind of meat, or combination of meats, cooked with chili peppers, various other spices and other ingredients, with the exception of thickening agents such as beans, spaghetti and so forth.

The winner of this year's chili roundup was Rufus Valdez, the contender from the Indian Nations. Mr. Valdez, a full-blooded Ute, had earned the right to compete when he won the Indian Nations' Cook-off at Gallup, New Mexico, last summer.

Understandably, perhaps, some of the observers at the contest were skeptical about the ability of anyone to judge, in a discriminating manner, more than thirty bowls of chili con carne at one sitting and that in less than an hour. Actually, it isn't all that difficult. Half the bowls of chili in the contest were markedly ordinary, evident at first taste. The remainder could be weighed on various valid counts: Are they too salty, too hot, too sweet, too bland; is the texture of the meat too soft and grainy; is there an excess of a single spice such as cloves or bay leaves?

By far the most famous recipe for chili is that for Pedernales River chili, so much favored by Lyndon Baines Johnson and so much publicized during his presidency. The end product of that recipe is a somewhat standard, run-of-the-mill item guaranteed not to offend anyone but dyed-in-the-wool chiliheads.

By far the most famous bowl of restaurant chili in the world is that made in the kitchen of Chasen's Restaurant in Los Angeles. It achieved worldwide notoriety, thanks to the enthusiasm for it shared by Elizabeth Taylor and Richard Burton. When in Rome they did as the Texans do; they dispatched a cable to Chasen's ordering ten quarts frozen to be sent to their address on the Via Appia Pignatelli.

Chasen's chili isn't bad, but then we esteem no chili to be bad provided it is honestly made with decent ingredients. Chasen's chili is just a bit innocuous, but for heaven's sake don't tell Maude Chasen that.

Some of the bowls of chili at the cook-off were prepared from "scratch," which is to say the cooks started with whole dried chili pods that were boiled and squeezed through a food mill to extract the chili pulp. Many of the contestants resorted to the much simpler chili powder.

Chili powder is not, as a few hundred thousand people seem to think, made of ground-up dried chilies, only that and nothing more. Almost all the chili powder bottled commercially today is composed of pulverized chilies, dried garlic, cumin, oregano, cloves, coriander and flaked or powdered dried onion. The chili itself lends heat plus a subtle flavor. What most people think of as *the* chili flavor is actually that of powdered cumin.

Although there is excellent source material in Frank X. Tolbert's book, we believe the finest essay on chili ever written came from the pen of Carter Rochelle in his criticism of a newly published tome, *The Chili Book*, some years back. The authors were Johnrae Earl and James McCormick, and Rochelle's commentary appeared in *The Houston Chronicle*. A part of his review follows:

"A preposterous little presumption called *The Chili Cook Book* has just been published in Los Angeles for the enrichment of a couple of Chicagoans; the further bewilderment of the unenlightened; and the incredulous irritation of people who know what chili really is.

"Johnrae Earl and James McCormick, who stirred up this agglomeration,

claim the 100 recipes in the book are selected from more than 600 they tested
and tasted from around the world. The mind boggles. The digestion reels.

"Maybe half a dozen palatable and veritable chili formulas are scattered
among these grotesqueries. The others are *not* chili. They are curries, slurries,
soups, gravies, sauces, chowders, ragouts, paprikashes, salamagundis,
kedgerees, slumgullions and the like."

Mr. Rochelle is marvelously outraged to think that what the authors list as
Houston's best chili contains flour, paprika, tomatoes and tomato juice. Among
other indignities Mr. Rochelle discovers are mutton, scallops, currant jelly,
cocoa, white bread, cornstarch and tomato soup. Plus macaroni, chicken gumbo
soup, onion soup, pickling spices, chicken fat, barley, raisins, sour cream and—
obscenity of obscenities—potatoes.

"Besides all that, there aren't 100 ways to make chili. . . . There is but
one, and since we've gone through all this together I'm going to give it to you
now."

There follows Mr. Rochelle's true Texas chili. We have substituted beef
broth for his water and bouillon cubes, and we hope the gentleman will find it
passably forgivable.

An Adaptation of Carter Rochelle's Real Texas Chili

3   *pounds boneless chuck or round steak*
⅓   *pound beef suet*
3   *cloves garlic, finely minced*
4   *to 6 tablespoons chili powder*
     Salt and freshly ground pepper to taste
8   *tablespoons masa harina (see note)*
6   *to 8 cups hot, rich beef broth (see note)*
2   *tablespoons vinegar*
2   *or more hot dried red chilies, or according to taste*

1. Cut the meat into ½-inch or even smaller cubes.

2. Cut the suet into cubes and add it to a heavy skillet or casserole. Cook, stirring, to render the suet of fat. Remove and discard the solid, rendered suet. Use all the liquid suet, or pour off some of it if you wish.

3. Heat the fat and add the meat and cook, stirring, until lightly browned. Add the garlic, chili powder, salt and pepper. Add the salt sparingly.

4. Cook, stirring, about 2 minutes and sprinkle in the masa harina. Stir to distribute the masa harina evenly. Add 6 cups of the beef broth and keep the remainder hot to add as needed. Add the vinegar and chilies.

5. Cook, partly covered, about 2 hours. Stir the chili occasionally and skim off surface fat as desired. If the chili becomes too thick, add more broth as necessary.

Yield: About 6 servings.

Note: Masa harina, a form of finely ground corn meal, is available in Spanish and Mexican markets in most metropolitan areas of the United States. In Mr. Rochelle's recipe, the liquid used is water combined with 2 teaspoons instant beef bouillon or 2 cubes of bouillon.

Pedernales River Chili

4   *pounds chopped beef*
3   *cups chopped onion*
1   *tablespoon finely minced garlic*
1   *teaspoon dried crushed oregano*
1   *teaspoon ground cumin*
2   *tablespoons chili powder, or more according to taste*
4   *cups canned tomatoes, crushed*
     Salt to taste
2   *cups beef broth or boiling water*

1. Combine the meat, onion and garlic in a skillet and cook, breaking up any lumps with the side of a heavy kitchen spoon, until lightly browned.

2. Sprinkle with oregano, cumin and chili powder and stir to blend. Add the tomatoes, salt and beef broth or water and bring to the boil. Cover and let simmer, stirring occasionally, about 1 hour.

Yield: 10 to 12 servings.

Rufus Valdez' World Championship Chili

4   large green chilies, preferably
     the Anaheim variety if avail-
     able (see note)
4   pounds flank steak
2   pounds center-cut pork chops
1   teaspoon ground cumin
1   teaspoon chopped fresh
     oregano, or the same amount
     dried
¼   cup rendered beef suet
4   cups chopped onions
½   cup chopped celery
4   cups chopped tomatoes
4   7-ounce cans chili salsa (see
     note)
2   cloves garlic, finely chopped
1   tablespoon mild New Mexico
     ground chili powder (see note)
1   tablespoon medium New Mex-
     ico ground chili powder
1   tablespoon hot New Mexico
     ground chili powder

1. Place the fresh green chilies under a broiler flame and cook, turning often, until blistered and brown all over. Drop the chilies into a bag and close the opening. This will let the chilies steam and facilitate peeling. If fresh green chilies are not available, use canned roasted green chilies to taste.

2. Grind half the flank steak. Cut the remainder into ½-inch or slightly smaller cubes. Cut the pork meat from the bones. Cut the meat into ¼-inch cubes. Discard the bones.

3. Add the beef to one skillet, adding a little fat if necessary, and cook, stirring often, using the side of a heavy kitchen spoon to break up any lumps. Add the pork to another skillet and cook, stirring often. When the meats start to brown, cover and let cook 45 minutes. Add half of the cumin and oregano to each skillet and stir. Continue cooking ½ hour.

4. Heat the suet in a 2-quart saucepan and add the onions and celery. Cook, stirring occasionally, about 30 minutes. Add the tomatoes and chili salsa and continue cooking 30 minutes.

5. Sprinkle the tomato mixture with the garlic and New Mexico chili powders. Peel the roasted chilies and chop them. Add them to the tomato mixture.

6. Combine the pork and beef. Add the tomato and spice mixture to the meats, stirring slowly. Cook slowly about 1½ hours. Stir every 10 minutes.

Yield: 10 to 12 servings.

Note: Anaheim green chilies and New Mexico chili powder are available in Spanish and Mexican markets. In New York, they are at Casa Moneo, 210 West 14th Street. Chili salsa is not standard bottled chili sauce but is available in many grocery stores under labels such as Ortega.

We have a recipe labeled "Chasen's Chili" sent to us by a friend in California and, although we cannot vouch for its authenticity, a note that precedes it states that it is "the exact recipe used by Dave Chasen at Chasen's Restaurant in Hollywood."

A Recipe for What Is Allegedly Chasen's Chili

1¼ cups pinto beans
3 cups cold water
Salt to taste
5 cups canned tomatoes, preferably imported Italian tomatoes
2 tablespoons peanut, vegetable or corn oil
4 cups chopped green peppers
4 cups chopped onions
2 tablespoons chopped garlic, more or less to taste
½ cup finely chopped parsley
8 tablespoons butter
2½ pounds ground beef chuck, preferably a coarse grind
1 pound ground pork, preferably a coarse grind
½ cup chili powder
1½ teaspoons ground pepper
2 teaspoons crushed cumin seed
½ teaspoon monosodium glutamate

1. Place the beans in a bowl and add the water. Let soak overnight.

2. Pour the beans and soaking water into a saucepan and bring to the boil. Cover and simmer until tender, about 1 hour. Stir occasionally to prevent scorching or burning. About 10 minutes before the beans are done, add salt to taste.

3. Drain the beans, but reserve both the beans and the liquid. Pour the liquid into a saucepan and add the tomatoes. Set the beans aside.

4. Bring the tomato mixture to the boil.

5. Heat the oil in a skillet and add the green peppers. Cook, stirring, about 5 minutes. Add the onions and continue cooking, stirring, until the onions are translucent. Stir in the garlic and parsley.

6. Meanwhile, heat the butter in a casserole large enough to hold all the ingredients. Add the beef and pork and cook, stirring to break up any lumps, about 15 minutes. Sprinkle with the chili powder and cook, stirring occasionally, about 10 minutes longer.

7. Add the green pepper mixture and the tomato mixture to the meat. Add salt to taste, ground pepper, cumin and monosodium glutamate. Cover and simmer about 1 hour. Stir often to prevent scorching or burning. A great deal of fat will rise to the top, but this will be skimmed off later.

8. Uncover and simmer 30 minutes longer, stirring occasionally. Add the beans.

9. Tilt the casserole and skim off and discard as much of the fat as possible. Serve piping hot with garlic bread.

Yield: About 3 quarts.

Note: We like this chili with a dollop of whipped sour cream seasoned with lime juice and salt to taste.

Winter's Epicurean Bargain

There's nothing out of the waters of the ice-blue Atlantic more likely to take the blahs out of winter menus than freshly caught cod. It has a sweetness of flavor and tenderness of texture unrivaled (in Northeast waters, that is) by any of God's other finned creatures. Moreover, for all of its elegance, it is not that expensive to come by—one of the few epicurean bargains around.

Cod, of course, is more freely associated with New England than any other region of America, and it is small wonder that it has frequently been referred to as Cape Cod turkey.

New England is abundantly inhabited by the descendants of Portuguese immigrants, and their influence on the region is undeniable. One source has seriously proposed that the association of the region with codfish is directly attributable to the Portuguese presence. The proposition is certainly fascinating and worth pondering, but a bit shaky.

Cod, if harvested in abundance anywhere in the world, would have undeniable appeal. (Or almost. One friend states that he loathes the stuff on the grounds that when he grew up in the region around Gloucester during the Depression, cod appeared on the table at least twice and sometimes three times a day.)

The kitchen uses to which cod may be put are seemingly endless. Cod takes well to grilling, broiling, poaching, frying and stewing. A simply poached cod steak with a basic lemon butter or a spoonful of hollandaise is superb. It is equally delectable in a complicated confection such as a mousse or in soups.

Here are recipes for fresh codfish indulged in over the years, the majority of them the creation of my colleague, Pierre Franey.

Cod and Potato Chowder with Saffron

1½   *pounds fresh, skinless, bone-less cod*
3   *ounces salt pork, chopped or cut into very small cubes*
1   *cup finely chopped onion*
1   *clove garlic, finely minced*
1   *bay leaf*
1   *teaspoon loosely packed stem saffron, crushed (optional)*
1   *pound potatoes, peeled and cut into ¾-inch cubes, about 3 cups*
4   *cups fish broth made with cod bones (see recipe), or use half bottled clam juice and half water*
¼   *cup finely chopped parsley Salt and freshly ground pepper to taste*
⅛   *teaspoon cayenne pepper*
2   *cups milk*

1. Cut the fish into 1-inch cubes. There should be 3½ to 4 cups. Set aside.

2. Cook the pork in a small kettle or large saucepan until it is rendered of fat and the particles of pork start to brown. Add the onion and stir. Cook until wilted. Add the garlic, bay leaf and saffron and cook, stirring, about 5 minutes.

3. Add the potatoes and stir. Add the fish broth, parsley, salt, pepper and cayenne. Bring to the boil and simmer about 30 minutes. Add the fish and return to the boil. Simmer about 30 seconds. Add the milk, bring to the boil and serve.

Yield: 4 to 6 servings.

Fish broth

1½   *pounds cod or other fish bones, broken and cleaned under cold running water*
4   *cups water*
3   *sprigs fresh parsley Salt to taste*
12   *peppercorns, crushed*

Bring all the ingredients to the boil in a saucepan and simmer about 5 minutes. Strain.

Yield: About 4 cups.

Poached Whole Cod

1   *8 to 10-pound codfish, cleaned and with head on but gills removed*
2   *cups dry white wine*
12   *cups water*
1   *teaspoon dried rosemary*
1   *bay leaf*
½   *cup coarsely chopped onion*
1   *hot red pepper*
4   *sprigs fresh parsley*
10   *sprigs fresh dill Salt to taste*
12   *peppercorns Orange and dill mayonnaise (see recipe), optional*

1. Prepare the cod and set it aside.

2. Combine the remaining ingredients in a fish cooker and bring to the boil. Simmer 15 minutes and let cool.

3. Add the codfish and bring to the boil. Simmer 15 to 20 minutes. Let stand until ready to serve. Serve with orange and dill mayonnaise.

Yield: 10 to 12 servings.

Orange and dill mayonnaise
(To be served with poached fish)

1   *egg yolk*
2   *tablespoons imported Dijon mustard*
    Salt and freshly ground pepper to taste
1   *cup olive oil*
¼   *cup chopped fresh dill*
    Juice of half an orange

1. Place the yolk in a mixing bowl and add the mustard, salt and pepper. Using a wire whisk, add the oil gradually while beating vigorously.

2. When thickened, add the dill and orange juice and beat to blend. Serve with poached fish.

Yield: About 1 cup.

Poached Cod Steaks with Butter Sauce

4   *cod steaks, about ¾ pound each*
½   *cup milk*
1   *bay leaf*
    Salt to taste
½   *small onion stuck with 1 whole clove*
12 *peppercorns, crushed*
⅛   *teaspoon or less cayenne pepper*
3   *parsley sprigs*
    Butter sauce with garlic (see recipe)
    Chopped parsley for garnish

1. Place the cod steaks in a stainless steel or enameled skillet and add water to barely cover. Add the milk,

bay leaf, salt, onion, peppercorns, cayenne and parsley sprigs.

2. Bring to the boil and simmer about 3 minutes. Remove from the heat. Using a pancake turner, carefully remove the steaks, one at a time, to a hot plate. Pour butter sauce over and sprinkle with chopped parsley.

Yield: 4 servings.

Butter sauce

8   *tablespoons butter*
    Salt to taste
1   *clove garlic, unpeeled but crushed*

Melt the butter and add salt and garlic. Let stand briefly. Heat until bubbling and remove the garlic. Serve hot over poached fish.

Yield: ½ cup.

Morue Boulangère
(Baked cod with potatoes)

10 *to 14 tablespoons butter*
    Salt and freshly ground pepper to taste
4   *cod steaks with skin on, each about 2-inches thick*
1½ *pounds baking potatoes, preferably Long Island or Maine potatoes*
1   *small onion, thinly sliced (about ½ cup)*
1   *small clove garlic, finely chopped*
3   *tablespoons chopped parsley*
3   *tablespoons fresh bread crumbs*

1. Preheat the oven to 400 degrees.

2. Butter a large metal baking dish with 2 or 3 tablespoons butter. The dish should be large enough to hold the fish and potatoes in one layer (we used an oval dish that measured 10 by 16 inches). Sprinkle with salt and pepper. Arrange the cod steaks in one layer on the bottom.

3. Peel and thinly slice the potatoes, plunging the slices immediately into cold water to prevent them from discoloring. Drain the potatoes in a colander.

4. Neatly scatter the potato slices around and between the pieces of fish, not on top. Scatter the onion slices over the potatoes. Salt and pepper the fish and vegetables.

5. Generously dot everything with the remaining butter. Do not add liquid; the fish provides its own.

6. Place the baking dish on top of the stove and bring to the boil. When it starts to boil, put the dish in the oven and bake uncovered for 15 minutes. Baste the fish and potatoes and continue baking 20 minutes longer, basting occasionally.

7. Meanwhile, combine the garlic, parsley and fresh bread crumbs in the container of an electric blender and sprinkle the mixture over the fish and vegetables. Bake 10 minutes longer, or until crumbs are brown.

Yield: 4 to 6 servings.

The Elegant Dacquoise

WITH PIERRE FANEY

It is, without question, one of the finest and most sought-after desserts in Manhattan. One of the first places we ever encountered it was at the distinguished Coach House on Waverly Place. One of the restaurants where we've most recently sampled it is the Windows on the World at the World Trade Center. The name of the dessert is dacquoise, and the origin of the name is elusive. It is not listed in any of the food dictionaries and encyclopedias that grace our kitchen bookshelves.

A dacquoise is a layered meringue dessert made with hazel or other nuts, the layers put together with a rich butter cream. One of the finest dacquoises we've ever sampled was prepared in our kitchen by our good friend and master pastry chef, Albert Kumin of the Culinary Institute of America in Hyde Park.

Albert Kumin's Dacquoise

5   egg whites, about ¾ cup
9   tablespoons granulated sugar
1⅓   cups ground hazelnuts,
        almonds or walnuts
        Butter cream (see recipe)
¼   cup confectioners' sugar,
        approximately

1. Preheat the oven to 250 degrees.

2. Select 1 or 2 baking sheets of sufficient size so that 3 9-inch circles can be traced on them without overlapping. Butter the baking sheet or sheets evenly. Sprinkle with flour and shake it around to coat the surface evenly. Shake off excess flour. Using a round-bottom 9-inch cake tin or false bottom and a pointed knife, outline 3 9-inch circles over the flour-coated baking sheet or sheets.

Outline circles over the baking sheet

3. Place the egg whites in the bowl of an electric beater. Beat until they stand in peaks, and gradually beat in half of the granulated sugar. Continue beating until stiff. Blend 1

cup of the nuts and remaining granulated sugar. Fold this into the meringue.

4. Outfit a pastry bag with a No. 4 star pastry tube. Add the meringue to the bag and squeeze out the meringue in a neat spiral to completely fill the 3 circles. Squeeze from the perimeter of each circle going toward the center or vice versa. Fill in any empty spots. Smooth over the meringue with a spatula. Do not discard any unused meringue, but squirt it out onto the baking sheet apart from the circles. This will be used later for garnish.

Squeeze out meringue in a neat spiral

5. Place the baking sheet in the oven and bake for 45 to 60 minutes, or until firm and set. Remove from the oven and gently run a metal spatula beneath the meringues to loosen them while still warm. Let cool.

6. Select the nicest of the 3 meringue circles for the top layer. Use a metal spatula and smoothly spread one of the circles with butter cream. Add a second circle and spread it similarly. Add the top circle. Spread a light layer of butter cream over the top. Smoothly spread the sides of the dacquoise with butter cream.

7. Blend any leftover pieces of meringue to make fine crumbs. Blend these with the remaining ⅓ cup ground nuts. Coat the sides of the cake with this and sprinkle any leftover mixture on top of the dacquoise. Sprinkle the top with confectioners' sugar.

Spread one circle with butter cream

8. Chill the dacquoise for an hour or longer to facilitate slicing. The dacquoise or leftover portions of it may be wrapped closely and frozen.

Yield: 12 or more servings.

Coat cake with meringue, nuts, and confectioners' sugar

Butter cream

6   egg whites, slightly more than ¾ cup
1¾   cups superfine sugar
1   pound sweet butter at room temperature

1. Combine the egg whites in the bowl of an electric mixer. Set the bowl in a basin of boiling water and start beating with a wire whisk. Gradually add the sugar, beating rapidly with the whisk. Continue beating until the mixture is somewhat thickened. Ideally, the temperature for the mixture should be about 105 degrees. In any event, a "ribbon" should form when the whisk is lifted.

2. Transfer the bowl to the electric beater and start beating on high speed. Continue beating about 20 minutes, or until the mixture is at room temperature. Gradually add the butter, beating constantly. This butter cream may be flavored variously (see flavored butter cream below).

Yield: 5 to 6 cups.

Flavored butter cream

Mocha butter cream: Blend 1 tablespoon or more of instant or freeze-dried coffee with 1½ tablespoons Cognac or rum. Blend this into the butter cream.

Chocolate butter cream: Melt 3 ounces of sweet chocolate with 1 tablespoon of water and blend it into the butter cream.

Ambrosial Fare of Childhoods Past

It was about fifteen years ago that I first read an unforgettable essay on the psychology of dining. It appeared in a magazine called *MD*, a publication whose audience was made up mostly of doctors. The article was titled "Prandial Psychology" and it remains vivid in my mind today. It contained a wealth of trenchant observations, numerous among them stemming from the thought that "many psychologic aspects of eating are not amenable to reason, probably because they were laid down in the prerational childhood years. . . .

"Saving the best tidbit for the last could be a childish expression of security; gobbling it up first or eating too rapidly expresses insecurity, either an unconscious fear that the tastiest morsel may be snatched away or an uncertainty about whether there will be a next meal. The habitual desire for a midnight snack reflects insecurity, or at least a desire for maternal reassurance at bedtime. . . ."

I am convinced that my craving, my absolute predilection for one certain category of dessert stems directly from the cradle and the years that immediately followed. First in a high chair, then sitting on a stack of Encyclopedia Brittanica (the telephone book in the town of my childhood was only a quarter-inch thick) to get the mouth and arms in an eating situation.

I am not basically a dessert man. At least not in the passionate way of certain friends and acquaintances. I find most European pastries toothsome enough—a well-made roulade au chocolat; variations on a genoise; Napoleons; éclairs; baked meringues; even baked Alaska. But these I can resist. Crêpes suzette have a certain appeal, but they do not interrupt my sleep with sweet anticipation.

No, it isn't these confections that make me salivate, that arouse the hounds of hunger at the conclusion of a meal. The dessert category that I find totally irresistible is purely and simply nursery desserts, those custards and mousses and glorious, sensual puddings and sauces based on egg and cream.

When I dine on such ambrosial fare, or even as I regard them, I am reminded of a childhood incident once related to me by a neighbor and friend. This, too, had to do with nursery foods (broadly speaking, nursery foods include things that can be eaten with a fork and/or spoon and for which a knife is not essential: noodles and any kind of spaghetti or pasta dish, creamed vegetables, cream soups and so on).

Anyway, this neighbor told me that in her high-chair days, her particular insatiable weakness was mashed potatoes. She simply couldn't get enough, and once on a birthday her mother decided to give her all the mashed potatoes she could possibly desire. After all, the dish is innocent and harmless enough.

My friend advised me that after the dozenth or so large spoonful had passed her lips and one more bite was obviously unthinkable, she took both her hands, dipped them into the bowl of potatoes and, quite without control or reason, massaged the remainder of the potatoes into the curls on top of her head.

Oeufs à la Neige

(Eggs in the snow)

4   cups milk
1¼   cups granulated sugar
1   vanilla bean, or 1 teaspoon
     vanilla extract
6   eggs, separated
½   teaspoon cornstarch
     Pinch of salt
     Kirsch or rum (optional)
¼   cup water

1. Bring the milk to the boil in a skillet. Add 6 tablespoons of the sugar and the vanilla bean or vanilla extract. Stir to dissolve the sugar.

2. Beat the egg whites until stiff. While beating, gradually add 6 tablespoons sugar, the cornstarch and the salt.

3. When the meringue is stiff, outfit a pastry bag with a star tube, No. 4. Fill it with the meringue and pipe it out in a 2-inch circle onto a baking sheet. Pipe out the meringue to make layer upon layer on the bottom circle. This will produce a small, roundish "beehive" pattern or, if you prefer, a kind of rosette about 2 inches high. Continue making rosettes until all the meringue is used. The meringue is sufficient to produce 16 to 18 rosettes or "eggs."

4. Using a metal spatula, transfer the rosettes, as many as the skillet will hold, into the milk.

5. Simmer about 30 seconds on one side, then, using a slotted spoon, gently turn the "eggs" over. Poach the other side 30 seconds.

6. Drain the "eggs," which should be quite firm by now, on paper toweling. Let cool while preparing the remainder of the recipe.

7. Strain the milk in which the "eggs" cooked. If a vanilla bean was used, remove it, rinse and wipe dry, then store in sugar for another use.

8. Beat the egg yolks until light and lemon colored. Gradually pour into the strained milk. Stir over low heat just until the custard coats the spoon.

9. The custard may be flavored with kirsch or rum. In any event, strain the custard into a wide, shallow serving dish and cover with the "eggs." Chill.

10. Combine the remaining sugar with the ¼ cup water in a saucepan. Cook until the caramel is dark amber in color, but do not let it burn.

11. Before the caramel has a chance to set, pour it in a thin thread all over the tops of the "eggs."

Yield: 10 or more servings.

Riz à l'impératrice

(A molded rice dessert)

1½ cups glacé fruitcake mix (candied citron, rind, cherries and so on, cut into small pieces)
1 tablespoon chopped candied ginger, optional
⅓ cup kirsch, mirabelle, framboise or other white liqueur
¾ cup raw Carolina rice
1 cup water
4 cups milk
1 vanilla bean, or 1 teaspoon pure vanilla extract
6 egg yolks
1¼ cups plus 1 tablespoon sugar
2 envelopes unflavored gelatin
1 cup heavy cream
Tangerine sections for garnish (see recipe), optional
Whipped cream for garnish
Apricot sauce (see recipe)

1. Place the candied fruit and ginger in a mixing bowl and add the liqueur. Let stand several hours or overnight.

2. Lightly oil an 8- or 9-cup decorative ring mold. Set aside.

3. Combine the rice with the water and bring to the boil. Drain.

4. Combine 3½ cups of milk and the rice in a small saucepan and bring to the boil. Add the vanilla bean, if it is to be used, and ¾ cup sugar. Stir and cover. Bring to the boil and simmer slowly about 25 minutes, or until milk is absorbed. Remove the vanilla bean if used. The bean may be washed well, dried and stored in sugar for another use. If the vanilla bean is not used, add the vanilla extract at this point.

5. Combine the egg yolks and ½ cup of sugar in a mixing bowl and beat with a whisk or electric beater until light and lemon colored. Beat in the gelatin.

6. Bring the remaining ½ cup of milk to the boil and gradually add it to the yolk mixture, beating. Bring to the boil, stirring constantly. At the boil, remove the mixture from the heat and stir in the fruitcake mix plus the liqueur in which it soaked. Add the rice. Let cool.

7. Whip the cream, adding 1 tablespoon of sugar as it is beaten. When stiff, fold this into the rice mixture. Pour the mixture into the prepared mold and chill until firm.

8. Unmold onto a round platter and garnish with tangerine sections and whipped cream. Serve with apricot sauce.

Yield: 8 to 12 servings.

Riz a l'imperatrice

Tangerine sections for garnish

Divide 2 tangerines into sections. Remove and discard the threadlike membranes attached to the sections. Combine ¼ cup water and ¼ cup sugar in a saucepan and bring to the boil. Add the tangerine sections. Cover and simmer about 5 minutes. Let cool in the syrup.

Apricot sauce

1   1-pound jar apricot jam or pre-
    serves
¼   to ½ cup water
¼   cup kirsch, mirabelle, fram-
    boise or other white liqueur,
    the same as used in the basic
    dessert, optional

1. Combine the apricot jam and the water in a saucepan. Cook, stirring, until blended. Strain through a fine sieve. Let cool.

2. Stir in the liqueur and chill.

Yield: About 2¼ cups.

Pouding au Liqueur

4   tablespoons butter
½   cup sugar
½   cup flour
½   cup milk
5   eggs, separated
1   tablespoon ricard, pernod,
    framboise, rum or other
    liqueur
    English custard (see recipe)

1. Preheat the oven to 400 degrees.

2. Melt the butter in a saucepan and add the sugar and flour, stirring with a whisk. Gradually add the milk, stirring rapidly with the whisk. When the mixture is thickened and smooth, remove it from the heat and add the yolks, one at a time, beating

vigorously after each addition. Add the liqueur.

3. Beat the whites and fold them in.

4. Generously butter a 6-cup charlotte mold and pour in the mixture. Set the mold in a basin of water and bring the water to the boil on top of the stove. Set the dish in the oven and bake 30 minutes. The pudding will rise like a soufflè and fall as it cools. Let stand until cool.

5. Run a knife around the inside rim of the mold. Unmold the pudding onto a serving dish. Serve with English custard flavored with the same liqueur as the pudding.

Yield: 6 to 10 servings.

English custard

5   egg yolks
⅔   cup sugar
2   cups milk
⅛   teaspoon salt

1. Place the yolks in a saucepan and add the sugar. Beat with a wire whisk until thick and lemon-colored.

2. Meanwhile, bring the milk almost, but not quite, to the boil.

3. Gradually add the milk to the yolk mixture, beating constantly. Use a wooden spoon and stir constantly, this way and that, making certain that the spoon touches all over the bottom of the saucepan. Cook, stirring, and add the salt. Cook until the mixture has a custardlike consistency and coats the sides of the spoon. Do not let the sauce boil, or it will curdle.

4. Immediately remove the sauce from the stove, but continue stirring.

Set the saucepan in a basin of cold water to reduce the temperature. Let the sauce cool to room temperature. Add a tablespoon of liqueur. Chill for an hour or longer.

Yield: 8 to 12 servings.

Bananas with Maltaise Pudding

3½   *cups milk*
     Peel from half an orange
½   *cup quick-cooking farina*
     (cream of wheat)
7   *tablespoons sugar*
3   *egg yolks*
½   *cup raisins*
1   *10-ounce jar apricot preserves*
3   *firm, ripe, unblemished bananas*
3   *tablespoons butter*
3   *tablespoons Grand Marnier, rum or cognac*
¼   *cup toasted, slivered, unsalted, blanched almonds*

1. Pour the milk into a saucepan and start to heat.

2. Peel the orange, eliminating as much of the white pulp as possible. Cut the yellow skin into very fine julienne strips. Add this to the milk and continue heating just to the boil.

3. Add the farina gradually, stirring constantly. Cook 5 minutes, stirring occasionally. Remove from the heat.

4. Immediately blend 5 tablespoons sugar with the egg yolks and add this to the hot farina, stirring rapidly with a whisk. Return briefly to the heat and, stirring constantly, bring just to the boil. Do not boil. Remove from the heat.

5. Spoon equal portions of the pudding mixture into 8 small, individual dessert bowls. Smooth over the top and let cool.

6. Meanwhile, place the raisins in a small bowl or cup and add boiling water to cover. Let stand until plumped.

7. Spoon the preserves into a saucepan and heat.

8. Peel the bananas and cut them first in half, then into quarters. Cut the pieces into cubes.

9. Heat the 3 tablespoons of butter in a skillet and add the cubed bananas. Sprinkle with remaining sugar and cook, stirring gently, about 2 minutes. Add the Grand Marnier and spoon this over the pudding.

10. Drain the raisins and add them to the heated preserves. Spoon this over all and sprinkle with almonds.

Yield: 8 servings.

Charlotte Plombiere

Charlotte Plombière

1½   cups glacé fruitcake mix
      (candied citron, rind, cherries
      and so on cut into small pieces)
¼   cup kirsch or other white
      liqueur
4   cups milk
1   vanilla bean, split, if avail-
      able, or use 1½ teaspoons pure
      vanilla extract
8   egg yolks
1   cup sugar
3   envelopes unflavored gelatin
⅓   cup water
16   to 18 "double" ladyfingers
2   cups heavy cream
      Apricot sauce or English cus-
      tard (see recipes)
      Whipped cream, optional

1. Soak the fruitcake mix in the kirsch for 1 hour or longer, stirring occasionally.

2. Bring the milk to the boil with the split vanilla bean. Do not boil further. If the bean is not to be used, add the vanilla extract later. Remove the vanilla bean, if used, rinse and dry it and reserve for later uses.

3. Place the yolks in a saucepan and add the sugar. Beat with a wire whisk until thick and lemon-colored.

4. Gradually add the milk to the yolk mixture, beating constantly. Use a wooden spoon and stir constantly, this way and that, making certain the spoon touches all over the bottom of the sauce. Cook until the mixture has a custardlike consistency and coats the sides of the spoon. Do not let the sauce boil, or it will curdle.

5. Soften the gelatin in the water and add it to the sauce, stirring to dissolve. Add the vanilla extract, if used, and strain the custard into a bowl. Let cool. When the mixture is cool, add the fruitcake mixture and the marinating liquid. Fold it in.

6. Line a 10- to 12-cup mold with the ladyfingers. To do this, separate the "double" ladyfingers. Arrange enough of them in a petallike, symmetrical arrangement over the bottom, cutting them to fit. Remember to place them smooth-surface down so that when the charlotte is unmolded, this surface will appear on top. Line the sides of the mold with ladyfingers, smooth-surface against the side of the mold. Arrange the ladyfingers close together and trim each ladyfinger as necessary so that they fit neatly, top and bottom.

7. Add the custard mixture and place in the refrigerator. Chill several hours or overnight, until the custard is set.

8. When ready to serve, dip the mold in hot water and remove immediately, A damp, hot cloth could also be used on the mold to help loosen it. Serve with apricot sauce or English custard, and, if desired, whipped cream.

Yield: 12 or more servings.

Rice Pudding

7   cups milk
1   vanilla bean, or 1 teaspoon
      pure vanilla extract
1   cup raw rice
1½   cups granulated sugar
¾   cup raisins
2   large eggs
1   tablespoon butter
½   teaspoon ground cinnamon
2   tablespoons confectioners'
      sugar

1. Pour the milk into a saucepan and add the vanilla bean or vanilla extract. Bring to the boil and add the rice and granulated sugar. Stir often from the bottom to prevent sticking. Cook until the rice is tender, about 40 minutes.

2. Add the raisins to a small bowl and pour boiling water over them. Let stand until rice is cooked.

3. Beat the eggs. Remove the rice from the heat and add the eggs, stirring rapidly.

4. Meanwhile, preheat the oven to 400 degrees.

5. Drain the raisins and add them to the cooked rice.

6. Grease a baking dish with the butter. We used an oval dish measuring 14-by-18-by-2-inches. Pour in the rice mixture. Sprinkle with cinnamon. Place the dish in a larger heat- and flame-proof dish and pour boiling water around it. Bring to the boil on top of the stove. Place the dish in the oven and bake 30 minutes, or until custard is set. Remove from the oven and sprinkle with confectioners' sugar. Serve hot or cold.

Yield: 8 to 10 servings.

Pouding de Semoule

(Semolina pudding)

4	cups milk
¾	cup sugar
1	cup quick cream of wheat
½	cup white raisins
1	teaspoon mint extract, or pure vanilla extract
3	egg yolks
1	cup heavy cream
	English custard (see recipe)
	Sweetened whipped cream

1. Place the milk and ½ cup of the sugar in a saucepan and bring to the boil, stirring with a wire whisk.

2. Immediately start adding the cream of wheat, stirring vigorously with the whisk. Add the raisins and mint or vanilla extract. Cook, stirring frequently, about 5 minutes.

3. Beat the yolks lightly. Turn off the heat beneath the cream of wheat mixture and immediately beat the yolks into the mixture. Reheat, while stirring, about 5 seconds and remove the saucepan from the heat. Spoon the mixture into a mixing bowl. Let cool, but do not let the mixture chill or it will harden.

4. Whip the cream with the remaining sugar until stiff. Fold the whipped cream into the cream of wheat mixture. Pour the mixture into a lightly oiled 2½-quart mold and chill until firm. Unmold and serve with English custard flavored with Pernod and more sweetened whipped cream.

Yield: 10 to 12 servings.

Mousse au Chocolat Sydney

(Chocolate mousse with candied ginger)

6	1-ounce squares semisweet chocolate
6	eggs, separated
⅓	plus ¼ cup sugar
1	cup heavy cream
1	teaspoon pure vanilla extract
3	ounces (1 small package) candied ginger

1. Place the chocolate squares in a small bowl and place the bowl in a larger receptacle containing very hot water. The chocolate should melt from the heat.

2. As the chocolate melts, put the egg yolks in a heavy saucepan and add ⅓ cup sugar, beating with a wire whisk. Set the pan in a skillet containing boiling water. Let the water continue to simmer while beating the egg yolks vigorously. Beat about 5 minutes until the yolks reach the rich, thickened "ribbon" stage. Fold the yolks into the chocolate.

3. Beat the whites with a whisk or electric beater until they start to become frothy. Add the remaining ¼ cup sugar and continue beating until they are stiff and meringuelike. Fold them into the chocolate and egg yolk mixture.

4. Whip the cream until it is stiff and add the vanilla. Fold the cream into the chocolate mixture. Chop the ginger fine and fold it in. Pour the mousse into 6 or 8 crystal glasses and chill in the refrigerator until thoroughly set. Serve, if desired, with more whipped cream on top.

Yield: 6 to 8 servings.

Pouding de Pain aux Pommes

(Bread pudding with apples)

1   *pound firm but sweet cooking apples*
2   *tablespoons butter*
1¼   *cups sugar*
¼   *cup currants or raisins*
¼   *cup Calvados or applejack, optional*
10   *to 20 slices French bread, each slice about ½-inch thick*
4   *egg yolks*
2   *whole eggs*
1   *teaspoon pure vanilla extract*
1   *cup heavy cream*
3   *cups milk*
     Confectioners' sugar

1. Preheat the oven to 400 degrees.

2. Peel the apples then core, quarter and slice them thinly. There should be about 4 cups.

3. Heat the butter in a heavy skillet and add the apple slices.

4. Sprinkle the apples with ¼ cup of sugar and add the currants. Sprinkle with Calvados and ignite it.

5. Arrange the bread slices, slightly overlapping, over the bottom of a baking dish. We used an 8-by-14-inch oval dish. Do not crowd the bread; use only enough to cover the bottom, slightly overlapping, in one layer.

6. Spoon the apple mixture evenly over the bread.

7. Blend the yolks, whole eggs, the remaining cup of sugar, vanilla, cream and milk. Beat lightly and pour it over all. Set the baking dish in a larger baking dish and pour boiling water around it. Carefully place it in the oven and bake 40 minutes. Carefully remove the pudding. When lukewarm, sprinkle the top evenly with confectioners' sugar put through a fine sieve. Run the pudding under the broiler until the top is nicely glazed.

Yield: 12 or more servings.

Bavarois à la Vanille

(Vanilla-flavored Bavarian cream)

4 cups milk
1 vanilla bean, split, if available, or use 1½ teaspoons pure vanilla extract
8 egg yolks
1 cup sugar
3 envelopes unflavored gelatin
⅓ cup water
¼ cup mirabelle, kirsch or other liqueur, optional
2 cups heavy cream
English custard (see recipe)
Whipped cream, optional

1. Bring the milk to the boil with the split vanilla bean. Do not boil further. If the bean is not to be used, add the vanilla extract later. Remove the vanilla bean, if used, rinse it off, dry it and reserve for later uses.

2. Place the yolks in a saucepan and add the sugar. Beat with a wire whisk until thick and lemon-colored.

3. Gradually add the milk to the yolk mixture, beating constantly. Use a wooden spoon and stir constantly, this way and that, making certain the spoon touches all over the bottom of the saucepan. Cook until the mixture has a custardlike consistency and coats the sides of the spoon. Do not let the sauce boil, or it will curdle. Add the vanilla extract, if used.

4. Soften the gelatin in the water and add it to the sauce, stirring to dissolve. Add the liqueur and strain into a bowl. Let cool.

5. Whip the heavy cream until stiff and fold it into the sauce.

6. Rinse out a 10- to 12-cup ring mold without drying. Sprinkle the inside with sugar and shake out excess.

Add the custard mixture and place in the refrigerator. Chill several hours or overnight until the custard is set.

7. When ready to serve, dip the mold into hot water and remove immediately. Wipe off and unmold. A damp, hot cloth could also be used on the mold. Serve with English custard flavored with the same liqueur used in the Bavarian cream and, if desired, whipped cream.

Yield: 12 or more servings.

Bread and Butter Pudding

½ cup dried currants
18 slices untrimmed French bread, each slice about ½-inch thick
4 tablespoons melted butter
3 egg yolks
3 eggs
1 cup sugar
3 cups milk
Confectioners' sugar for garnish

1. Preheat the oven to 350 degrees.

2. Select an oval, heat-proof baking dish (a recommended size is one that measures 14-by-18-by-2-inches). Scatter the currants over the bottom.

3. Slice the bread. Preferably, the diameter of the bread should not exceed 3 inches. If much larger, cut the pieces in half. Cut off enough slices to cover the bottom of the dish neatly, the slices slightly overlapping top to bottom, arranging them in two or three rows as necessary. Butter each slice on one side only and arrange them buttered-side up.

4. Beat the yolks, eggs and sugar until smooth. Stir in the milk until well blended. Strain this through a sieve over the bread.

5. Set the baking dish in a heatproof basin or larger baking dish. Add about 1 inch of water. Bring the water to the boil on top of the stove. Place in the oven and bake 40 minutes to 1 hour, or until custard is set. Remove, place on a rack and cool. Serve sprinkled with confectioners' sugar.

Yield: 8 to 12 servings.

Tapioca Pudding

6   *cups milk*
½   *cup minute tapioca*
1   *vanilla bean, or 1 teaspoon*
    pure vanilla extract

½   *cup sugar*
3   *egg yolks*

1. Combine the milk, tapioca and vanilla bean in a saucepan and bring to the boil, stirring constantly with a wooden spoon. Let cook 6 to 7 minutes.

2. Combine the sugar and yolks in a mixing bowl and beat rapidly with a wire whisk until light and lemon-colored. Add a little of the hot tapioca mixture to the egg yolk mixture, stirring constantly. Return this mixture to the saucepan and, when it begins to boil, continue cooking, stirring constantly, about 1 minute. Remove the vanilla bean. Pour the pudding into a serving dish and let cool. Chill until ready to serve.

Yield: 8 to 12 servings.

Bread and butter pudding

February

I T IS A LONG WAY from Bangkok to the banks of the Delaware, but the columns that ran in February ran precisely that gamut. There was a celebration of the fiery hot food of a Thai kitchen, and a celebration of the arrival of that incredible prespringtime delicacy—the first shad and shad roe.

Legend has it that 100 years ago shad was considered, in America at least, "trash fish." Particularly in the South, where it was abundant, it was never eaten by the white aristocracy. It was food for slaves and at times was used as fertilizer. That conception, or misconception, about the delicate nature of the fish and the roe in particular is gone forever. Like leeks, which were for centuries called "the poor man's asparagus," shad and shad roe are costly commodities whether they grace the tables of the rich or the poor.

Another celebration of the month was a welcoming in of the Chinese New Year—that year to be known as the year of the snake. And for dessert, there was a marvelous creation by Pierre Franey, a glorious chocolate mousse.

Thai Cuisine: Hot, Hot, Hot

The current and well-entrenched American enthusiasm for highly spiced foods—dishes that in truth would please Beelzebub's palate—is a relatively recent thing. It is a rage that can fairly well be pinpointed to the opening of the first Szechwan restaurants in Manhattan when New Yorkers were introduced to the seductive delights of dishes flavored with chili paste and garlic, oil-seared red peppers, slivered or chopped fresh green peppers, and so on. The first of these restaurants to achieve considerable popularity was the Szechuan Taste on Chatham Square in Chinatown in 1968.

Spicy foods were not entirely unknown in town, of course, prior to that date. There were a few Mexican restaurants here and there that served what might be called four-alarm chili, and there was a small audience that knew the joys of hot green chilies. Indian restaurants were relatively few in number and, besides, these establishments would dish up hot curries only when they were assured that the guests who requested same were genuine afficionados of peppery seasonings.

A liking for spicy foods is not unusual, nor is it an uncommon phenomenon in various parts of the world. In addition to the Mexican and Indian kitchens, the Japanese in certain dishes have a fondness for sprinklings of ground red pepper. Much of native African cooking would be at a loss for want of chilies, including one of the best-known and delectable of African dishes, couscous, which is almost invariably served with harissa, a powerfully hot sauce made with chilies.

Creole cooking in this country relies heavily on highly spiced foods, and Tabasco sauce is mother's milk to masses of southerners. In a recent trip to the Caribbean we breakfasted each morning on the glorious island of St. Bartholomew on chili-sharpened Creole boudins noirs, or blood sausages. The chilies in the Caribbean enliven the flavors of a fantastic assortment of Creole dishes, including fish soups and stuffed crabs.

The most recent addition to the roster of restaurants in Manhattan that serve devilishly hot foods are those that specialize in Thai cookery. Although we relished the food of Thailand on a trip to Bangkok about ten years ago, we had never been intimately acquainted with its preparation until we learned of a young couple who live on the East Side of Manhattan. He is Thai, she is American-born, and the food served at their table is primarily Thai-inspired. When we were invited to share a meal and participate in its preparation, we accepted with more than a little enthusiasm. The couple's names are Karen and Wanchai Sriuttamayotin.

"I am Denver-born," Karen said over a scrumptious, irresistibly hot and spicy shrimp soup her husband had just served, "but I was raised in New York. I've never been to Thailand but, because of Wanchai, my taste buds go there often. I love the food."

In the course of that day and that meal we learned that the home cooking of Thailand is quite remarkably different and good, easily made and certain to appeal to that vast and ever-widening breed of New Yorkers who delight in zestier fare than steak béarnaise.

One of the most impressive of the dishes was a cold romaine, onion and tomato salad with thin slivers of freshly broiled beef on top and a fiery-hot yet oddly refreshing dressing made with fresh lime juice, fish sauce and powdered hot red chilies. The meal ended with a sensuously good tapioca pudding with rambutan fruit, a typical Thai fruit.

Two of the most interesting flavors in that meal were the lemon grass (it smacks of lemon peel but is more astringent to the taste) and makrut leaves, also called kaffirlime leaves. These are the leaves of special lime trees.

"Anyone familiar with the Chinatown shopping scene," Karen observed, "would have no difficulty in obtaining the necessary ingredients. Many Chinatown groceries stock at least some Thai products, including spices, fish sauce and tapioca." Basic tapioca that has not been converted into a minute version is a rare commodity in United States groceries these days.

"One of the best outlets," she continued, "is the Southeast Asia Food and Trading Company at 68A Mott Street with a full line of the essentials. The Chinese American Trading Company at 91 Mulberry Street also has a good selection of Thai products."

Since lunch in their home I have shopped at both sources and they offer a lavish number of ingredients for Southeast Asian cookery. The proprietor of the Southeast Asia store was particularly helpful in pointing out the necessary foods.

The Sriuttamayotins also live only a block away from an entire complex of Indian stores and markets situated between 28th and 30th Streets on Lexington Avenue. Here, too, are available excellent supplies of fresh coriander, ginger and hot green chilies, herbs that are indigenous to both Thai and Indian cooking.

"Thai cooking," the couple noted, "relies heavily on Chinese and Indian for basic forms and techniques. It is the pungent condiments such as fish sauce, or nam pla; baked curry, called nam prik pao; and fresh coriander, called pakchi, that add much. We also serve a pork satay which is originally Indonesian."

The menu of that day included a distinctive and consummately good shrimp soup, a pork satay with a peanut and curry sauce, a delectable platter of chicken with dried basil leaves and beef with Chinese broccoli and oyster sauce.

Wanchai is an artist who works both privately and commercially in his field. Karen is a biology student. They both cook, she during the week, he on weekends. Their hobbies include not only cooking but music and gardening. She plays the piano; he plays jazz flute.

In midwinter they grow numerous herbs for the kitchen, including basil, sweet marjoram, rosemary and two herbs essential to the Thai kitchen: by krapow, which is sometimes called "hot basil," metbangrap, or lemon basil; and melissa, or lemon balm.

In summer they participate in a sort of communal plot of ground near their apartment in the mid 30s. Their "vacant lot plot" measures about 6 by 9 feet and generally flourishes. Last year someone gave them a prized lemon grass plant so vital to Thai cooking, but it died.

The couple were asked if chopsticks were used in private homes in Thailand, and they stated that they are not, other than in the homes of Chinese who live there. The usual dining implements are a fork and spoon and no knives. Beer is a favored beverage and freshly cooked hot rice is an essential.

Before the meal ended the guests were insisting that the Sriuttamayotins should open their own restaurant. They stated that cooking was too much fun at home. Why spoil it?

Tom Yam Kung
(Thai shrimp and herb soup)

1½ pounds neck bones of pork
6   cups water
2   teaspoons dried lemon grass (see note), or use 1 teaspoon grated lemon peel
2   dried makrut leaves, also called kaffirlime leaves (see note)
2   or more tablespoons fish sauce (see note)
1   pound small-to-medium-size shrimp in the shell
¾   cup thinly sliced fresh mushrooms
3   tablespoons or more lemon juice to taste
1   tablespoon chili paste with oil (see note)
¼   teaspoon or more powdered Thai red chili pepper to taste
8   sprigs fresh coriander leaves, coarsely chopped (see note) Shredded hot, green, fresh chilies
¼   cup chopped green onions

1. Place the bones in a kettle and add the water. Bring to the boil without salt and simmer about 1 hour, or until the liquid is reduced to 4 cups. Strain the liquid into a 2- or 3-quart saucepan and bring to the boil. Discard the bones. Add the lemon grass, makrut leaves and fish sauce. Do not add salt. The fish sauce is quite salty. Simmer 15 minutes to abstract the flavor of the herbs. Strain.

2. Meanwhile, peel and devein the shrimp but leave the last tail segment intact. Bring the soup to the

boil. Add the shrimp to the boiling soup. Simmer about 10 minutes and add the mushrooms. Simmer about 2 minutes longer.

3. Add the lemon juice, chili paste with oil and powdered red chili pepper. Serve piping hot in individual bowls with the chopped coriander, shredded green chilies and chopped onion as garnishes.

Yield: 4 to 6 servings.

Note: All the unfamiliar ingredients listed here are available at the Southeast Asia Food and Trading Company, 68A Mott Street; Chinese American Trading Company, 91 Mulberry Street, or at other Oriental stores in Chinatown.

Grilled Beef and Romaine Salad Thai-Style

The salad

1   *large head romaine lettuce, about 1½ pounds*
1   *large or 2 medium-size cucumbers, peeled and thinly sliced, about 1 cup*
1   *red onion, peeled and sliced*
10   *to 12 firm radishes, trimmed and thinly sliced, about 1 cup*
2   *red ripe tomatoes, cored and cut into eighths, or sliced*
1   *bunch scallions, trimmed and cut into 1-inch lengths, about ¾ cup*
16   *mint leaves*
16   *basil leaves*
½   *cup loosely packed fresh coriander leaves (also known as Chinese parsley and cilantro)*

The sauce

½   *cup fish sauce (see note)*
⅓   *cup freshly squeezed lime juice*
1   *tablespoon finely chopped garlic*
2   *teaspoons grated fresh ginger*
½   *to 1 teaspoon hot red powdered chilies (see note) or hot red pepper*

The meat

8   *thin slices top round, sirloin or club steak, about 1½ pounds Salt and freshly ground pepper to taste*
¼   *cup peanut, vegetable or corn oil*

1. Prepare a charcoal or other grill for cooking the meat. This should be done before starting to prepare the ingredients.

2. Prepare all the greens as indicated.

3. Combine all the ingredients for the sauce and blend well. Set aside.

4. Sprinkle the meat with salt and pepper. Grill the meat on both sides, about 2 minutes to a side or longer, depending on the desired degree of doneness.

5. Quickly, while the meat is still hot, cut the slices into ½-inch strips and add them to the greens. If there are any accumulated meat juices, add them to the sauce. Pour the sauce over all and toss. Serve immediately with hot rice or long loaves of bread.

Yield: 8 servings.

Note: Fish sauce and powdered red pepper are widely available in Chinese markets in Chinatown, including the Southeast Asia Food and Trading Company, 68A Mott Street and the Chinese American Trading Company, 91 Mulberry Street. Also at Sunflower, 2445 Broadway (between 90th and 91st Streets).

Note: Unfamiliar ingredients are available at the Southeast Asia Food and Trading Company, 68A Mott Street, Chinese American Trading Company, 91 Mulberry Street, or at other Oriental stores in Chinatown.

Gy Pad By Krapow

(Chicken with straw mushrooms and dried basil leaves)

1¼	*pounds chicken breast (1 large whole breast)*
3	*tablespoons peanut oil*
2	*tablespoons coarsely chopped garlic*
2	*teaspoons mushroom-soy, available in bottles (see note)*
2	*canned bamboo shoots, cut into thin slices*
2	*tablespoons dried by krapow leaves (see note)*
2	*or more tablespoons fish sauce (see note)*
6	*to 10 canned straw mushrooms (see note), drained and sliced in half lengthwise*

1. Remove and discard the skin and bones of the chicken breast. Cut the meat into thin, bite-size slices. The slicing is facilitated if the meat is partly frozen in advance. Set aside.

2. Heat the oil in a wok or skillet and add the garlic. Cook until garlic is nicely browned, a bit darker than golden. Add the chicken and stir-fry quickly until chicken is cooked through.

3. Add the mushroom-soy, bamboo shoots, by krapow leaves and fish sauce, stirring constantly over high heat. Add the mushrooms and cook briefly, stirring. Serve hot.

Yield: 4 to 6 servings.

Nua Pad Kanha

(Beef with Chinese Vegetables)

1	*pound lean round steak*
2	*tablespoons corn oil*
2	*tablespoons coarsely chopped garlic*
3	*or more tablespoons bottled oyster sauce (see note)*
3	*cups Chinese broccoli, Chinese cabbage or other Chinese vegetable, cut on the bias into large bite-size pieces*
1	*teaspoon fish sauce (see note)*

1. Cut the meat into thin, bite-size pieces. This is facilitated if the meat is partly frozen in advance.

2. Heat the oil in a wok or skillet and cook the garlic until it is nicely browned, a bit darker than golden. Add the beef and stir-fry quickly until the meat is cooked through.

3. Add the oyster sauce, stirring. Add the Chinese vegetable and cook, stirring, about 1 minute. Cover and cook about 1 minute. Uncover, add the fish sauce and continue cooking about 2 minutes.

Yield: 4 to 6 servings.

Note: Unfamiliar ingredients are available at the Southeast Asia Food and Trading Company, 68A Mott Street, Chinese American Trading Company, 91 Mulberry Street, or at other Oriental stores in Chinatown.

Happy Year of the Snake

What would you like for the next twelve months? Health? Wealth? Happiness? An untroubled, carefree life? Or perhaps a combination of all these things? Well, as the year of the dragon lumbers out and the year of the snake slithers in, these perquisites and more can be yours according to Chinese tradition and most of the Chinese cooks we know.

If you eat large bean sprouts, for example, "no matter how rough the road, your path will be smoothed." Should you choose braised duck, "all money will come to you." And how about a bite of casserole pork belly? That would provide "all happiness." Or perhaps a personal favorite, both from the standpoint of flavor and prophecy: whole fish with hot bean sauce means that "everything you have is more than you have, or in other words, everything we do is head and tail, there is no half way."

I was tutored in the fine points of the Chinese New Year by Virginia Lee, a colleague, good friend and one of the finest Chinese cooks in Manhattan, during a recent two-day session in my home as she picked over the large bean sprouts, made casserole dishes and cooked shrimp balls, pork balls and fish balls for a delectable Chinese fire pot to be offered guests at the end of a feast should they still feel pangs of hunger (as it turned out, most of the fire pot was left unconsumed and made a splendid midday feast the following day).

Mrs. Lee stated that the food for a Chinese New Year's feast in her homeland might best be compared with the Thanksgiving dinner in America when foods traditionally appear on the table in superabundance.

"But there are no set dishes, such as a turkey and cranberry sauce. Not like Easter when there's ham, or Christmas when there's goose. The foods would vary from region to region."

In her own home, she stated, there was rarely a large, planned formal banquet to celebrate the day.

"The menu would vary. But it would be based mostly on what you might call casserole dishes; that is, dishes that could be prepared well in advance like casserole pork belly and jellied lamb. There would be certain dishes for good fortune. We would almost always have a whole fish. That stands for a lot—lots of descendants, success, a long life and happiness."

The New Year's feast that Mrs. Lee prepared in my kitchen was for eight people. Because the more dishes you serve the more you honor the guests at table, she offered, in addition to the casserole dishes and good luck foods such as the fish with hot bean sauce, two stir-fry dishes made at the last minute. And the meal ended with a traditional Chinese fire pot.

Basically, any well-made and carefully prepared menu would serve. The Chinese fire pot alone, as one guest said recently, would be "super." Although it was made in a traditional fire pot, it could be made in an electric skillet.

Chinese New Year Bean Sprouts

3 cups large bean sprouts
10 dried black mushrooms
1 or 2 pieces bamboo shoot
3 tablespoons plus 1 teaspoon peanut, vegetable or corn oil
½ cup chicken broth
¼ teaspoon monosodium glutamate, optional
1½ teaspoons salt
1 tablespoon shao hsing or dry sherry wine
1 teaspoon sugar
½ teaspoon dark soy sauce

1. Rinse the bean sprouts and drain well.

2. Pour boiling water over the mushrooms and let stand about 20 minutes. Drain and squeeze dry. Trim off stems.

3. Cut the bamboo shoots into 12 pyramid shapes, each about 1½ inches tall. Rinse and drain.

4. Heat 3 tablespoons oil in a wok or skillet and add the bean sprouts. Cook about 30 seconds and add the mushrooms. Cook 20 seconds and add the bamboo shoots. Add the chicken broth, monosodium glutamate, salt, wine, sugar and dark soy sauce. Cook over high heat, stirring, about 6 minutes. Turn off heat.

5. Arrange the pieces of bamboo shoots in an oval on a small oval serving dish. Arrange the bean sprouts in the center. Leave the mushrooms in the wok.

6. Add remaining 1 teaspoon of oil to the wok and cook the mushrooms about 45 seconds. Arrange the mushrooms over the bean sprouts and serve.

Yield: 8 banquet servings.

Virginia Lee prepares Chinese New Year's feast

Casserole Pork with Spinach

1¾ pounds pork belly with bones, available in pork stores, particularly those in Chinatown and in Chinese markets
5   cups cold water
¼   cup dark soy sauce
5   large chunks rock sugar (see note), about 3 ounces total weight
1½ teaspoons salt
1   pound fresh spinach in bulk, or 1 10-ounce package
1   cup chicken broth

1. Place the pork in a casserole and add water to cover. Bring to the boil and cook 2 hours. Drain and let cool.

2. Return the pork to a clean, not too large casserole and add the 5 cups of water, dark soy sauce, rock sugar and salt. Bring to the boil and simmer 4 hours. The pork may be cooked to this point and left to stand until about an hour before serving.

3. Return to the boil and cook 30 minutes or until skin and fat are fork tender. Remove the pork and cook down the sauce over high heat to about ¾ cup. It should be quite syrupy.

4. Meanwhile, pick over the spinach. Discard any blemished leaves and tough stems. Drop the spinach into boiling water to cover and return to the boil. Drain well.

5. Place the spinach in a saucepan and add the broth. Bring to the boil and simmer 5 minutes. Drain.

6. Cut the hot pork into ½-inch-thick slices. Arrange on a serving dish with the spinach around it. Strain the hot sauce over and serve.

Yield: 8 banquet servings.

Bean Sauce Hot Fish

1   cup fermented rice (see recipe)
1   1¾- to 2-pound red snapper Peanut, vegetable or corn oil for deep frying
½   pound ground pork
½   cup finely chopped ginger
2½ tablespoons finely chopped garlic
¼   pound hot, fresh, red peppers, seeded and chopped, about ¾ cup
1½ tablespoons chili paste with garlic (see note)
½   cup bean paste (see note) Salt to taste
1½ cups water
1   cup chopped scallions

1. Prepare the rice the day before as indicated in the recipe.

2. Rinse the fish and pat dry.

3. Heat the oil in a wok or casserole large enough to hold the fish. When it is almost smoking, add the fish and cook about 1 minute. Drain and set aside. Pour off and reserve the oil.

4. Heat ½ cup of reserved oil in a wok or skillet and add the pork, stirring to break up lumps. When the meat changes color, add the ginger, garlic and red pepper, stirring. Add the chili paste and bean paste. Cook about 1 minute and add the cup of fermented rice and salt. Cook, stirring, over high heat and add ½ cup of water. Cook over high heat, stirring, about 10 minutes.

5. Meanwhile, heat 2 tablespoons of oil in a pan, preferably an oval pan, large enough to hold the fish, and add the fish. Add remaining 1 cup of water and cover. Steam 8 to 10 minutes. Drain. Transfer the fish to a serving dish.

6. Add the scallions to the pork sauce and pour the sizzling hot sauce over the fish. Serve.

Yield: 8 banquet servings.

Fermented Rice

¾   *pound glutinous rice*
½   *wine ball, or wine cube*
1½ *teaspoons all-purpose flour*

1. Soak the rice overnight in cold water to cover, then drain.

2. Line a steamer top or a colander with cheesecloth and add the drained rice. Cover and steam 1 hour.

3. Crush the wine ball or cube on a flat surface, using a mallet or rolling pin. When it is crushed fine like a powder, blend well with the flour. Set aside.

4. Rinse the rice delicately in lukewarm water, working gently with your hands to separate the grains. The rice should be at about body temperature when it is ready. If it is too warm at this time, it will ferment too quickly. If it is cold, it will not ferment.

5. When the rice is right, drain it well. Sprinkle with the wine ball and flour mixture and work gently with your fingers to mix thoroughly. Spoon the rice into a thin bowl and smooth the top with the fingers.

6. Using your fingers, make a hole or well in the center, about 1

inch in diameter. Pat the top of the rice with wet fingers to smooth it, but do not disturb the hole. You will see later when you uncover the rice that the hole accumulates liquid as the rice stands.

7. Cover the bowl well and then carefully wrap it in blankets. Set the blanket-covered bowl in a warm (but not too warm) place and let it stand for 24 hours. If properly made and all the elements are right, liquid will have accumulated in the hole.

8. Spoon the rice and liquid into mason jars and seal loosely. Let stand until room temperature, then refrigerate. The fermented rice keeps for weeks in the refrigerator, but you should loosen the tops occasionally to make sure too much gas is not accumulating inside the jars.

Yield: 1½ pints.

Yuan Pao
(Braised duck with leeks)

1   *5-pound duck, preferably with head left on, available in Chinese poultry markets*
6   *tablespoons dark soy sauce*
6   *cups oil*
6   *tablespoons shao hsing or dry sherry wine*
6   *cups water*
1   *tablespoon plus 1 teaspoon salt*
2   *tablespoons plus 1 teaspoon sugar*
6   *leeks*

1. Remove and discard any cavity fat from the duck. Cut off the wing tips but leave the main wing bone and second joint intact.

2. Slice the skin of the duck from head to tail. Using a sharp cleaver, hack the duck's backbone from head to tail to open up the inside of the duck.

3. Open up the duck's inside, placing it skin-side down on a flat surface. Trim and pull away dark pulpy matter, veins and so on. Rinse the duck and drain. Pat dry.

4. Place the duck skin-side up and, using a small trussing needle, skewer the skin of the tail section together neatly and firmly. Brush the duck skin all over with 3 tablespoons dark soy sauce. If the head is still on, loop a long, heavy string around the neck to facilitate turning it in hot oil.

5. Heat the oil in a wok or other utensil large enough to hold the duck with the body flattened. Add the duck, skin-side down, and cook over high heat about 3 minutes. Turn, spooning oil over the head so that it cooks, too. Cook 3 minutes longer and remove. Pour out the oil and wipe out the wok. Reserve the oil. Return the duck to the wok, skin-side up. Add the wine. Turn the duck skin-side down and add 2 tablespoons of dark soy sauce and 6 cups of water. Add 1 tablespoon of salt and 2 tablespoons of sugar. Cover and cook over low heat about 45 minutes. Turn duck and cook 1 hour. (The duck may be cooked to this point and left to stand.)

6. Meanwhile, trim off the ends of the leeks. Cut off the tops of the leeks but leave leeks 7 or 8 inches long. Split leeks in half and rinse well under cold water. A spoonful of salt added to the water helps in cleaning. Drain the leeks.

7. Heat reserved oil for deep fat frying in a wok or kettle and add the leeks. Cook about 4 minutes. Remove and drain.

8. About ½ hour before serving, reheat the duck and add the leeks. Cover and cook 15 minutes.

9. Remove the duck to a platter skin-side up and remove the string from the neck. Cover the duck with the leeks. Add remaining tablespoon of dark soy sauce, remaining 1 teaspoon salt and remaining teaspoon sugar to the sauce and boil down until syrupy. Pour it over the duck and serve hot.

Yield: 8 banquet servings.

Crystal Fish

½	pound shrimp
2	tablespoons cornstarch, plus cornstarch for dredging
½	egg white (beat the egg white lightly and measure it)
2½	teaspoons salt
½	teaspoon sugar
¼	teaspoon monosodium glutamate, optional
1	tablespoon shao hsing or dry sherry wine
1½	tablespoons finely chopped scallions
1½	tablespoons finely diced, soaked, black mushrooms
2	flounder fillets, about ¾ pound total weight
2	tablespoons crab roe, optional
2	large rectangles (about 14- by-11-inches) cawl fat, available in pork stores
11	tablespoons flour

4 teaspoons peanut, vegetable or
   corn oil, plus oil to cover fish
1 tablespoon baking powder
9 tablespoons water, approximately
   Chinese parsley sprigs for garnish
   Szechwan peppercorn dip (see
   recipe)

1. Shell and devein the shrimp. Chop to a pulp on a flat surface or blend in a food processor or electric blender. Spoon into a bowl and add 1 tablespoon cornstarch, ½ egg white, 1 teaspoon salt, sugar, monosodium glutamate and wine. Blend well. Add scallions and mushrooms and blend again. Set aside.

2. Place the flounder fillets, skinned-side down, on a flat surface. Brush the top side liberally with cornstarch. With dampened fingers, smear each fillet with equal amounts of the shrimp mixture. Smooth over with a rubber spatula.

3. Dot the top of both with bits of crab roe.

4. Lay out 2 rectangles of cawl fat and place one fillet, shrimp side up, in the center of each. Carefully and neatly fold the edges of cawl fat over the fillet to enclose it completely.

5. Combine the flour, remaining 1 tablespoon cornstarch, remaining 1½ teaspoons salt, 4 teaspoons oil and baking powder in a mixing bowl. Add enough water to make a smooth but not too thin paste, about 9 table-spoons.

6. Dip the coated fish in the batter, using the fingers to coat top and bottom liberally.

7. Heat enough oil to barely cover the fish. Add one fillet and ladle the oil over, turning the fish as necessary so that it cooks evenly. Cook about 5 minutes. Remove and drain. Add other fish and cook. Drain.

8. Cut the fillets widthwise into 1½-inch rectangles. Serve hot, garnished with sprigs of Chinese parsley. Serve the Szechwan peppercorn mixture on the side as a dip.

Yield: 8 banquet servings.

Szechwan peppercorn dip

1 tablespoon finely ground
   Szechwan peppercorns
1 tablespoon salt
1 tablespoon sugar
¼ teaspoon monosodium glutamate, optional

Combine all the ingredients and use as a dip for crystal fish.

Yield: About 3 tablespoons.

Steamed Chinese Bread

1 envelope granular yeast
2 tablespoons sugar
1 tablespoon warm but not
   melted lard
3 cups flour plus additional as
   necessary for kneading
1 cup cold water
1 teaspoon baking powder

1. Place the yeast, sugar, lard, ½ cup of flour and ½ cup of water in a mixing bowl. Blend. Let stand 5 minutes.

2. Add 2½ cups more flour and remaining ½ cup of water. Stir to blend. Knead with floured fingers (use up to ¼ cup more for kneading but as little flour as possible). Knead until the dough does not stick to the board or fingers.

3. Shape the dough into a ball and place it in a mixing bowl. Cover with a damp cloth. Let stand in a warm place about 3 hours, or until doubled in bulk.

4. Remove the cloth and punch the dough down. Add the baking powder and continue kneading, using up to ¼ cup of flour but as little as possible. Knead vigorously about 10 minutes.

5. Line a steamer at least 11 inches in diameter with a damp cloth. Shape the dough into an oval loaf about 8½ inches long. Place this on the damp cloth in the steamer, cover with the steamer lid and let rise in a warm place about 45 minutes. Place the steamer basket over boiling water in the steamer bottom and steam 20 minutes. When cooked, the loaf will be pure white but firm to the touch. Let cool.

6. When cool, slice the loaf lengthwise down the center. Cut crosswise into about 22 slices, each about ¾-inch thick. Let stand in the steamer basket.

7. Five minutes before serving, cover and heat over boiling water about 5 minutes. Serve with pork and duck dishes.

Yield: 8 banquet servings.

About Chinese Fire Pots

Authentic fire pots are available at certain stores in Chinatown, including the Oriental Country Store, 12 Mott Street. The costs vary, but a thirteen-inch fire pot at the Country Store is priced at $69.95.

Electric skillets can be used in place of a genuine fire pot. Or use any utensil you normally use for making sukiyaki.

If you use an authentic fire pot with charcoal, make certain the room in which you cook is well ventilated because of the fumes from the charcoal. Also make certain the fire pot is placed on a heat-proof pad. Do not place it directly on a fabric or wooden surface. It may be placed on a wooden table provided there is insulation between the fire pot and the table top. The commercial pad known as a Flame-tamer makes an excellent pad or insulation for the fire pot.

Chinese fire pot

If you do not intend to make the fire pot, remember that the fish balls, shrimp balls and pork balls are delicious when added to simmering chicken broth. To the same soup you may add sprigs of watercress, spinach and so on.

How to assemble ingredients for an eight-person Chinese fire pot

Arrange a layer of precooked Chinese cabbage on the bottom of the round food and liquid basin of a Chinese hot pot. Arrange drained bean thread over this. Arrange groups of precooked shrimp balls, fish balls, pork balls, sliced boned chicken, shrimp in the shell, rectangles of ham, soaked, drained black mushrooms, and quail eggs. Unless the fire pot is quite large, do not add all the ingredients at once, but add more as the portions are eaten.

When ready to cook, add a well-seasoned chicken broth to barely cover the ingredients. Add the clams. Cover with the fire-pot lid. Add burning charcoal to the fire-pot chimney and let the broth come to the boil. Sprinkle, if desired, with fresh coriander leaves. Serve with small bowls of rice and chopsticks.

Shrimp balls for a Chinese fire pot

½   pound shrimp in the shell
1   tablespoon cornstarch
½   egg white (empty white into a bowl, beat it lightly and measure it)
1   teaspoon salt
½   teaspoon sugar
1   tablespoon shao hsing or dry sherry wine

1. Peel and devein the shrimp. Combine all the ingredients in the container of a food processor. Blend thoroughly. Or chop finely with a knife or cleaver on a flat surface.

2. Fill a casserole about 2 inches deep with cold water. Gather a mass of the mixture into the hand. Close the fist slowly, squeezing a ball of the mixture out the top between the thumb and forefinger. Empty this into a wet spoon, scooping it neatly to form a more or less round ball. Drop the balls as they are made into the cold water. Continue until all the balls are formed.

3. Bring the water to the boil slowly. When the balls rise to the surface, remove them with a slotted spoon and drop them into a bowl of cold water. Let stand until ready to use in the fire pot. These balls can be refrigerated in cold water for a day or so longer and, when drained, may be served in clear chicken soup.

Yield: 10 to 12 balls.

Fish balls for a Chinese fire pot

½   pound fresh fish fillets, preferably yellow pike, or use another white-flesh, nonoily fish
1½   teaspoons salt
¼   cup water
1   egg white
1   tablespoon lard at room temperature, optional
1   tablespoon shao hsing or dry sherry wine
1   tablespoon finely chopped scallions
2   tablespoons finely minced cooked ham, preferably Smithfield
½   tablespoon chopped fresh ginger
    Freshly ground pepper to taste

1. The flesh of the fish should be firm. Trim away and discard any thin, flabby stomach flesh. Cut the fish into cubes and place in the container of a food processor. Blend thoroughly. Or chop finely with a knife or cleaver on a flat surface.

2. Add the salt, water, egg white and lard and blend.

3. Scrape the mixture into a mixing bowl and add the wine, scallions, ham, ginger and pepper.

4. Follow the instructions for shrimp balls for shaping and cooking. These balls may be kept refrigerated in cold water for a day or longer and may be used later in soup.

Yield: 10 to 12 balls.

Pork balls for a Chinese fire pot

½ *pound ground pork*
1 *egg yolk*
½ *egg white (empty white into a bowl, beat it lightly and measure)*
3 *tablespoons finely chopped water chestnuts*
1 *tablespoon grated fresh ginger*
1 *tablespoon finely chopped scallion*
1½ *teaspoons salt*
1 *tablespoon shao hsing or dry sherry wine*
½ *teaspoon sugar*
1 *tablespoon cornstarch*

1. Place the pork in a bowl and add the remaining ingredients. Stir in a circular fashion to blend. The more the mixture is stirred, the looser the meat will become and the pork balls will be more tender when cooked.

2. Follow the instructions for shrimp balls for shaping and cooking. These balls may be kept refrigerated in cold water for a day or longer and may be used later in soup.

Yield: 10 to 12 balls.

Miscellaneous ingredients for a Chinese fire pot

Trim off and discard the root end of one small head of Chinese cabbage (bok choy). Cut the cabbage leaves into 3-inch pieces. Drop into boiling water and cook about 8 minutes. Remove the pieces but reserve the liquid for cooking bean thread. Set cabbage aside.

Drop 2 ounces of bean thread (sometimes called Chinese vermicelli and cellophane noodles) into the boiling liquid in which the cabbage cooked. Or drop into boiling water. Simmer about 3 minutes. Add cold water to the kettle to stop the cooking action. Set aside until ready to use.

If 12 fresh quail eggs can be found (they are not common in local markets), put them in a skillet and add hot water to cover. Bring to the boil and simmer 30 minutes. Drain and peel. Or use 12 canned quail eggs directly from the can.

Drop 12 small-to-medium shrimp in the shell into boiling water and let water return to the boil. Let simmer 1 minute and let cool in the cooking liquid. If you want to be fastidious, prior to cooking the shrimp, make a small gash in the top shell of each shrimp and, using a small needle, insert it under the vein of each shrimp. Carefully lift out and discard the dark vein. Set shrimp aside.

Place 8 large dried black mushrooms in a mixing bowl and pour boiling water over them. Let stand until cool. Drain. Squeeze out most of the moisture. Cut or trim off the tough stems. Slice diagonally and set aside.

Cut ¼ pound bone-and-fat-free cooked ham, preferably Smithfield or Virginia ham, into 8 to 12 thin, bite-size rectangles. Reassemble the slices and set aside.

Cut 1 large or 2 small bamboo shoots into 12 thin bite-size slices. Reassemble the slices and set aside.

Scrub 16 littleneck or cherrystone clams. Arrange them on top of all the other ingredients in the fire pot. Cover and cook until clams open.

The Finest Chocolate Mousse

WITH PIERRE FRANEY

Once in a rare while, we discover a formula for a dish that seems the ultimate, the definitive, the ne plus ultra of its kind. Over the years we have printed recipes for a score or more desserts called mousse au chocolat, or chocolate mousse. We are convinced that the finest chocolate mousse creation ever whipped up in our kitchen is the one printed here. As if you didn't know, mousse means foam in French. This mousse is the foamiest.

Mousse au chocolat

(Chocolate mousse)

½   pound sweet chocolate
6   large eggs, separated
3   tablespoons water
¼   cup sweet liqueur such as chartreuse, amaretto, mandarine or Grand Marnier
2   cups heavy cream
6   tablespoons sugar
    Whipped cream for garnish
    Grated chocolate for garnish

1. Cut the chocolate into ½-inch pieces and place the chocolate in a saucepan. Set the saucepan in hot, almost boiling water and cover. Let melt over low heat.

2. Put the yolks in a heavy saucepan and add the water. Place the saucepan over very low heat while beating vigorously and constantly with a wire whisk. Experienced cooks may do this over direct heat such as a low flame or electric burner. It may be preferable, however, to use a metal disc such as a Flame-tamer to control the heat. In any event, when the yolks start to thicken, add the liqueur, beating constantly. Cook until the sauce achieves the consistency of a hollandaise or a sabayon, which it is. Remove from the heat.

3. Add the melted chocolate to the sauce and fold it in. Scrape the sauce into a mixing bowl.

4. Beat the cream until stiff, adding 2 tablespoons of the sugar toward the end of beating. Fold this into the chocolate mixture.

5. Beat the whites until soft peaks start to form. Beat in the remaining sugar and continue beating until stiff. Fold this into the mousse.

6. Spoon the mousse into a crystal bowl and chill until ready to serve. When ready to serve, garnish with whipped cream and grated chocolate.

Yield: 12 or more servings.

Spring Means Shad

WITH PIERRE FRANEY

There is one sign of spring infinitely more welcome to a dedicated and fish-loving gastronome than the first robin on the lawn, the first jonquil under the trees. That is the succulent shad and, it goes without saying, shad roe. The sad thing about the shad season is its uncommon brevity. Whereas most fish in Atlantic waters may be had in one quantity or another throughout the year, shad comes in like a grace note or a rainbow and seems to disappear just as quickly.

Shad and shad roe, properly prepared, are delectable in any form. Shad roe, in particular, is perfection when poached in butter, turning once, until done, then served with a little melted butter, parsley and lemon juice. That plus toast.

Perhaps the ultimate way with shad and the roe are to cook them together in one glorious dish as outlined here. The shad fillets are filled sandwich-fashion with the roe and a fish mousse. When cooked, the dish is sliced and served with a white wine sauce.

Shad Stuffed with Shad Roe

  2   *shad fillets*
3½ *cups mousse of fish (see recipe)*
  1   *pair shad roe*
  5   *tablespoons butter*
  2   *tablespoons finely chopped shallots*
      Salt and freshly ground pepper
  1   *cup dry white wine*
  2   *cups cream sauce for stuffed shad (see recipe)*

1. Preheat the oven to 400 degrees.

2. Place the 2 shad fillets skin-side down on a flat surface. Open up

the "flaps" of each fillet and spoon half
the fish mousse down the center of
1 fillet, smoothing it over.

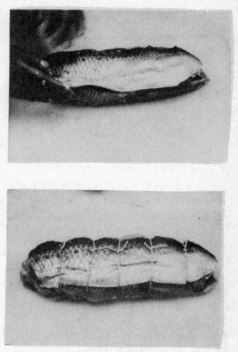

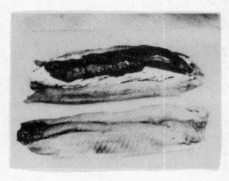

3. Separate the 2 sections of 1
pair of shad roe and arrange them
neatly lengthwise over the mousse.

6. Tie the package neatly to keep
it intact.

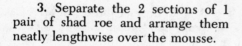

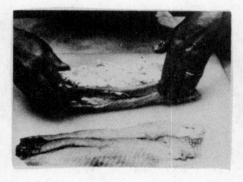

4. Spoon the remaining mousse
over the roe, smoothing it over. Bring
up the "flaps" of the filled fillet to
make "sides."

5. Carefully place the other shad
fillet, skin-side up and flaps down, to
completely enclose the filling.

7. Grease a baking dish (our oval
dish measured 10- by-16-inches) with 3
tablespoons butter and sprinkle with 2
tablespoons finely chopped shallots.
Sprinkle with salt and pepper to taste
and lay the fish in the dish.

8. Sprinkle the fish with salt and pepper and dot with 2 tablespoons butter. Pour the white wine over the fish and cover with foil. Bring to the boil on top of the stove and place in the oven. Bake 45 minutes.

9. Cut off and discard the strings. Pour the liquid from the fish into a saucepan and prepare the sauce. Keep the fish warm. Cut into crosswise slices and serve with the sauce.

Yield: 8 or more servings.

Mousse of fish

1 *pound fillet of flounder, sole or rockfish*
  Salt and freshly ground pepper
1 *large egg*
1½ *cups heavy cream*
.3 *tablespoons chopped chives*

1. Cut the fish into cubes and place in the container of a food processor or electric blender. If a blender is used, it may be necessary to do this in 2 steps, dividing the ingredients before blending.

2. Add salt and pepper to taste and process the fish until smooth, but without overblending.

3. Add the egg and blend briefly. Gradually add the cream while blending. Spoon the mixture into a mixing bowl and add the chives.

Yield: About 3½ cups.

Cream sauce for stuffed shad

In a saucepan, boil the liquid from the cooked fish over high heat until reduced by half. Add 1½ cups heavy cream. Cook 10 minutes and strain (if liquid accumulates from the fish as it stands, add this to the saucepan). Cook the sauce down about 5 minutes longer and add 1 tablespoon of lemon juice. Swirl in 1 tablespoon of butter and add salt and pepper to taste.

Yield: About 2 cups.

March

THE ZIGZAG of subjects that appeared in March might have been to some minds curious. The columns ranged from the "odd parts" of animals to the brilliant talents of Alain Chapel, considered by some to be the greatest chef in all of France; from the uses of leftover foods and inexpensive dishes to deep-fried bread boxes filled with creamy delights—a palatal pleasure recalled from years ago on a visit to Le Grand Véfour restaurant. We have often stated that a "gourmet" dish is beyond definition, except to say that it is any food well and honestly made—one that tempts the appetite and gratifies the soul when it is partaken. Such would be those fabulous and rich bread boxes filled with a shrimp in tomato cream sauce. We also find a great deal of sensual gratification in something as humble and delectable as shepherd's pie.

Special mention should be made of Alain Chapel's devastatingly good baked mousse of chicken livers, listed on his menu in Mionnay, France, as gateau de foies blonds. This is one of the most beautiful, tempting and sublime foods ever conceived in a French kitchen. It is gluttonously rich in calories, but the kind of dish, once tasted, to be remembered forever.

Chitterlings and Other Odd Parts

Confession is not only balm for a critic's soul. It acts as a hedge against the slings and arrows of readers who would pick up paper and pen and accuse you of shallow memory.

Thus, I confess that whenever the odd parts of an animal are the subject at hand, there is an irresistible urge to quote an observation found years ago in the *Wise Encyclopedia of Cookery* (William H. Wise & Company, 1971). It should, in fact, be added to any list of "Great Quotations about Food."

Specifically, the quotation has to do with tripe, but it is pertinent to those splendid, enormously edible odd parts of the animal that are also known as offal, innards, variety cuts, variety meats and so on.

"Tripe," the unknown author wrote, "like certain alluring vices, is enjoyed by society's two extremes, the topmost and the lowermost strata, while the multitudinous middle classes of the world look upon it with genteel disdain and noses tilted. Patricians relished tripe in Babylon's gardens, plebeians have

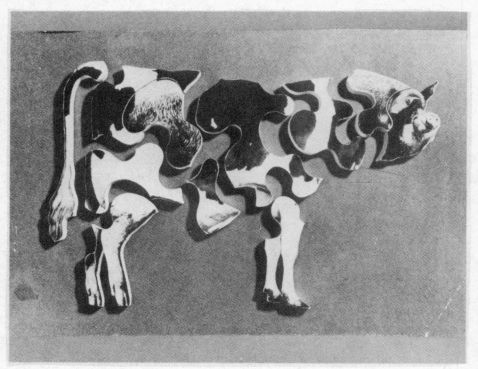

always welcomed it as something good and cheap, and always the peasant cook has taught the prince how to eat it."

Volumes could be written in praise of the scores of odd parts that can be purchased in Manhattan (and throughout America one would suppose) and turned into toothsome feasts for the knowledgeable.

The list is endless and includes one of our personal cravings, the famed French sausage known on home territory as andouillettes. These are made with chitterlings, the much publicized "soul food" of American blacks.

Chitterlings, the small intestine of swine, are available in many pork stores in America and, if you know of a good and conscientious butcher, he should be able to order them for you. To make them you need not only the chitterlings but the casings as well. These are thick and are known as hog bunk ends. Both the chitterling and casings are available at G. Esposito and Sons, 500 Ninth Avenue (at 38th Street). The cost of the hog bunk ends is 75 cents each (they are about thirty-six inches long).

Queue de Boeuf Forestière

(Oxtail ragout with mushrooms)

6 pounds oxtail cut into pieces
  Salt and freshly ground pepper to taste
2 cups coarsely chopped onion
2 cups coarsely chopped celery with leaves
2 cloves garlic, finely minced
1 teaspoon dried thyme
1 bay leaf
6 tablespoons flour
1 bottle (3 cups) dry red burgundy
2 cups water
3 cups fresh or canned beef broth
1 cup whole tomatoes, peeled and crushed
4 whole cloves
6 sprigs fresh parsley
10 or 12 whole carrots, about 1¼ pounds
1 pound mushrooms, preferably button mushrooms
2 tablespoons butter

1. Preheat the oven to 375 degrees.

2. The oxtail pieces should be well trimmed, leaving only a light layer of fat all around each piece. Sprinkle with salt and pepper. Use one or two large, heavy skillets and add the oxtail pieces, fat-side down. It is not necessary to add additional fat. Brown the pieces well on all sides, turning the pieces often, 40 to 45 minutes.

3. Transfer the pieces to a large, deep casserole or Dutch oven and continue cooking without adding liquid or fat about 10 minutes longer, stirring and turning the pieces in the casserole. Pour off any fat that accumulates.

4. Add the onion, celery, garlic, thyme and bay leaf and stir to distribute the ingredients. Sprinkle the flour evenly over the surface and stir to coat the ingredients. Add the wine, water, beef broth, tomatoes, salt, pepper, cloves and parsley.

5. Cover and bring to the boil on top of the stove. Place the casserole in the oven and bake 2 hours.

6. Meanwhile, trim and scrape the carrots. Quarter the carrots lengthwise and cut the pieces into 1½-inch lengths. There should be about 4 cups. Drop the carrots into boiling salted water to cover and cook about 5 minutes. Drain and set aside.

7. If button mushrooms are not used, quarter or slice the mushrooms according to size. Heat the butter in a skillet and add the mushrooms, with salt and pepper to taste. Cook, stirring, about 5 minutes. Set aside.

8. When the oxtail is tender, remove the pieces to another large bowl. Add the carrots and mushrooms. Put the sauce in which the oxtails cooked through a fine sieve, pushing the solids through as much as possible. Add the sauce to a casserole, add the oxtails and vegetables and cook briefly until piping hot. Serve hot with buttered noodles.

Yield: 8 to 12 servings.

Andouillettes

(French chitterling sausages)

10	*pounds ready-to-cook chitterlings (see note)*
½	*cup powdered mustard*
1	*cup finely chopped shallots*
½	*teaspoon nutmeg*
	Salt to taste
1	*teaspoon freshly ground pepper*
½	*cup dry white wine*
3	*to 4 yards sausage casings known as hog bunk ends (see note)*
½	*teaspoon dried thyme*
1	*large bay leaf*
1	*large onion, peeled*
2	*cloves garlic, peeled*
6	*whole cloves*
12	*peppercorns*
	Prepared mustard, preferably imported, such as Dijon or Düsseldorf

1. The chitterlings should be cleaned and ready to cook. Rinse them in numerous changes of cold water and drain well in a colander. Squeeze to extract much of the moisture. Pour the chitterlings into a large mixing bowl.

2. Add the powdered mustard, shallots, nutmeg, about 3 tablespoons of salt, the pepper and wine. Mix well with the hands.

3. Tie the end of a yard or so of hog bunk ends. Stuff the sausage casings with the seasoned chitterlings and tie the open end. Continue stuffing until all the chitterlings are used.

4. Put the sausages in a large kettle and prick each in several places with a needle. Add cold water to cover, thyme, bay leaf, onion, garlic, cloves, salt and peppercorns. Cover and bring to the boil. Simmer 2 hours. Drain.

5. Weight the sausages down with heavy, flat weights for at least 2 hours. Remove the weights and refrigerate. When ready to cook, grill the sausages, as many as necessary, about 20 minutes. The sausages may be grilled under the broiler but preferably they should be grilled over a charcoal or gas grill. Remember that before grilling the sausages are already cooked, so it is necessary to grill them just until they are golden brown on the outside and piping hot inside. Serve with mustard.

Yield: 24 or more servings.

Note: The chitterlings and hog bunk ends are available where specialty pork products are sold, including G. Esposito and Sons, 500 Ninth Avenue (at 38th Street).

Langue Ecarlate aux Epinards

(Boiled smoked tongue with spinach purée)

1 3½-pound smoked beef tongue
Spinach purée (see recipe)
Sauce piquante (see recipe)

1. Place the tongue in a kettle and add water to cover. Bring to the boil and simmer 40 minutes to the pound, about 2 hours and 20 minutes, or until the tongue is thoroughly tender.

2. Drain the tongue and, using a two-pronged fork to hold it, skin the tongue and neatly trim the base of the tongue with a sharp slicing knife. Cut the tongue against the grain to produce thin, neat, rectangular slices.

3. Serve hot with spinach purée and the hot sauce piquante spooned over the sliced tongue.

Yield: 8 or more servings.

Spinach purée

3 pounds or 3 10-ounce packages fresh spinach
4 cups water
Salt to taste
2 tablespoons butter
Freshly ground pepper to taste
½ cup heavy cream
⅛ teaspoon freshly grated nutmeg

1. Pick over the spinach. Tear off and discard any tough stems. Discard any blemished leaves. Rinse the spinach well and drain.

2. Bring the 4 cups of water to the boil and add salt to taste. Add the spinach and cook, stirring often, about 5 minutes. Drain well and let cool. Squeeze the spinach between the hands to remove the excess moisture. Divide it into 4 balls. Blend in a food processor or electric blender. There should be about 3 cups.

3. Heat 2 tablespoons butter and add the spinach, salt, pepper and cream. Add the nutmeg and serve piping hot.

Yield: 8 or more servings.

Sauce piquante
(A mustard and pickle sauce for tongue)

2 tablespoons butter
⅓ cup finely chopped onion
1 clove garlic, finely minced
1 tablespoon wine vinegar
½ bay leaf
1⅓ cup brown sauce, or canned beef gravy
½ cup fresh or canned beef broth
⅓ cup thinly sliced sour pickles, preferably imported cornichons, available where fine imported delicacies are sold
1 teaspoon prepared mustard, such as Dijon or Düsseldorf

Melt half the butter in a saucepan and add the onion and garlic. Cook until wilted and add the vinegar. Cook about 2 minutes and add the bay leaf, brown sauce, beef broth and pickles. Simmer 10 minutes and stir in the mustard. Swirl in the remaining tablespoon of butter. Serve hot with tongue or pork.

Yield: About 2¼ cups.

Deviled Pigs' Feet

4   pigs' feet, preferably large ones.
    Salt to taste
1   bay leaf
1   small onion, peeled and stuck with 2 cloves
2   sprigs parsley
12 crushed peppercorns
2   carrots, trimmed and scraped
3   ribs celery, rinsed and quartered
3   tablespoons imported mustard, such as Dijon or Düsseldorf
2   tablespoons dry white wine
    Freshly ground pepper to taste
2   cups fresh bread crumbs
8   tablespoons peanut, vegetable or corn oil
    Mustard

1. Place the pigs' feet in a kettle and add water to cover, salt, bay leaf, onion, parsley, peppercorns, carrots and celery. Bring to the boil and simmer about 3 hours, or until the pigs' feet are quite tender. Let stand until cool.

2. Preheat the oven to 400 degrees.

3. Remove the pigs' feet. Blend the 3 tablespoons of mustard with wine, salt and pepper to taste. Brush the pigs' feet with this. Roll the pigs' feet in fresh bread crumbs and arrange them on a rack. Dribble 2 tablespoons of oil over each pigs' foot. Bake

30 minutes or until crisp and golden brown. Serve with mustard on the side.

Yield: 4 servings.

Tripes Lyonnaise

(Tripe sautéed with onions)

1¾ pounds cleaned, ready-to-cook tripe
    Salt and freshly ground pepper to taste
4   whole allspice
2   whole cloves
2   sprigs fresh thyme, or 1 teaspoon dried
1   bay leaf
3   small ribs of celery, trimmed
1   carrot, trimmed and scraped
3   sprigs fresh parsley
1   large onion, peeled
3   tablespoons butter
1   clove garlic, finely minced
1   or 2 tablespoons red wine vinegar
2   tablespoons finely chopped parsley

1. Cut the tripe into 3 or 4 pieces and place it in a kettle. Add water to cover, salt, pepper, allspice, cloves, thyme, bay leaf, celery, carrot and parsley sprigs. Bring to the boil. Partly cover and simmer until tender. This may vary from a few minutes to an hour depending on the tripe. Test often. When cooked, the tripe should be quite tender but not mushy. Drain.

2. When the tripe is cool, shred it with a knife.

3. Chop the onion. There should be about 3 cups.

4. Heat the butter in a heavy skillet and add the tripe, salt and pepper. Cook, stirring, about 10 minutes. Add the onion and continue cooking and stirring often, shaking the skillet to prevent sticking. Cook until nicely browned or golden. Sprinkle with garlic, salt and pepper and stir. Sprinkle with vinegar and serve sprinkled with chopped parsley.

Yield: 2 to 4 servings.

Three-Star Chef

When Alain Chapel, generally acknowledged to be one of the ten or twelve finest chefs of France, arrived in my kitchen, he looked disconsolate.

"You will never know what happened," he explained. "I asked for calves' ears. They sent me three cows' heads."

This curious dilemma had its genesis a few days ago when he was invited to come into my kitchen to cook and to prepare any dish traditionally served in his famed restaurant in Mionnay, a small town only a few kilometers removed from Lyon, often called the gastronomic capital of France.

Chef Chapel had made considerable news in the world of food a few years ago when, in the short space of five years, his restaurant had gone meteorlike from one to three stars in the Guide Michelin. Three stars is, of course, the ultimate number awarded by the Guide.

When it was learned that Mr. Chapel had arrived in Manhattan for a three-week stint of cooking at the Four Seasons restaurant, it was with considerable enthusiasm he was invited to visit us. And early one morning he telephoned, his voice alive with excitement, to state that he had located a fantastic source for calves' ears and thus he would be pleased to prepare one of the dishes most in demand by visitors to his restaurant, oreilles de veau, persil frit, or stuffed calves' ears with fried parsley.

It was good news for we knew the dish by reputation to be one of his finest, most admired and talked-about creations. The cooked calves' ears are stuffed with a fantasy mixture and the whole thing breaded and baked until crisp.

"But the cows' heads arrived this morning and it was too late to go shopping. Those heads. They weighed eighty pounds apiece and the horns were still on, but the ears were missing."

In his frustration, he decided to prepare a main course of young chicken stuffed with truffles and served with a foie gras sauce and sea salt. This, too, would be a compromise, for he had really wanted to prepare another of his well-known specialties, poulette en vessie, which is the same truffle-studded chicken tightly enveloped in a well-cleaned pork bladder and cooked in a rich chicken broth. Even the most sophisticated butcher in this country does not sell vessie.

But Mr. Chapel would make many things on his visit. In addition to the chicken he would prepare what surely must be his ultimate triumph, one of the absolute cooking glories of this generation, his gateau de foies blonds, a blissfully silken, creamy, mousselike creation made with puréed chicken livers and the marrow of beef bones. It is indecently rich and served with a sinfully seductive sauce of lobster and cream.

As he went about his labors (he arrived at 11:30 in the morning) guests sat down to dine on the first course of sole with oysters four hours later), Mr. Chapel told us that he is married but has no children. He is 39 years old and began his kitchen training when he was 15 at his family's establishment. He told us that the greatest influence on his life—other than the chefs he had worked under—were the writings of Lucien Tendret, who lived in the late nineteenth century and who was, oddly, a lawyer, but a man with a consummate interest in dining well. From Tendret's works, the chef added, he had derived ideas for about 45 percent of the dishes for which his restaurant is noted, including the chicken liver gateau and the stuffed calves' ears.

Asked about the curious name of his family establishment, La Mère Charles, he stated it was owned by a woman who was married to a man named Charles. He said that as he approached his fortieth birthday, one of the things that gives him the greatest pleasure is that from now on there will be no La Mère Charles in Mionnay. It is now called Alain Chapel and all the guidebooks this year will make note of the fact.

Poulette Gros Sel

(Chicken with truffles)

5   *quarts chicken broth, or enough to cover 2 3-pound chickens*

2   *3-pound chickens, cleaned and ready for stuffing but with livers and chicken fat reserved*

3   *large fresh truffles, or 4 large canned truffles*
    Salt and freshly ground pepper to taste

3   *tablespoons water*

5   *or 6 very white and tender center ribs of celery with leaves*

6   *small leeks, trimmed, split and rinsed*

¾   *pound carrots, preferably about 20 baby carrots*

6   *turnips, peeled*

6   *tablespoons butter*

1   *cup heavy cream*

¼   *cup whipped cream*
¼   *cup fresh or canned foie gras*
    Sea salt

1. A day in advance, if desired, prepare the broth and have it ready.

2. Using the fingers, insert the hand between the skin and body of each chicken, starting at the neck cavity. Run the fingers between the breast, thighs and legs to separate the skin and flesh. This is easily done.

3. Should fresh truffles be available, peel them with a knife but reserve the parings. It is not necessary to peel canned truffles. Thinly slice the 3 fresh truffles or 3 of the canned truffles. Insert equal numbers of truffle slices between the skin and flesh of each chicken, stuffing into the thighs and legs as well.

4. Add the chicken livers to the container of a food processor. Add the truffle peelings (if fresh truffles are

used) or the remaining canned truffle, coarsely chopped. Add salt and pepper to taste and purée to make a fine thin paste.

5. Meanwhile, add the chicken fat and water to a small saucepan and cook, uncovered, until water evaporates and the solids give up the liquid chicken fat. Remove the solids.

6. Add the puréed liver mixture and cook briefly, stirring, just until liver loses its red color, about 45 seconds. Remove from the heat. Let cool.

7. Add half the liver mixture to the cavity of each chicken. Truss the chickens neatly and securely with string. If time permits, place the chickens in a dish and cover closely with a clean, damp but wrung-out cloth. Refrigerate overnight.

8. When ready to cook, bring the chicken broth to the simmer.

9. Cut both the celery ribs and leeks into thin, lengthwise julienne strips. There should be about 2 cups of celery and 4 cups of leeks. Place the shredded vegetables into separate saucepans. Add 3 cups of water to the leeks, add 2 cups of water to the celery.

10. If the carrots are small, simply trim and scrape them and add them to a saucepan. If large, quarter them lengthwise and cut them into 2-inch lengths. Cut the turnips into similar shapes. Place the carrots and turnips in separate saucepans. Add 2 cups of water to each.

11. Add to each saucepan with vegetables 1½ tablespoons butter and salt to taste. Bring them all to the boil and simmer about 5 minutes. To each saucepan add ½ cup of the chicken broth. Continue cooking until each

vegetable is tender but not mushy. Cooking times will vary. Set aside.

12. Meanwhile, remove the chickens from the refrigerator. Drain and discard any liquid that has accumulated in the bowl. Add the chicken to the simmering broth and bring to the boil. If the chickens are not wholly submerged, add more broth or water to cover. Partly cover and simmer 35 to 40 minutes. Remove from the heat and let stand 10 minutes.

13. As the chickens cook, ladle out 3 cups of the broth and bring to the boil over high heat. Cook down about 20 minutes, until only ¾ cup remains.

14. Add ½ cup of cream to this and cook about 5 minutes. Stir in the whipped cream.

15. Blend the foie gras to a paste, using a blender or food processor. Stir this into the sauce and add another ½ cup of cream. Bring to the boil and strain. Reheat briefly.

16. When ready to serve, remove the chickens. Remove and discard the trussing string.

17. Drain the vegetables. Spoon the carrots and turnips over the bottom of a large serving dish. Add the chickens and spoon the shredded celery and leeks over the top. Serve the chickens carved with equal portions of the vegetables spooned over. In addition, spoon over a little hot broth and the sauce. Serve with sea salt, preferably in a hand grinder, or serve with kosher salt.

Yield: 8 to 10 servings.

Gateau de Foies Blonds

(A baked mousse of chicken livers)

The mousse of chicken livers

¼ *pound firm, fresh marrow (see note)*
⅔ *pound chicken livers, picked over to remove any veins and connecting tissue*
1 *very small clove garlic*
1 *cup whole eggs, about 4*
⅔ *cup egg yolks, about 8*
2⅔ *cups heavy cream*
Salt and freshly ground pepper to taste

The sauce

1 *cooked 2-pound lobster (see recipe)*
¼ *cup butter, preferably lobster butter (see recipe)*
Salt and freshly ground pepper to taste
3 *tablespoons cognac or armagnac*
1 *cup heavy cream*
¼ *cup whipped cream*
3 *egg yolks*
2 *tablespoons water*
½ *pound melted butter*

1. Preheat the oven to 350 degrees.

2. It will take about 1½ pounds of marrow bones to produce about ¼ pound of marrow. To make the mousse, blend the marrow with the chicken livers and garlic clove in the container of a food processor. Beat lightly the whole eggs and egg yolks and stir the chicken liver mixture into the egg mixture. Add the cream, salt and pepper to taste and strain the mixture through a very fine sieve.

3. Butter a 6-cup mold and pour in the mixture (2 three-cup molds could be used). Line a deep baking dish large enough to hold the mold or molds with a layer of paper. Alain Chapel used one section of the *New York Times*. Pour in boiling water. Place the mold in the dish and place in the oven. Bake 1 hour or longer until the custard is slightly firm in the center. A straw inserted in the center will come out clean when withdrawn.

4. As the custard cooks, prepare the sauce.

5. Remove the meat from the tail and claws of the lobster and cut the meat into slices.

6. Heat the butter in a saucepan and add the lobster slices, salt and pepper. Add the cognac and ignite. Add the heavy cream and whipped cream and bring just to the boil.

7. Prepare the egg yolks like a hollandaise. Place them in a saucepan and add the water. Cook, beating vigorously over high heat or hot water until they are thickened and pale yellow. Gradually spoon the clear liquid from the melted butter into the sauce, beating constantly. Pour out the white milky residue. Stir this into the lobster and heat without boiling.

8. Unmold the mold and spoon the lobster sauce over each serving.

Yield: 8 to 10 servings.

Note: If you wish to butcher your own, buy marrow bones and carefully crack them with a cleaver so that they break in half and the marrow can be easily removed.

Boiled lobster

4 *quarts water*
3 *onions, peeled and quartered*

3 carrots, scraped and quartered
4 cloves garlic, unpeeled and
   lightly crushed
6 sprigs fresh parsley
2 sprigs fresh thyme, optional
   Salt to taste
12 peppercorns, crushed
1 bottle (3 cups) dry white wine
1 2-pound live lobster

1. Combine the water, onions, carrots, garlic, parsley, thyme, salt and peppercorns in a kettle large enough to hold the lobster and bring to the boil. Simmer 10 minutes.

2. Add the wine and return to the boil. Cook 5 minutes.

3. Add the lobster and simmer 20 minutes, covered. Remove from the heat and let stand 10 minutes longer. Drain.

Lobster butter

1 cooked lobster carcass, plus
   any excess trimmings, coral
   and so on

¾ pound butter at room temperature
6 cups water, approximately

1. Pound the carcass with a mallet and/or chop it finely with a cleaver. Add it to the container of a food processor and add the butter. Blend well.

2. Scrape the mixture into a saucepan and heat, stirring. Cook, stirring, until a nice "brown" or nutty smell comes from the saucepan. Add water to cover to a depth of about 1 inch over the top of the butter mixture. Bring to the boil and remove from the heat.

3. Strain the mixture through a fine sieve, using a wooden spoon to extract as much liquid from the solids as possible.

4. Let cool, then chill. The butter will harden on top. Remove the butter and discard the water. This butter will keep for more than a week in the refrigerator and can be frozen.

Yield: About ¾ pound.

The Virtues of Leftovers

WITH PIERRE FRANEY

There are many people of taste in this world who prefer a cold turkey sandwich to a freshly carved bird, or hunger more for cold sliced steak with mustard than a slab of sirloin hot from the grill. Leftovers, we aver, have virtues all their own and can be an end in themselves. Our enthusiasm is evidenced by the heartily endorsed recipes on this page. One is for leftover chicken or turkey metamorphosed into croquettes to be served with a fresh mushroom sauce; the other for leftover ham transmuted into another variety of croquette, this to be served with a simply made tomato sauce. What's more, with a bit of ingenuity, other leftover foods may be substituted in these recipes for the chicken or ham.

Chicken or Turkey Croquettes

3½ cups coarsely chopped cooked chicken or turkey meat, including skin
2 tablespoons butter
3 tablespoons finely minced onion
3 tablespoons flour
1½ cups chicken broth
Salt and freshly ground pepper
¼ teaspoon freshly grated nutmeg
3 drops Tabasco sauce
3 egg yolks
Flour for dredging
1 egg lightly beaten
3 tablespoons water
1½ cups fine, fresh bread crumbs
Peanut, vegetable or corn oil for deep frying
Mushroom sauce (see recipe)

1. Prepare the chicken or turkey and set aside. The chopped pieces, incidentally, should be no more than ¼ inch in diameter.

2. Melt the butter in a saucepan and add the onion, stirring to wilt. Sprinkle with flour and stir with a wire whisk until blended. Add the broth, stirring rapidly with the whisk. Stir in the chicken. Add salt and pepper to taste, nutmeg and Tabasco. Remove the sauce from the heat and add the yolks, stirring vigorously with the whisk. Cook briefly, stirring, and remove from the heat.

3. Spoon the mixture into a dish (a dish measuring 8-by-8-by-2-inches is convenient) and smooth it over. Cover with a piece of buttered wax paper and refrigerate, preferably overnight.

4. Remove the paper and, using the fingers, divide the mixture into 12 to 14 portions. Shape into balls and roll lightly in flour. The portions may

be shaped finally into balls or cylinders. When smooth on the surface and neatly coated with flour, dredge in the whole egg combined with the 3 tablespoons water, and then in bread crumbs. Arrange on a rack and chill until ready to cook.

5. Heat the oil and, when it is hot, add the balls or cylinders, a few at a time. Cook 2 or 3 minutes or until golden and cooked through. Serve hot with mushroom sauce.

Yield: 6 to 8 servings.

Mushroom sauce

1   tablespoon butter
2   tablespoons finely minced
    onion
4   medium-size mushrooms,
    about ¼ pound, cut into small
    cubes
    Salt and freshly ground pepper
2   tablespoons flour
1   cup chicken broth, fresh or
    canned
½   cup heavy cream

1. Melt the butter in a saucepan and add the onion. When wilted, add the mushrooms and cook until they give up their liquid. Cook until liquid evaporates and sprinkle with salt and pepper to taste.

2. Sprinkle with flour, stirring with a wire whisk. When blended, add the broth, stirring rapidly with the whisk. When blended and smooth, continue cooking, stirring occasionally, about 15 minutes. Add the cream and simmer about 5 minutes longer.

Yield: About 2 cups.

Ham Croquettes

4   cups coarsely chopped cooked
    ham (or leftover beef, lamb,
    pork)
3   tablespoons butter
3   tablespoons finely chopped
    onion
¼   cup flour
1½ cups milk
3   egg yolks
¼   teaspoon freshly grated nut-
    meg
    Salt and freshly ground pep-
    per
    Flour for dredging
1   egg lightly beaten
3   tablespoons water
1½ cups fine, fresh bread crumbs
    Peanut, vegetable or corn oil
    for deep frying
    Tomato sauce (see recipe)

1. Prepare the meat and set it aside. The chopped pieces, incidentally, should be no more than ¼ inch in diameter.

2. Melt the butter in a saucepan and add the onion, stirring with a wire whisk. Add the flour, stirring to blend. When blended, add the milk, stirring rapidly with the whisk. When blended and smooth, add the meat. Bring to the boil and remove from the heat.

3. Add the yolks, stirring rapidly with the whisk. Return to the heat and cook briefly. Add the nutmeg, salt (if the ham is salty, do not add salt) and pepper to taste. Spoon the mixture into a dish and cover closely with buttered wax paper. Refrigerate, preferably overnight.

4. Remove the paper and, using the fingers, divide the mixture into 12 to 14 portions. Shape into balls and roll lightly in flour. The portions may be shaped finally into balls or cylinders. When smooth on the surface and neatly coated with flour, dredge in the whole egg combined with 3 tablespoons water and then in bread crumbs. Arrange on a rack and chill until ready to cook.

5. Heat the oil and, when it is hot, add the balls, a few at a time. Cook 2 or 3 minutes, or until golden and cooked through. Serve hot with tomato sauce.

Yield: 6 to 8 servings.

Tomato sauce

2   *tablespoons butter*
1½ *tablespoons finely chopped onion*
½   *teaspoon finely minced garlic*
2   *cups canned tomatoes that have been blended or sieved*
¼   *bay leaf*
    Salt and freshly ground pepper

1. Melt 1 tablespoon butter in a saucepan and add the onion and garlic, stirring. When wilted, add the tomatoes, bay leaf, salt and pepper to taste and cook, stirring occasionally, about 30 minutes.

2. Swirl in the remaining butter and serve hot.

Yield: About 2 cups.

Economy Fare

Rich man, poor man, fin bec or glutton, who would not save pennies at food markets and rejoice in his cunning? To be sure, truffles and cockscomb and plover's eggs offer undeniable delights. Foie gras, caviar and nightingale's tongues all have their place—if not in the kitchen at least in the literature. The mouth can salivate at the thought of a grouse ragout enriched with the aromas of La Tache and Romanée-Conti.

But who could grouse about a conscientiously, imaginatively made Swiss steak simmered with a bit of thyme and the least trace of a good and inexpensive dry white wine? A splendidly made shepherd's pie dating from the days beyond the Tudors is something to tempt the palate of any good shepherd who knows his potatoes as well as his sheep. Hamburgers lyonnaise or Salisbury steak? What's the difference? By one name or the other they can be delectable.

The trouble is the image of Salisbury steak in the American mind, an image that stems perhaps from a recipe that, I am told, was seriously used in the kitchen of one of New York's most famous hostelries—the recipe reads, "one pound ground beef, one pound bread crumbs, one pound water, one pound chopped onions and two eggs. Salt and pepper to taste."

There are many things to consider in economy cookery. Chicken is and seems always to have been the symbol of what to eat in times that test men's pocketbooks. And what a marvelous bird it is, a point that doesn't really require elaboration.

Many economy dishes link meat with starches such as potatoes and beans, and this is no mean thing where taste is concerned. Such a marriage is the basis for some of the finest peasant or country cooking on this earth, and name me the chef who, on a day-to-day basis, would not choose to dine on such fare rather than his silken sauces. The latter are for fêtes and special occasions.

An haricot of lamb or lamb stew with beans can be, in its own way, sublime. And speaking of lamb, breast of lamb when available is one of the principal bargains at meat counters today. We recently purchased a three-and-one-half-pound stuffed ready-to-cook breast of lamb and the cost was $3.33. Topped with a few bread crumbs, chopped parsley and a little garlic during the final few moments of baking, it was elegant to the taste and served six amply.

To speak of bargains, however, the ragout of chicken giblets outlined here beats all. Less than two pounds of gizzards and hearts (cost, $1.59) simmered with potatoes and other vegetables in a light tomato sauce served eight. And where inexpensive dining is concerned, sauerkraut with pork hocks and sausages can be a winner.

Shepherd's Pie

2½ pounds raw or cooked ground lamb
3   tablespoons butter
2   cups chopped onion
2   teaspoons finely chopped garlic
½   teaspoon thyme
1   bay leaf
    Salt and freshly ground pepper to taste
2   tablespoons flour
1   cup crushed tomatoes
½   cup water
¼   cup finely chopped parsley
2   pounds potatoes
2   cups milk
½   cup grated Gruyère or Swiss cheese

1. Prepare the lamb and set it aside.

2. Heat 1 tablespoon butter in a casserole and add the onion, garlic and thyme. Cook briefly until onion wilts. Add the meat and bay leaf. Cook, stirring to break up lumps in the meat. Add salt and pepper to taste and sprinkle with flour. Add the tomatoes and water, stirring. Cover and cook 30 minutes. Add the parsley.

3. Meanwhile, peel the potatoes. Cut them into quarters and add them to a saucepan. Cover with cold water and salt to taste. Bring to the boil and simmer until tender, about 20 minutes.

4. Drain the potatoes and put them through a food mill. Bring the milk to the boil. Add the milk to the potatoes and beat in the remaining butter.

5. Spoon the lamb stew into a baking dish (a dish measuring about 8½-by-13½-by-2-inches is a suitable size). Top with the mashed potatoes and smooth them over. Sprinkle with cheese.

6. When ready to cook, preheat the oven to 400 degrees.

7. Bake 20 minutes. Run under broiler to glaze. Serve hot.

Yield: 6 to 8 servings.

Hamburgers Lyonnaise

2   tablespoons butter
¾   cup finely chopped onion
2   pounds ground beef
1   cup bread crumbs
1   egg, lightly beaten
    Salt and freshly ground pepper to taste
¼   cup heavy cream or water
2   tablespoons oil
1½ cups thinly sliced onions
1   clove garlic, finely minced
1   tablespoon flour
2   cups fresh or canned beef broth
½   bay leaf

1. Heat half the butter in a skillet and add the chopped onion. Cook until starting to brown.

2. Put the meat in a mixing bowl and add the bread crumbs, egg, salt, pepper and chopped onion. Blend well, adding the cream gradually.

3. Shape the mixture into 6 oval patties. Flatten them. They should be about 1 inch thick.

4. Heat the oil in a heavy skillet large enough to hold the patties in one layer. Add the patties and brown well on one side. Turn and brown on the other side, cooking about 10 minutes on the second side.

5. Meanwhile, heat the remaining butter in a saucepan and add the sliced onion and garlic. When browned, add the flour and stir. Add the broth, stirring rapidly with the whisk. Add the bay leaf, salt and pepper to taste. Cook 10 minutes.

6. When the hamburgers are cooked, transfer them to a hot platter. Pour the fat from the skillet in which they cooked. Add the onion sauce to the pan, stirring to dissolve the brown particles that cling to the bottom and sides of the pan. When piping hot and boiling, pour the sauce over the meat and serve.

Yield: 6 servings.

Ragout of Chicken Giblets

1¾	*pounds combined chicken gizzards and hearts*
2	*tablespoons butter*
	Salt and freshly ground pepper to taste
1	*cup finely chopped onion*
1	*clove garlic, finely minced*
2	*tablespoons flour*
½	*cup dry white wine*
3	*cups water*
2	*tablespoons tomato paste*
2	*sprigs fresh thyme, or 1 teaspoon dried*
1	*bay leaf*
2	*turnips, about ½ pound, cut into eighths*
2	*ribs celery, trimmed, halved and cut into 1½-inch lengths*
3	*carrots, trimmed, quartered and cut into 1½-inch lengths*

2	*potatoes, about 1 pound, cut into 1½-inch pieces to resemble french fries.*

1. Pick over the giblets. Rinse and drain well.

2. Heat the butter and add the giblets, salt and pepper. Cook about 10 minutes, stirring occasionally. Add the onion and garlic and cook briefly. Sprinkle with flour and stir in the wine, water, tomato paste, thyme and bay leaf.

3. Cover and cook about 5 minutes. Add the remaining ingredients, cover again and let simmer about 1 hour, or until tender.

Yield: 8 servings.

Parsleyed Roast Stuffed Breast of Lamb

1	*3¼- to 4-pound stuffed breast of lamb, available at times in many supermarkets*
	Salt and freshly ground pepper to taste
¼	*cup bread crumbs*
1	*clove garlic, finely minced*
1	*tablespoon finely chopped parsley*
1	*tablespoon finely chopped shallots*
½	*cup fresh or canned beef broth, or water*

1. Preheat the oven to 400 degrees.

2. Sprinkle the lamb with salt and pepper and place it flat-side down in a baking dish. Place in the oven and bake 1½ hours.

3. Blend the bread crumbs, garlic, parsley and shallots. Remove the lamb from the oven and sprinkle it uniformly on top with the crumb mixture.

4. Return the lamb to the oven and cook about 10 minutes longer, basting often.

5. Remove the lamb and pour off fat. Add the broth to the pan and stir to dissolve the brown particles that cling to the bottom and sides of the pan. Serve sliced with the pan gravy.

Yield: 6 servings.

Navarin d'Agneau

(A ragout of lamb)

2¼ *pounds lean shoulder of lamb, cut into 2-inch cubes and including a few rib bones*
 Salt and freshly ground pepper to taste
2 *carrots*
2 *ribs celery*
1 *or 2 white turnips*
2 *potatoes*
2 *cups water*
½ *cup chopped onion*
1 *clove garlic, finely minced*
½ *cup dry white wine*
2 *tablespoons tomato paste*
1 *bay leaf*
2 *sprigs fresh thyme, or ½ teaspoon dried*
½ *cup frozen peas (reserve the remaining peas for another use)*

1. Sprinkle the meat with salt and pepper and set aside.

2. Trim the carrots, celery, turnips and potatoes, peeling as necessary. Quarter the carrots and cut them into 1½-inch lengths. Cut the celery into pieces of the same size. Cut the turnips into ½-inch slices. Cut the slices into pieces the same size as the carrots.

3. Cut the potatoes into ½-inch slices. Cut the slices into "sticks" the size of french fried potatoes. Drop into cold water.

4. Heat a skillet large enough to hold the meat in one layer. Do not add fat. The meat has enough fat. Add the cubes of meat and cook to brown well on all sides, turning as necessary as the pieces give up fat. The browning will take from 10 to 15 minutes.

5. Transfer the pieces of meat to a heavy casserole and heat briefly, stirring.

6. Pour off the fat from the kettle in which the meat was browned. Add 1 cup of water and stir to dissolve the brown particles that may cling to the bottom and sides of the kettle. Set aside.

7. Add the onion and garlic to the meat and stir. Add the wine and cook briefly. Add the skillet liquid. Add the remaining cup of water, tomato paste, bay leaf and thyme. Bring to the boil and cook 1 hour.

8. Meanwhile, cover the carrots, celery and turnips with cold water and bring to the boil. Drain and set aside.

9. Drain the potatoes. Add them to a saucepan, cover with cold water and bring to the boil. Drain.

10. When the stew has cooked 1 hour add the carrot, celery and turnips. Cook 20 minutes.

11. Add the potatoes and cook 5 minutes longer.

12. Add the peas and continue to cook 5 minutes or until the potatoes are tender.

Yield: 6 to 8 servings.

Haricot d'Agneau

1   *pound small white dried beans, preferably California small white beans or Minnesota pea beans*
2¼ *pounds lean shoulder of lamb, cut into 2-inch cubes and including a few rib bones*
    Salt and freshly ground pepper to taste
¾   *cup chopped onion*
2   *cloves garlic, finely minced*
1   *14-ounce can tomatoes with tomato paste*
2   *sprigs thyme, or ½ teaspoon dried thyme*
1½ *bay leaves*
1   *small onion stuck with 2 cloves*
1   *large carrot, trimmed and scraped*

1. Soak the beans overnight in cold water to cover to a depth of 2 inches.

2. Sprinkle the lamb with salt and pepper. Heat a skillet large enough to hold the meat in one layer. Do not add fat. The meat has enough fat. Add the cubes of meat and cook to brown well on all sides, turning as necessary as the pieces give up fat. The browning will take from 10 to 15 minutes.

3. Transfer the pieces of meat to a heavy casserole and sprinkle with onion and garlic. Cook briefly. Add the tomatoes, 2 cups water, thyme, 1 bay leaf, salt and pepper. Cover and cook about 1½ hours.

4. Pick over the beans to remove any foreign material. Put the beans in a saucepan and add 8 cups water, half a bay leaf, onion stuck with cloves and whole carrot. Bring to the boil and simmer 1 to 1½ hours, skimming the surface as necessary. Test for doneness.

5. When the lamb is tender and cooked, drain the beans and remove the bay leaf and thyme sprigs. Remove and reserve the carrot.

6. Cut the carrot into ½-inch dice. Add the beans and carrot to the lamb stew. Cover and cook 10 minutes.

Yield: 8 servings.

Sauerkraut with Gin

3   *slices bacon, cut into small strips*
1   *clove garlic, finely minced*
1   *cup chopped onion*
3   *pounds pig's knuckles, cut crosswise through the bone into pieces about 1½ inches thick*
    Salt and freshly ground pepper to taste
2   *pounds sauerkraut*
1½ *cups chicken broth*
1   *cup dry white wine*
6   *small carrots, or 2 large carrots cut into quarters*
1   *bay leaf*
2   *tablespoons gin*
6   *peeled potatoes, about 1 pound*
1   *pound kielbasa (Polish sausage), or frankfurters*

1. Put the bacon in a deep skillet, Dutch oven or casserole and add the garlic and onion. Cook until wilted and arrange the pieces of pig's knuckles over in one layer. Sprinkle with salt and pepper.

2. Drain the sauerkraut well and add it. Add the broth, wine, carrots, bay leaf and gin. Cover and cook 30 minutes.

3. Add the potatoes, cover and cook 30 minutes longer. Turn the pieces of knuckles.

4. Cover and cook 10 minutes or until pork meat is tender. Add the kielbasa, cover and cook about 5 minutes. Turn off the heat and let stand about 15 minutes or until kielbasa is heated through.

Yield: 6 servings.

French Bread Boxes

It would be far easier to extricate a lure from the mouth of a game fish than eradicate the sights and flavors of certain dishes from my mind. These would include the first taste of a charlotte russe as a child; a breakfast of that utterly delectable fish listed on menus in Hawaii as mahi-mahi; a first platter of couscous with its mutton and vegetable stew one long-ago supper in Morocco; the spaghetti like baby angulas or eels served sizzling from the stove in a bath of olive oil and garlic and hot pepper.

The list would most assuredly include a dish that left us wild-eyed in our elation in Paris almost thirty years ago. The circumstances that surrounded that meal could not have diminished the pleasure of the evening.

I had been in Paris for several weeks taking a language course at the well-known Alliance Francaise on the Boulevard Raspail. As with most of my colleagues, my spending money was scarce and I thought twice before taking the metro. Far cheaper to walk. I had never had enough sous to entertain even a remote fantasy about dining in one of the luxury restaurants of Paris. And then one morning a miracle occurred in the form of a sizable and wholly unexpected check. Excitedly, I cornered a friend or two and invited them to join me for dinner at Le Grand Véfour, then at the height of its fame and an establishment known to us only by its international reputation.

In any event, the thing about that evening at Le Grand Véfour, the snare that has clung so tenaciously in my mind, was the first course, listed on the menu as Toast de Crevettes Rothschild, a crisp, buttery, hollowed-out bread filled with very small shrimp in a delicate cream, white wine and tomato sauce.

A short while ago, my friend and collaborator, Pierre Franey, and I set about duplicating that dish in my East Hampton kitchen. The first efforts were excellent in all but one respect. We used a store-bought loaf of bread to cut out the toast "boxes" or casings, and while the appetizer filled with shrimp in the tomato and cream sauce was eaten with gusto by those assembled around the table, we decided that a homemade loaf of bread would be infinitely preferable both from the standpoint of flavor (American white bread is far too sweet) and texture.

It was at about this time that we dined one evening with friends on Shelter Island, Clifton and Jane Phalen. She served cubes of toasted bread that were remarkable. Jane Phalen told us that she had made the bread herself from a recipe given to her by the chef-owner of a small hotel, the Chateau Philip, in St. Nicolas de la Balerme. The hotel's restaurant rates one star in the Guide Michelin.

The bread had been baked in special pans, traditional in France, which she had purchased at the Bridge Kitchenware Corporation in Manhattan. They are black tin pans with sliding lids and the bread baked in them comes out of the oven golden brown all over and in a loaf shape.

Mrs. Phalen gave us the recipe (it was listed in grams and liters and was sufficient to bake a dozen or more loaves, enough for a hotel dining room).

We availed ourselves of the Bridge bread pans and over the next few weeks we must have made a dozen or more experiments with the recipe. We tailored the recipe to fit two pans (the bread the pans produce, incidentally, is known in France as pain de mie). We also used it for long loaves baked in long French bread molds.

The bread dough as printed here is the most easily made and produces some of the best bread we've ever encountered from home ovens. We offer the recipes for various loaves and instructions for making hollowed-out "boxes" to be baked for various fillings.

French Bread Dough

7 cups flour, approximately
½ cup milk
2 cups water
1½ tablespoons salt
4 tablespoons butter
2 envelopes granular yeast

1. Place the 7 cups flour in a mixing bowl or, preferably, in the bowl of an electric mixer outfitted with a dough hook.

2. Combine the milk and 1¾ cups of water in a saucepan. Add the salt and butter and heat, stirring, just until the butter melts. Do not boil. Let cool.

3. Combine the yeast with the remaining ¼ cup of lukewarm water and stir to dissolve. Add the yeast to the flour, stirring constantly with the dough hook or with a wooden spoon.

4. Add the liquid, stirring constantly with the dough hook or beating vigorously with the spoon. Knead with the dough hook about 5 minutes. Or turn the dough out onto a lightly floured board and knead about 10 minutes, adding flour as necessary, but always using as little flour as possible.

5. Shape the dough into a ball and put it in a large, clean mixing bowl. Stretch plastic wrap over the bowl and place in a warm place until doubled in bulk, 2 to 3 hours.

6. Shape and bake the dough according to any method outlined below.

Yield: 2 loaves.

French bread loaves baked in oval molds

Prepare the dough as outlined. When doubled in bulk, turn it out onto a lightly floured board and knead briefly. Divide it in half or into thirds and shape it into 2 or 3 long ropes, approximately the same length as the bread molds.

Grease the molds lightly and arrange one length of bread in each. Cover loosely with a clean dry kitchen towel and let rise in a warm place until double in bulk. Remove the towel and give the dough 3 parallel and diagonal slashes across the top with a razor or very sharp knife.

Meanwhile, preheat the oven to 450 degrees. Bake 45 minutes for the double-loaf mold or 40 minutes for the triple-loaf mold, turning the molds as necessary so that the loaves brown evenly. Remove from the oven and remove the loaves. Place on a rack to cool.

Yield: 2 or 3 loaves.

Note: This bread is improved by introducing steam into the oven. You may use a pan on the bottom of the oven and pour boiling water into it the moment the mold is placed in the oven.

French sandwich loaves

Prepare the dough as outlined. When doubled in bulk, turn it out onto a lightly floured board and knead briefly. Divide it in half and shape into 2 oval loaves. Place each of these into buttered sandwich bread pans (see note), measuring about 10½-by-3¾-by-3½-inches, and seal with the lids. Let rise until pan is filled with dough, about 1 hour. Do not open the pans, but slide lid gently just a fraction of an inch and you can tell if dough is sticking to the top. Meanwhile, preheat the oven to 450 degrees. Bake 45 minutes. Remove cover, unmold onto a rack and let cool.

Yield: 2 loaves.

Note: French sandwich bread pans are available at the Bridge Kitchenware Corporation, 212 East 52nd Street. The cost is $11.95 each.

French bread rolls

Prepare the dough as outlined. When doubled in bulk, turn it out onto a lightly floured board and knead briefly. Sprinkle two baking sheets liberally with corn meal. Cut or pull off pieces of dough, about ½ cup or slightly more in volume. Shape these into smooth rounds and arrange them on the baking sheets. Cover loosely with a clean, dry towel. Let rise until double in bulk.

Meanwhile, preheat the oven to 450 degrees.

Remove the towel. Using a razor or very sharp knife, cut a cross in the top of each bread roll. Place in the oven and bake until browned and cooked through, 35 to 40 minutes. Remove from the oven and remove the rolls. Place on a rack to cool.

Yield: 16 to 20 bread rolls.

Note: These rolls are improved as they bake by introducing steam into the oven. You may use a pan on the bottom of the oven and pour boiling water into it the moment the baking sheets are placed in the oven.

Crevettes Belle Aurore

(Shrimp with tomato cream sauce)

6   *unbaked bread casings (see instructions)*
¾   *pound shrimp, about 24 medium-size*
2   *tablespoons butter*

2 tablespoons finely diced carrot
2 tablespoons finely minced onion
2 tablespoons finely minced celery
2 tablespoons finely minced shallots
1 tablespoon flour
½ cup dry white wine
2 tablespoons tomato paste
1 cup milk
   Salt and freshly ground pepper to taste
1 cup heavy cream
   Tabasco sauce to taste
2 tablespoons cognac

1. Prepare the bread casings and set aside for baking later.

2. Peel and devein the shrimp. Set aside.

3. Heat half the butter and add the carrot, onion, celery and 1 tablespoon of shallots. Cook about 3 minutes and sprinkle with flour. Stir in wine and tomato paste.

4. Bring the milk to the boil and add it, stirring with a wire whisk. Add salt and pepper to taste and cook 10 minutes. Add the cream and Tabasco and cook down over high heat about 20 minutes.

5. Heat the remaining butter and add the remaining shallots. Add the shrimp, salt and pepper to taste and cook about 3 minutes, or just until the shrimp turn red. Add the cognac and ignite it. Blend the sauce with the shrimp.

6. Bake the bread casings according to instructions. Fill with equal portions of the hot shrimp mixture and serve immediately.

Yield: 6 servings.

Bread casings

1 1-pound loaf unsliced white bread
4 tablespoons butter

1. Neatly slice off the ends of the loaf. Cut the center of the loaf into 4 1½-inch-thick slices.

2. Neatly trim off the sides of each slice to make a square. Use excess pieces of bread to make bread crumbs. Refrigerate or freeze the crumbs for future use.

3. Arrange the squares of bread on a flat surface. Use a sharp, serrated knife and carefully cut around the inside of the squares to make a "wall" or border about ½-inch thick or slightly less. Slice down to about ½ inch from the bottom of the square.

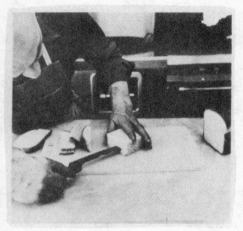

4. Hold the knife parallel to the work surface. Insert it into the bread ½ inch from one side of the bread or the other. Slice through to within ½

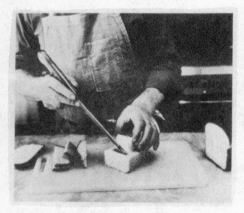

inch of the other side. This should produce a removable center square of bread. Remove this. Use it also to make bread crumbs for some other use. At this point the bread should be ready to bake and fill.

5. Brush the casing all over with 1 tablespoon of butter or slightly more.

6. Preheat the oven to 350 degrees. Place the buttered casings on a baking sheet and bake until golden brown on top, 8 minutes or longer. Turn the casings bottom side up and continue baking until nicely browned all over.

Yield: 4 toast casings.

Hachis de Volaille

(Creamed chicken)

6	*unbaked bread casings (see instructions)*
¾	*pound boneless, skinless chicken breast*
¼	*cup dry white wine*
1	*cup chicken broth*
3	*tablespoons chopped onion Salt and freshly ground pepper to taste*
½	*bay leaf*
3	*tablespoons butter*
3	*tablespoons flour*
1	*cup heavy cream*
⅛	*teaspoon nutmeg Pinch of cayenne pepper*
3	*large mushrooms, cut into ½-inch cubes*
½	*tablespoon finely chopped shallots*
1	*egg yolk*
½	*tablespoon lemon juice*
12	*asparagus tips, each about 3 inches long*
¼	*cup grated Parmesan cheese*

1. Prepare the bread casings and set aside for baking later.

2. Place the chicken in a saucepan and add the wine and broth, onion, salt, pepper and bay leaf. Bring to the boil and simmer 10 minutes. Let cool in the cooking liquid.

3. Remove the chicken and strain the liquid into another saucepan. Bring to the boil and cook down to 1 cup.

4. Cut the chicken into ½-inch cubes.

5. Heat 2 tablespoons of butter and add the flour, stirring with a wire whisk. When blended, add the reserved cup of liquid, stirring vigorously with the whisk. When thickened, simmer 10 minutes, stirring occasionally. Add ¾ cup of heavy cream. Add the nutmeg and cayenne.

6. Heat remaining 1 tablespoon of butter and add the mushrooms, shallots, salt and pepper. Cook until mushrooms are wilted and add remaining ¼ cup of heavy cream. Add the cubed chicken.

7. Add half the cream sauce to the mushroom and chicken mixture.

8. Add the egg yolk to the remaining sauce and stir. Cook about 30 seconds, stirring vigorously. Add the lemon juice.

9. Place the asparagus tips in a skillet and add cold water to cover. Bring to the boil and simmer 30 seconds. Drain.

10. Bake the bread casings as directed in the instructions for making them. Remove from the oven and heat the broiler.

11. Fill the casings with the hot creamed chicken mixture. Spoon the remaining sauce over. Garnish each serving with 2 asparagus tips. Sprinkle with Parmesan cheese and run briefly under the broiler.

Yield: 6 servings.

April

T S. ELIOT to the contrary, April was by no means the cruelest month. Come to think of it, it was one of the most joyous. It was a marvelous opportunity to sing the praises of the Swiss cheese known as gruyère, a cheese that is infinitely superior to that commonplace one with a hole traditionally known as Swiss.

April was also a time to give credit to John Montagu (through research we learned that he was something less than a gentleman in his private manners, morals and ethics, but as the fourth Earl of Sandwich, he did become the father of a kind of dish without which the world would be an infinitely poorer place).

In April we elaborated on the uses of leftover ham, we reported on the joys of dining on freshly caught trout, pan-fried over a charcoal fire in the Catskill mountains. But most of all, there was the pleasure of reminiscing on an Easter feast celebrated years ago in Athens in the great good company of our friends Leon and Aphrodite Lianides.

Ham Bonuses

WITH PIERRE FRANEY

In the next few days, the remains of that once plump and clove-studded Easter ham may loom rather large in the refrigerator. And while there is much to recommend in a cold ham sandwich—particularly when smeared with home-made mayonnaise or hot mustard—the moment may come when that, too, palls on the palate.

Leftover ham is, fortunately, a highly versatile kitchen commodity, yielding itself to wondrous variations. Ham and sauerkraut balls (they can also be made with leftover corned beef or a combination of ham and corned beef) are delicious; a well-made ham loaf with a sour cream and paprika sauce could tempt the most jaded appetites; and baked mushrooms, noodles and ham in a Mornay sauce is as edible as it is economical.

Ham and Sauerkraut Balls

4	teaspoons butter
1½	tablespoons flour
½	cup milk
½	pound cooked ham
½	pound sauerkraut
¼	cup finely chopped onion
½	teaspoon caraway seeds
2	teaspoons dry mustard
	Freshly ground pepper
2	egg yolks
1	egg
¼	cup water
	Salt
	Flour for dredging
1½	cups fresh bread crumbs
	Oil for deep frying
	Lemon wedges
	Hot mustard (see recipe), optional

1. Melt 3 tablespoons butter in a very small saucepan and add the flour, stirring with a wire whisk. Add the milk, stirring rapidly with the whisk. When blended and smooth, the sauce should be quite thick. Remove from the heat.

2. Chop the ham finely on a flat surface or grind it, using the medium blade.

3. Press the sauerkraut to extract most of the liquid.

4. Heat the remaining teaspoon of butter and add the onion. Cook, stirring, until wilted. Add the sauerkraut and cook briefly, stirring. Add the ham, caraway, dry mustard and pepper to taste. Add the white sauce. Blend thoroughly. Add the egg yolks, stirring rapidly. Cook about 1 minute, stirring, and remove from the heat.

5. Spoon into a mixing bowl and

smooth over the top. Cover with foil or plastic wrap and chill.

6. Using the fingers, shape the mixture into 28 or 30 balls.

7. Beat together the egg, water, salt and pepper to taste. Set aside.

8. Dredge the balls lightly all over with flour. Dip the balls into the egg mixture to coat well and finally in bread crumbs. Arrange on a rack.

9. When ready to cook, heat the oil for deep frying and cook the balls, turning as necessary, until golden brown and piping hot to the center. Drain and serve hot with lemon wedges and, if desired, hot mustard.

Yield: 28 or 30 balls.

Hot mustard

⅓   cup powdered mustard
2   tablespoons cold water, white wine, milk or beer
     A touch of salt

Blend together all the ingredients. Let stand at least 15 minutes to develop flavor before you use it.

Yield: ¼ cup.

Ham Loaf with Sour Cream and Paprika Sauce

1½   pounds cooked ham
1   tablespoon butter
1   clove garlic, finely minced
1   cup finely chopped onion
¼   pound mushrooms, cut into very small cubes, about 1¾ cups
½   cup finely chopped celery
     Freshly ground pepper

1   cup chicken broth
2   cups fine bread crumbs
2   whole eggs, lightly beaten
1   egg yolk
¾   cup heavy cream
¼   teaspoon finely ground nutmeg
2   tablespoons chopped parsley
     Sour cream and paprika sauce (see recipe)

1. Preheat oven to 400 degrees.

2. Cut the ham into cubes and grind it, using the medium blade of a food grinder or a food processor. Spoon it into a mixing bowl and set aside.

3. Heat the butter in a skillet and add the garlic, onion, mushrooms, and celery. Cook briefly until vegetables are wilted. Sprinkle with pepper to taste and cook about 15 minutes.

4. Add the chicken broth and cook about 3 minutes. Spoon the mixture into the bowl with the ham. Add the bread crumbs, the eggs beaten with the yolk, cream, nutmeg and parsley. Blend well.

5. Butter a 9-by-5-by-2¾-inch loaf pan and add the ham mixture. Smooth over the top and bake 45 minutes to 1 hour. Remove from the oven and let stand at least 30 minutes before serving. This is not a firm loaf, but it can be sliced. Serve sliced with sour cream and paprika sauce.

Yield: 6 to 8 servings.

Sour cream and paprika sauce

1   tablespoon butter
1   small clove garlic
¼   cup finely chopped onion
¾   cup finely chopped green pepper
2   teaspoons paprika

1   *tablespoon flour*
¾   *cup chicken broth*
½   *cup fresh or canned cooked*
    tomatoes
1   *cup sour cream*
    Salt
2   *tablespoons finely chopped*
    parsley

1. Heat the butter in a saucepan and add the garlic, onion and green pepper. Cook until vegetables are wilted and add the paprika and flour, stirring with a wire whisk. Add the broth and tomatoes and stir rapidly until thickened and smooth.

2. Stir in the sour cream and salt to taste and heat thoroughly, stirring. Stir in the parsley and serve hot.

Yield: About 2 cups.

Baked Mushrooms, Noodles and Ham, Mornay

3   *tablespoons butter*
3   *tablespoons flour*
3   *cups milk*
    Salt and freshly ground pepper
⅛   *teaspoon ground nutmeg*
⅛   *teaspoon cayenne pepper*
½   *pound grated cheddar cheese*
1   *cup heavy cream*
¼   *cup finely chopped onion*
¼   *pound mushrooms, cut into*
    small cubes, about 2 cups

½   *pound cooked ham, cut into*
    ½-inch cubes, about 1 ¾ cups
¾   *pound broad noodles*
2   *tablespoons port wine*
¼   *cup grated Parmesan cheese*

1. Preheat the oven to 450 degrees.

2. Heat 2 tablespoons of butter in a saucepan and add the flour, stirring with a wire whisk. When blended, add the milk, stirring rapidly with the whisk.

3. Add salt and pepper to taste, nutmeg, cayenne and the cheddar, stirring until the cheese melts. Add the cream and bring to the boil. Remove from the heat.

4. Melt the remaining 1 tablespoon of butter in a skillet and add the onion, stirring. When wilted, add the mushrooms and cook until wilted. Add the ham and heat through.

5. Meanwhile, cook the noodles according to package directions until tender. Take care not to overcook, for they will cook briefly later.

6. Add the cheese sauce to the ham mixture and add the wine. Bring to the boil. Drain the noodles well and add them to the mixture. Stir gently to blend.

7. Put the mixture into a baking dish (an oval dish measuring about 8-by-14-inches is appropriate). Sprinkle with the grated Parmesan. Bake 5 to 10 minutes. Run briefly under the broiler until nicely glazed. Serve immediately.

Yield: 6 to 8 servings.

A Greek Easter Feast

There is conceivably no religious festival on earth that is not in some way related to the eating of food and the drinking of wine. Historians are generally agreed that until a few centuries ago, most such celebrations were seasonally inspired and sacred by nature. We learned as children that the earliest of these ceremonies were agrarian in nature, when pagan man tilled the soil yet found himself helpless in the face of flood and drought and other caprices of nature. It was then that he appealed to and attempted to appease whatever gods might be out there.

Several years ago in Athens I found myself a most willing participant in the celebration of Easter, Greek-Orthodox fashion, with my friend Leon Lianides, the proprietor of New York's much esteemed Coach House restaurant, and his wife, Aphrodite.

It was Holy Saturday and a night of brilliant stars and moonlight. As midnight approached we strolled through otherwise darkened streets to a tiny church in an area of the city I no longer recall. Hundreds of other "pilgrims" had preceded us to the small plaza in front of the church to await the tolling of the bells that would signify the arrival of Easter morning. In the darkness someone handed us candles and as bells were tolled the priest emerged bearing a candle with which he kindled the candle of the closest member of those assembled.

"Christos anesti," he declared. "Christ is risen." The second candle illuminated a third, the third a fourth, individual to individual, chain-reaction fashion, until moments later that entire square was awash with light.

The second event of that evening remains equally vivid in memory. The Lianideses and I joined a Greek artist, Jannis Spyropolous, and his wife for a traditional Greek Easter feast. It consisted merely of soup and bread, but it was an incredibly delicious spread, including one dish with which I had had no prior knowledge. Of course, in years past, I had dined on avgolemono soup, that typical Hellenic specialty made of an abundantly rich broth thickened and flavored with lemon and eggs. But on this occasion I was told that the soup was named mayeritsa avgolemono and that in that moment in thousands and thousands of households throughout the island, celebrants would be dining on this particular soup made with the head of lamb and assorted other odd parts of the animal including the neck, knuckles and liver, all bones removed and the meats chopped fine. This, too, was flavored with egg and lemon.

The Easter bread was made with a lightly sweetened egg and yeast dough of surpassing flavor and texture. Red-dyed Easter eggs were offered the guests and these, too, are traditional, representing both the rebirth of the season and the resurrection of Christ. And those three elements were the sum and substance of that meal.

Earlier, when asked why the mayeritsa soup was so traditional in Greek homes at the beginning of Easter, Leon explained that roast baby lamb is the almost inevitable main dish for the principal feast of Easter day.

"In Greece," he said, "nothing is wasted. Tomorrow," he said, "we will dine here again and they will use the tripe of the lamb in another soup, avgolemono-style."

Later in the afternoon of that day we returned to the artist's home to devour another fine meal, a menu that seems throughout Greece to be fairly rigid in its structure. There was, in addition to the tripe and avgolemono soup, the roast lamb with artichokes, roast potatoes with fresh mint, a Greek salad and assorted rich desserts.

In the years that have ensued, we have often dined with the Lianideses in their handsome apartment in Riverdale. Both Leon and Aphrodite (his real name, by the way, is Napoleon and they have been called the Beauty and the Power) are marvelous cooks, and on occasion they have reproduced that memorable Easter menu. Aphrodite told us recently that on the occasion when the roast lamb was a bit too large for one oven, she would have it divided in half before roasting. She would roast one half and send the other to her sister's apartment to have it cooked. It would be served on a large platter with a garnish to disguise the earlier and necessary cleavage.

The Greek Easter recipes that follow are those the Lianideses have shared many times over the years with friends and all who have requested them.

Bourekakia

(Cheese puffs)

½ pound feta cheese, grated
1 3-ounce package cream cheese
1 tablespoon cream or rich milk
2 egg yolks
   Dash of nutmeg
½ pound phyllo pastry (see note)
½ pound sweet butter, melted

1. Preheat the oven to 350 degrees.

2. Combine the feta cheese, cream cheese, cream and egg yolks in a blender or whip until smooth in a bowl. Add nutmeg.

3. Remove the phyllo pastry from wrapping and place between heavy plastic wrap to prevent pastry from drying out.

4. Place one sheet of phyllo pastry on a flat surface and brush with melted butter and fold in half crosswise.

5. Cut folded pastry into 5 strips approximately 2-by-8-inches. Put ½ teaspoon of cheese mixture at one corner of each strip and fold to opposite side to form a triangle. Continue to fold each strip, keeping the

triangle shape. Continue until all pastry sheets and cheese mixture is used. Place on cooky sheet and bake for 15 minutes, or until golden brown.

Yield: About 50 puffs.

Note: These cheese puffs can be made in advance and frozen before baking. Place in 350-degree oven while still frozen and bake about 25 minutes.

Phyllo pastry is available at many specialty shops and stores that sell Greek foods, including Poseidon Confectionery Co., 629 Ninth Avenue (between 44th and 45th Streets) and Kassos Brothers, 570 Ninth Avenue (between 41st and 42nd Streets).

Greek Easter Bread

¾   *cup plus 1 tablespoon luke-warm milk*
½   *cup sugar*
2   *envelopes dry yeast*
5½ *to 6 cups flour*
1   *teaspoon salt*
½   *pound sweet butter, melted*
5   *eggs, lightly beaten*
1   *cooked red egg (see note)*
1   *egg yolk*

1. In a bowl combine ¾ cup luke-warm milk, sugar and yeast and let stand in a warm place for 10 minutes.

2. In a large bowl, combine 5½ cups flour and salt. Make a well in the center and add cooled melted butter and eggs. Add yeast mixture and blend to form a soft sticky dough. Knead, adding a little more flour as necessary, about 5 minutes, until dough is smooth and satiny. Place in a buttered bowl and stretch a sheet of plastic wrap over the bowl. Set in a warm, draft-free place to rise until double in bulk, about 1½ hours.

3. Punch down dough and knead for 5 minutes. Cut off 4 pieces, each piece about the size of a large egg. Place remaining dough into a round pan 10 inches in diameter and 2 inches high. Shape the small pieces of dough into twists about 5 inches long. Arrange the 4 twists from the center of the dough radiating to edge of dough. Put in a warm place to rise again, until double in bulk, about 1 hour. Place the red egg in the center of the bread.

4. Preheat the oven to 375 degrees.

5. Brush entire surface of bread with a wash made from the egg yolk and remaining tablespoon milk. Bake for 30 minutes until bread is a deep golden brown and sounds hollow when tapped. Transfer to rack and cool.

Yield: 12 or more servings.

Note: Color a hard-cooked egg with red Easter-egg dye according to package instruction.

Mayeritsa Avgolemono

The liver, neck, knuckles and head from a 12- to 14-pound baby lamb
5   *quarts water*
3   *to 4 pounds meaty veal bones*
4   *ribs celery, coarsely chopped*
2   *onions, sliced*
2   *sprigs parsley*
    Salt to taste
3   *bunches fresh scallions, minced*

1   *cup minced leeks*
¼   *pound butter*
1   *cup fresh minced dill*
½   *cup raw rice*
5   *eggs*
    Juice of 2 lemons
    Freshly ground pepper to taste

1. Soak the lamb's head in cold water to cover for 3 hours. Drain. In an 8-quart kettle, combine the 5 quarts of water with the head, liver, knuckles and neck of lamb, the veal bones, celery, onions, parsley and salt to taste. Bring to the boil and simmer for 20 minutes.

2. Remove the liver with a slotted spoon and reserve. Simmer the remaining mixture for 1 hour or until meat is tender, skimming off the scum that rises to the surface. Strain the broth and reserve. Remove as much meat as possible from the lamb's head and bones. Discard the bones and chop the meat and liver very fine.

3. In a skillet, sauté the scallions and leeks in the butter until transparent. Add the dill and meat and sauté about 10 minutes. Add the rice and sauté another 5 minutes.

4. Reserve 1 cup of the strained broth. Bring the remaining broth to a boil. Add the sautéed ingredients and then simmer until rice is tender. Remove from the fire.

5. In a bowl beat the eggs until they are light and frothy. Add juice of 2 lemons in a stream, beating constantly until sauce is thickened. Whisk in the reserved cup of broth and stir the sauce into the soup. Add salt and pepper to taste and serve.

Yield: 12 or more servings.

Roast Baby Lamb with Artichokes

1   *12- to 14-pound baby lamb*
½   *cup butter at room temperature*
    Juice of 6 lemons
2   *cloves garlic, minced, optional*
2   *tablespoons oregano*
    Salt and freshly ground pepper to taste
    Boiling water
8   *large artichokes*
¼   *cup flour*
    Chopped fresh dill
    Parsley sprigs for garnish

1. Preheat the oven to 500 degrees.

2. Wipe the lamb with a damp cloth. Rub all over with butter, juice

Leon Lianides carves traditional roast baby lamb

of 2 lemons, garlic, oregano, salt and pepper to taste. Place lamb in a large roasting pan and place in the oven. Bake 30 minutes. Reduce the temperature to 350 degrees and bake for about 2 hours, basting frequently, until the leg moves freely from the body. Keep adding boiling water so that there will be about 2 to 2½ cups drippings.

3. Meanwhile, as the lamb roasts, prepare the artichokes. Trim the artichokes at the base, leaving about 1 inch of stem. Remove all tough outer leaves. Cut off about 1 inch from the top. Cut each artichoke in half lengthwise and scrape away the fuzzy choke. Pare around the stem. Rub the cut portions with juice of 1 lemon. Place each half in a large saucepan of salted cold water to which is added the juice of the remaining 3 lemons and the flour. Bring to the boil and simmer about 10 minutes until slightly tender.

4. Remove the lamb and set aside in a warm place. Gently place each artichoke half in pan with lamb drippings. Bake the artichokes about ½ hour until tender but not overcooked. Sprinkle with dill and garnish with parsley sprigs.

Yield: 12 or more servings.

Roast Potatoes with Fresh Mint

24   small potatoes
     Salt and freshly ground pepper to taste
     Juice of 1 lemon
 1   cup natural gravy from roast lamb

¼   pound butter
    Sprigs of fresh mint

1. Preheat the oven to 400 degrees.

2. Peel the potatoes, leave whole and rinse. Place in a baking pan and add salt and pepper to taste and lemon juice.

3. Add hot gravy and butter and bake until tender. Garnish with mint leaves and serve.

Yield: 12 or more servings.

Greek Salad

     Salt
 1   clove garlic
 2   heads Boston lettuce, shredded
 1   romaine lettuce, shredded
 3   celery hearts, diced
 6   radishes, sliced
 1   bunch scallions, sliced
 1   cucumber, thinly sliced
 1   green pepper, cut into thin rings
12   oil-cured black olives
 ½   pound feta cheese, diced
 ½   cup olive oil
     Juice of 2 lemons
     Salt and freshly ground pepper to taste
 ½   teaspoon oregano
 1   tablespoon minced parsley
 8   anchovy fillets
 3   tomatoes, cut into wedges
     Parsley sprigs for garnish

1. Rub a large salad bowl with salt and garlic. Discard the garlic.

2. In the salad bowl, combine the

lettuce, celery, radishes, scallions, cucumber, green pepper, olives and cheese.

3. Beat the olive oil with the lemon juice and pour over the salad. Toss and season with salt and pepper. Sprinkle the salad with the oregano and parsley.

4. Arrange the anchovy fillets radiating from the center with the tomato wedges. Garnish with parsley sprigs.

Yield: 12 or more servings.

Galaktoboureko

(A rich milk and egg pastry)

2	quarts plus 1 cup milk
10	large eggs
1	cup sugar
⅔	cup fine semolina, or cream of wheat
2	teaspoons vanilla
1	pound sweet butter
1	pound phyllo pastry (see note)

The syrup

18	ounces sugar
12	ounces water
1	stick cinnamon
	Few drops of lemon juice

1. In a saucepan scald the 2 quarts of milk and set aside to cool.

2. In a bowl, beat the eggs until they are frothy. Gradually beat in the sugar and semolina and beat about 2 minutes more. Add vanilla and remaining cup of cold milk and add the mixture to the warm milk.

3. Cook over low heat, stirring constantly, until mixture thickens and coats the spoon. Do not allow mixture to boil. Remove from heat and add 4 tablespoons butter, cut into pieces, and continue stirring until butter melts. Cool the custard, cover with wax paper and chill for 3 hours.

4. Preheat the oven to 400 degrees.

5. Melt the remaining butter. Butter a 16-by-11-by-12-inch pan and add half the phyllo pastry, one leaf at a time, and brush each leaf with butter as it is added. Have the pastry overlap the edges of the pan. Keep the remaining leaves covered with plastic wrap.

6. After half the leaves have been placed in the pan, pour in the custard, spreading it evenly, and fold the edges of the leaves over the custard. Arrange remaining phyllo leaves over the custard in the same manner and brush each leaf with melted butter. Trim the edges to 1 inch and fold them inward and under.

7. Cut the top layers of leaves, down to the custard, into strips about 2 inches wide and then cut strips diagonally to form diamond patterned pieces. Bake for 15 minutes and then reduce the oven heat to 350 degrees. Bake for 45 minutes longer, or until top of pastry is golden brown and flaky.

8. While pastry is baking prepare the syrup. In a saucepan combine the sugar, water, cinnamon and lemon juice. Bring to the boil over low heat, stirring constantly until syrup thickens and coats the spoon. Cool the syrup and pour over warm pastry.

Yield: About 40 pieces.

Note: Phyllo pastry is available at many specialty shops and stores that sell Greek foods, including Poseidon Confectionery Co., 629 Ninth Avenue (between 44th and 45th Streets) and Kassos Bros., 570 Ninth Avenue (between 41st and 42nd Streets).

Walnut and Almond Torte

3   cups ground walnuts
3   cups ground almonds
16 pieces zwieback, ground
    Grated rind of 1 orange
½   teaspoon cinnamon
¼   teaspoon ground cloves
12 eggs, separated
1½ cups sugar
1   teaspoon vanilla

The syrup

4   cups water
3   cups sugar
1   slice of lemon

1. Preheat the oven to 350 degrees.

2. Blend the nuts, zwieback, orange rind, cinnamon and cloves in a mixing bowl and set aside.

3. Beat the egg yolks with the sugar until light and lemon-colored, about 15 minutes. Add vanilla and fold into the nut mixture.

4. Beat the egg whites until stiff but not dry and gently fold into the batter.

5. Butter a 12-by-15-by-3-inch pan and pour in the batter. Bake for exactly 1 hour, without opening the oven door.

6. While the torte is baking make the syrup. Combine the water, sugar and lemon slice in a saucepan and simmer about 20 minutes.

7. Pour the warm syrup over the torte immediately upon removing the torte from the oven. Let the torte stand for 24 hours. Cut into 3-inch squares and serve topped with whipped cream.

Yield: 20 pieces.

Easter Cookies

½   cup sweet butter, at room temperature
½   cup confectioners' sugar
1   egg
¼   cup heavy cream
2   tablespoons orange liqueur, or brandy
3   cups flour
½   teaspoon salt
1   teaspoon baking powder
1   egg yolk
    Sesame seeds

1. Preheat the oven to 350 degrees.

2. In a bowl, cream the butter and add the sugar. Beat until creamy. Add the egg, cream and orange liqueur and beat the mixture for 5 minutes.

3. In another bowl sift together the flour, salt and baking powder and blend into the butter mixture, ½ cup at a time, to form a soft dough.

4. Form the dough into 1½-inch balls and shape into twists. Brush the twists with egg yolk and sprinkle with sesame seeds. Place on cookie sheets and bake for 30 minutes, or until they turn a light golden color.

Yield: About 48 cookies.

Aphrodite Lianides displays assorted rich desserts

A Trout Treat
in the Catskills

Up here, a two-and-one-half-hour drive from Manhattan, there is a territory known as the Catskills. To some of the citizens and visitors hereabouts, it is also known as a transplant of the French Pyrenées, for the French, mostly American citizens who come here by the score, say that is what it reminds them of. And for many of those who have settled here the Pyrenées is, or was, home.

Those who come here to ski or climb on Hunter Mountain, who hunt in the hills and fish in the Eposus and other rivers and streams are varied in their occupations. There are waiters and chefs and restaurant owners. There are vintners and perfumers and construction men and hair dressers, and they have been coming here for nearly a quarter of a century.

I came to visit for one reason expressly. I had heard of a legendary fisherman, a Frenchman and former restaurant owner, who still dabbles to an uncommon and fascinating degree in food. Besides, it was trout season and the thought of a freshly caught rainbow or speckled brown trout sizzling in a skillet on a spring morning whetted the appetite.

The man is Pierre Larré, 57 years old, slightly built, born in New York but taken to France by his parents where he was raised in a small town halfway between Pau and Lourdes in the Pyrenées.

For many years, Pierre was a partner with his four brothers in Larré's Restaurant, 50 West 56th Street in Manhattan, one of those dining establishments almost invariably detailed in any list of relatively inexpensive French restaurants in New York. He retired to his mountain home four years ago, when management of the business fell to his nephew, Jean Larré, 39, and his son, Jean, 25.

We gathered on a frosty morning over crusty rolls and coffee and tea in the Auberge des Quatre Saisons.

"It's a bad day for trout," he said gloomily, he who is celebrated among his friends as a man who fishes every day permitted by law and never returns home without his legal limit.

"Last night there was a full moon," he told us. "The fish have been up all night eating. They won't be hungry. Besides, the water's too cold. The fish won't be moving." He looked honestly worried. "I promised you fish for lunch. Perhaps I should get some neighbors to help me just in case." At this point we were joined by his son, Jean, who had the day off.

A few moments later Pierre and his son descended with poles down the banks of a small, rock-ridden stream, the water gushing over rapids. We remarked on the turbulence.

"That's why the name of that town over there is Shandaken. It's Indian for 'rapid waters.' " Seconds later a trout caught his hook and that was one for lunch. Another. And another. These fish obviously hadn't been up all night eating their breakfast by the light of the moon.

Back into automobiles, down more river banks and by noon the bags were full to the limit.

At midday, the sun was still brooding behind lead-gray skies, and Pierre warmed the day and friends with glasses of ricard, the anise-flavored drink of the Midi region of France. We had arrived with a bag of charcoal and an iron fry-pan at a flat, stony terrain on the banks of a stream lined with pussywillows.

Pierre unloaded his oil and flour, salt, pepper, butter, partly cooked potatoes and an onion and proceeded to build a fire. First, a group of flat stones was assembled, the stones overlapping in circular fashion to make a ringed fire pit, three feet wide. Into the center went dried sprigs, pieces of driftwood and charcoal, and moments later the fire was ablaze.

As he worked Pierre told us that he cures his own hams and that they are just as good as he remembered them from the Pyrénées, which is celebrated for its ham.

"I bury it in a dry cure of salt and pepper and let it stand one day for each pound. After that I rub it with garlic, put it in a clean cloth and hang it in a ventilated shack next to my home. I even cure hams in August."

He also raises rabbits and chickens and pheasants. In late summer he gathers cepes and girolles, those woodland mushrooms so cherished in the Pyrénées.

"I know a place, a field of yellow, where in mid-September you can pick up twenty pounds of girolles or chanterelles," he stated. The streams around here, incidentally, produce what appears to be acres of fresh peppery watercress.

As he spoke, Pierre went about his business of heating oil in the flat grill, dusting the fish with salt, pepper and flour and cooking it until deliciously brown. As the fish cooked the potatoes were sliced onto the grill along with thin slices of onion. A touch of salt and pepper was added.

"The French started coming here in 1955," he said. "That was the year Dadou Labeille opened the Auberge des Quatre Saisons or the Inn of the Four Seasons. He hadn't intended to attract a lot of Frenchmen, but he did. He opened the place and the French started coming. It really does look like the Pyrénées except the mountains are not as high here as they are there."

The trout cooked bankside by Pierre were pure ambrosia—sweet, tender, crisp skin and moist juicy inner texture. And marvelously complemented by the potatoes and onions.

There follows an assortment of recipes for trout. In addition to the outdoor version of Pierre Larré's pan-fried trout, there are numerous dishes from traditional French cookery. These recipes work equally well with trout directly from a stream or those freshly purchased at fish dealers.

Truites Pierre Larré
(Pan-fried trout)

4　trout, 8 to 10 ounces each, cleaned but with head and tail on
　　Salt and freshly ground pepper to taste
　　Flour for dredging
⅓　cup peanut, vegetable or corn oil
3　partly cooked, peeled potatoes, cut into ¼-inch slices, about 3 cups
1　small onion, peeled and sliced
　　Lemon wedges

1. Sprinkle the trout on all sides with salt and pepper. Dredge lightly in flour.

2. Meanwhile, heat the oil in a large iron skillet over a hot charcoal fire. Or heat it on the stove.

3. When the oil is hot and almost smoking, add the fish and cook until crisp and golden brown on one side. Turn and cook until crisp and golden on the other side. Continue cooking until the fish is cooked through. Cooking time will depend on the size of the fish.

4. As the fish cook, push them to one side and add the potatoes and onions. Cook, turning the potatoes and onion slices, until browned and golden on both sides. Remove the fish and serve with lemon wedges. Serve with the potatoes and onions.

Yield: 4 servings.

Truites Jean Vergnes
(Trout meunière with pecans)

4　10-ounce trout (see note)
¼　cup milk
　　Salt and freshly ground pepper to taste
½　cup flour
¼　cup peanut, vegetable or corn oil
5　tablespoons butter
½　cup pecan halves
　　Juice of 1 lemon
2　tablespoons finely chopped parsley

1. Using a pair of kitchen shears, cut off the fins from the back and sides of the trout. Leave the head and tail intact.

2. Place the trout in a large pan and add milk, salt and pepper. Turn the trout in the mixture.

3. Remove the trout without patting dry and dredge on all sides in flour seasoned with salt and pepper.

4. Heat the oil and 1 tablespoon of the butter in a large, heavy skillet and add the trout, lining them up neatly in the pan. Cook about 8 minutes, or until golden and cooked on one side. Turn and cook 8 minutes longer. Baste often. The basting is important to keep the trout juicy.

5. Remove the trout to a warm platter. Sprinkle with salt and pepper.

6. Pour off the fat from the pan and wipe out the skillet. Add the remaining 4 tablespoons of butter and, when melted, add the pecans. Cook, shaking the pan and stirring, until the butter becomes the color of hazelnuts. Do not burn. Add the lemon juice and pour the sauce over the fish. Serve sprinkled with chopped parsley.

Yield: 4 servings.

Note: The 10-ounce weight specified here is arbitrary. Larger or smaller trout may be cooked in the same manner, but adjust the cooking time accordingly.

Truites Frites

(Deep-fried trout)

4 10-ounce trout (see note)
¼ cup milk
   Salt and freshly ground pepper to taste
½ cup flour
   Oil for deep frying
   Tartar sauce
   Lemon wedges for garnish

1. Using a pair of kitchen shears, cut off the fins from the back and sides of the trout. Leave the head and tail intact.

2. Place the trout in a large pan and add milk, salt and pepper. Turn the trout in the mixture.

3. Remove the trout without patting dry and dredge on all sides in flour seasoned with salt and pepper.

4. Heat the oil for deep frying, about 325 degrees. Add the trout and fry until golden brown and cooked through, about 8 minutes.

5. Remove the trout. Drain on absorbent toweling. Sprinkle with salt and serve with tartar sauce on the side and lemon wedges as a garnish.

Yield: 4 servings.

Note: The 10-ounce weight specified here is arbitrary. Larger or smaller trout may be cooked in the same manner, but adjust the cooking time accordingly.

Truite en Gelée

(Trout in aspic)

The court bouillon

¼ cup chopped celery
¼ cup small onion cut into rings
¼ cup thin carrot rounds
¼ cup chopped leeks
1 clove garlic, peeled
6 peppercorns
1 bay leaf
2 sprigs fresh parsley
2 sprigs fresh thyme
2 cups water
2 cups dry white wine
   Salt to taste

The fish

6 10-ounce ready-to-cook trout (see note)

The aspic

Liquid from the cooked fish, about 2 cups
¼ cup coarsely chopped parsley
1 envelope unflavored gelatin
¼ cup wine
2 egg whites, lightly beaten until frothy
2 egg shells, crushed

The decorations

Green part of leeks, scallions, cucumber skin cut in strips, pimentos, black olives or truffles, hard-cooked egg whites, etc.

Garnishes

Cucumber rings
Cherry tomatoes

1. Combine all the ingredients for the court bouillon in a saucepan and bring to the boil. Remove from the heat and let cool.

2. Preheat the oven to 350 degrees.

3. Using a pair of kitchen shears, cut off the fins from the back and sides of the trout. Leave the head and tail intact. Arrange the fish in one layer in a large heat-proof baking dish. Pour the cooled court bouillon with the vegetables over the fish and place on top of the stove. Bring to the boil. Cover with foil and place in the oven. Bake 15 minutes. Remove. Let cool and chill.

4. When chilled, the cooking liquid will set. Warm up the liquid gently, just until melted. It should not be hot. Pour the liquid into a saucepan.

5. Add the parsley, gelatin, wine, egg whites and crushed egg shells. Stir until gelatin is softened. Put over low heat and cook about 15 minutes, stirring gently on occasion. Be sure to stir until gelatin is melted and stir to prevent sticking and burning on the bottom. Let stand briefly. Strain and let cool. Do not chill or it will set.

6. Using a paring knife, prepare the trout for decoration. Neatly and carefully pull away the skin from the sides of each trout. Leave the heads and tails intact.

7. Using sharp, small knives and fancy cutters, make cutouts of leaves, petals, stamens and so on, using any or all of the indicated decorations. If cucumber skins are used, drop them into boiling water about 3 seconds and drain. Let cool. Working with aspic is easy. Remember that the food to be coated with aspic must be well chilled before each layer of liquid aspic is added. Remember, too, that the aspic must always be cool but still liquid before applying. Cutouts should be dipped in aspic before applying to the foods to be decorated.

8. Arrange the trout on a rack. Chill well. Arrange any desired design on one side of the trout, using cutouts as indicated above. Chill thoroughly. When the pattern is made, neatly and carefully spoon aspic over. Add about 5 or 6 coatings of aspic, chilling well before each coating.

9. When the final coating sets, arrange the fish on a serving platter such as a silver tray. Spoon the remaining aspic between the fish onto the bottom of the try and chill until set. Garnish the platter, if desired, with cucumber rings and cherry tomatoes. Serve with mayonnaise or a variation of mayonnaise on the side (see recipe for mayonnaise with herbs).

Yield: 6 servings.

Note: The 10-ounce weight specified here is arbitrary. Larger or smaller trout may be cooked in the same manner, but adjust the cooking time accordingly.

Mayonnaise with herbs

½ *cup mayonnaise*
2   *teaspoons finely chopped dill*
1   *tablespoon chopped scallions*
1   *teaspoon prepared, imported mustard, such as Dijon or Düsseldorf*
Lemon juice to taste

Blend all the ingredients and serve with cold fish, poultry and so on.

Yield: About ½ cup.

Truite en gelee

Truites au Bleu

(Trout cooked in court bouillon)

4   *10-ounce trout (see note)*
4   *quarts water*
1   *cup white vinegar*
1   *bay leaf*
    Salt to taste
10 *peppercorns*
    Lemon wedges
    Melted butter or hollandaise
    sauce (see recipe)

1. Using a pair of kitchen shears, cut off the fins from the back and sides of the trout. Leave the head and tail intact.

2. Using a long needle such as a trussing needle, run a string through the eyes of the trout, then through the tail. Tie the head and tail together. The reason for this is simply appearance. When trout are freshly caught, they are killed and dressed and dropped into boiling water immediately. These trout will curve naturally through muscle and nerve reaction.

3. Combine the water and vinegar in a fairly wide casserole. There should be enough liquid to cover the trout when they are added. Add the bay leaf, salt and peppercorns. Bring to the boil and simmer 10 minutes.

4. Drop the trout into the simmering water. Simmer 5 minutes. Drain the trout and serve with lemon wedges and hot melted butter or hollandaise sauce.

Yield: 4 servings.

Note: The 10-ounce weight specified here is arbitrary. Larger or smaller trout may be cooked in the same manner, but adjust the cooking time accordingly.

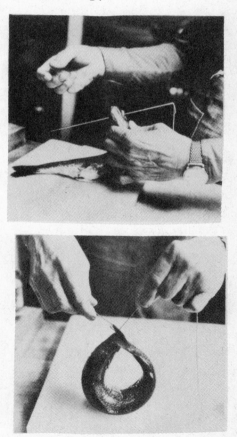

Hollandaise sauce

12   *tablespoons butter*
3   *egg yolks*
2   *tablespoons cold water*
    Salt to taste
2   *teaspoons lemon juice*
⅛   *teaspoon cayenne*

1. Place a skillet on the stove and add about ½ inch of water. Bring the water to the simmer. Have ready a 1½-quart saucepan.

2. Place the butter in another saucepan and place it over very low heat (perhaps using an asbestos pad or a Flame-tamer).

3. Set the 1½-quart saucepan in the simmering water in the skillet.

Place the egg yolks in the saucepan. Add the cold water, salt and half the lemon juice. Start beating the egg yolks with a wire whisk, stirring in a back-and-forth and circular fashion, making certain that the whisk covers the bottom of the saucepan so that the yolks do not stick. It is imperative that the heat beneath the saucepan be moderate.

4. When the egg yolks become custardlike and thickened, start adding the melted butter.

5. Continue beating, stirring constantly and vigorously, until all the butter is added. Add the remaining lemon juice and cayenne. The sauce is now ready to be served.

Yield: About 1 cup.

Say Gruyère

WITH PIERRE FRANEY

Although much has been made by food historians of the revolution in the American kitchen and American taste in general, there are still a surprising number of people in this country who do not know that one of the greatest cheeses of Switzerland is not what is known generically in all English-speaking countries as "Swiss" cheese. That cheese, the one with the holes, is known in its country of origin as Emmental and comes from Emmental, or Valley of the Emme.

Good cooks know that a superior cheese, a cheese more sophisticated, full-bodied in flavor and with more character all around is gruyère, which comes from three Swiss cantons: Fribourg, Neufchâtel and Vaud.

Although it is becoming increasingly well known in this country, and is available in most fine shops that specialize in cheeses, gruyère is thought of by most people as that dreadful processed stuff that comes in small triangles wrapped in foil. The stuff served on airlines along with the fruit basket. A real gruyère comes in a large round loaf with a firm texture much like that of "Swiss" or Emmental cheese.

The virtues of gruyère are limitless, although its chief uses are in a fondue and for gratinéed onion soup (for these dishes it is infinitely more respectable than ordinary Swiss). Gruyère is a marvelous addition to cheese sauces (any calling for Swiss), as a topping for many casseroles and at its best makes an excellent "dessert" cheese to be served on the platter right alongside brie and camembert.

Cheese Fondue

3 pounds gruyère cheese
1 clove garlic
2½ cups dry white wine
¼ cup kirsch
4 teaspoons cornstarch
   Salt, optional
1 loaf French bread
   Freshly ground pepper

1. Grate or shred the cheese or cut into small cubes.

2. Rub the inside of a fondue pot (see note) with the clove of garlic. Add the wine and heat without boiling. This is probably best done at the stove, using a Flame-tamer or other heat-proof pad to prevent sticking on the bottom.

3. Add the cheese and stir with a

wooden spoon without stopping until the mixture is runny. Blend the kirsch and cornstarch and add it to the mixture, stirring. The cornstarch should bind the mixture and make it smooth. If desired, add a touch of salt to the fondue. The saltiness of gruyère varies. When the fondue is boiling and smooth, it may be transferred to a fondue cooker with a flame for serving at table.

4. Cut the French bread into 1-inch cubes. Serve with fondue forks, first spearing a cube of bread and dipping it into the hot fondue. Serve with a peppermill on the side. If desired, add more kirsch to taste.

Yield: 6 to 8 servings.

Note: Prior to using an earthenware fondue pot or casserole, rub the inside and outside unglazed surface with a clove of garlic. Preheat the oven to 400 degrees. Fill the pot with water and place in the oven. Let simmer about 1 hour. Fondue pots can be used over direct flame but it is chancy. There is less danger of breakage if the pot is placed over a heat-proof pad to insure equal distribution of heat.

Onion Soup Gratinée

2	pounds large yellow onions
4	tablespoons butter
1	teaspoon finely minced garlic
2	tablespoons flour
5	cups fresh or canned beef broth
3	cups water
	Salt and freshly ground pepper
1	bay leaf
1	cup dry white wine

12	thin slices French bread
½	pound gruyère cheese, grated

1. Peel the onions and slice them thinly with a sharp knife. Or slice them in a food processor.

2. Heat the butter in a deep casserole or kettle and add the garlic and onions. Cook, stirring often, until nicely browned, about 15 minutes. Sprinkle with flour and stir. Add the broth and water, salt to taste and a generous amount of black pepper. Add the bay leaf and wine. Cook 30 minutes.

3. Meanwhile, preheat the oven to 400 degrees and bake the bread until browned and crisp.

4. Ladle the boiling soup into 6 individual soup crocks, each with about a 2-cup capacity. Cover each serving of soup with 2 slices of bread and sprinkle with cheese.

5. Arrange the crocks on a baking pan and bake 30 minutes or until golden on top and bubbling throughout.

Yield: 6 servings.

Cheese Crusts Fribourgeoise

2	teaspoons butter
1	tablespoon flour
½	cup milk
	Salt and freshly ground pepper
1	egg, lightly beaten
½	pound grated gruyère cheese, about 2½ cups
¼	teaspoon grated nutmeg
	Pinch of cayenne pepper
2	tablespoons dry white wine

¾   teaspoon finely chopped garlic
12   slices French bread cut on the
     bias

1. Melt the butter in a small saucepan and stir in the flour, using a wire whisk. Add the milk, stirring rapidly with the whisk. Add salt and pepper to taste and let cool.

2. Preheat the oven to 400 degrees.

3. Spoon the white sauce into a mixing bowl and add the egg, cheese, nutmeg, cayenne, wine and garlic. Blend well with a fork.

4. Toast the bread lightly on both sides and spoon equal amounts of the cheese mixture on one side. Smooth it over. Place the toast on a baking sheet and bake 10 minutes.

Yield: 4 servings.

Homage to the Sandwich

England's greatest contribution to gastronomy has nothing to do with Brussels sprouts, toad in the hole, bubble and squeak or roast beef and Yorkshire pudding. It is purely and simply the Sandwich, that portable edible whose consumption in America alone must total in the billions in the course of a year.

The legend of the origin of the name is almost as familiar as that of George Washington, the cherry tree and his moral incapacity to tell a lie.

Almost any schoolboy can tell you that the sandwich was named for John Montagu, the fourth Earl of Sandwich, who, in his desire not to leave the gambling table, requested his manservant to bring him meat between bread to assuage his hunger.

What that schoolboy will not be able to tell you is that the fourth Earl of Sandwich was far better known in his day as a scoundrel, a rogue and a scandalous blackguard, a reputation well recorded in our favorite source book, the eleventh edition of the Encyclopedia Brittanica.

Montagu held his posts in his day. He was at one time or another postmaster general of the British Isles, secretary of state and the first lord of the Admiralty.

"For corruption and incapacity," the encyclopedia reveals, "Sandwich's administration is unique in the history of the British Navy." Under his direction, the book adds, "offices were bought, stores were stolen, and, worst of all, ships, unseaworthy and inadequately equipped, were sent to fight battles of their country."

Not a line in praise of the father of the BLT; the Monte Cristo; the Reuben; pan bania; the club; mozzarella en carrozza; the croque monsieur and the croque madame and those tall-stacked and inspired creations of the Stage Deli. No heroes? No submarines? Without him the residents of New England might well have been spared something I have only heard of by reputation, sandwiches made with baked beans!

There is no end, of course, to what sandwiches can be and are made of, and connoisseurs of the open, single-, double- or triple-deckers have strong opinions about how they should be made. Should they be buttered or does mayonnaise suffice? I personally plump for no butter with lots of mayonnaise, preferably homemade and, depending on the filling, one slice smeared with mustard. A hamburger would be an exception to that rule in my kitchen. I like a hamburger on a lightly toasted, buttered bun and, occasionally, an English muffin. No mayonnaise, no mustard, but a slice of onion and lots of ketchup with the bottle left on the table, diner fashion.

Some people don't trim the crusts of sandwiches made with sandwich bread. I demur. Don't serve me an untrimmed sandwich, please. I will stand in my kitchen making sandwiches for hours and munch at times on the trimmings, but an untrimmed sandwich is to my eyes vulgar, crude and uncouth.

Have you ever tried a pan bania, that marvelous sandwich from Provence made with a filling that is the equivalent of a salade nicoise? Or mozzarella en carrozza with its anchovy sauce?

There is a weighty sandwich board of recipes here including several of those already mentioned plus basic salad creations with variations. I also repeat a few personal favorites including the Reuben, croque monsieur and Irma Rhode's onion sandwiches. A roundup of sandwiches would not be complete without them.

Pan Bania

(A provençale sandwich)

6   *crusty hard rolls, or two loaves French bread*
2   *tablespoons vinegar*
    Salt and freshly ground pepper to taste
1   *clove garlic, finely minced*
¾   *cup olive oil*
¼   *pound romaine lettuce leaves*
6   *thin tomato slices*
1   *small red onion, peeled and sliced*
1   *7-ounce can tuna packed in oil, undrained*
2   *hard-cooked eggs, thinly sliced*
6   *black olives, preferably Italian or Greek olives packed in brine*
1   *tablespoon drained capers*
¼   *cup finely chopped parsley*
1   *green pepper, cored, seeded and chopped*
1   *2-ounce can flat anchovies*
4   *small sprigs fresh basil, chopped*

1. Slice the rolls or French bread in half. With the fingers, pull out some of the white center of each roll. Use for bread crumbs or feed to the birds.

2. Combine the vinegar, salt, pepper, garlic and olive oil in a small bowl and stir to blend.

3. Cut or tear the romaine into 1- or 2-inch pieces as for salad. Add it to a bowl.

4. Add the tomato slices, onion slices, tuna and eggs.

5. Pit the olives and cut in half. Add them to the bowl. Add the capers, parsley and green peppers.

6. Drain the anchovies and cut them in half. Add them. Add the basil.

7. Brush the cut and slightly hollowed-out center of the hard roll halves with a little of the oil and vinegar mixture.

8. Pour the remaining oil and vinegar mixture over the salad. Toss well. Use the salad mixture as a sandwich filling for the hard rolls.

Yield: 6 sandwiches.

Note: There are many people in Provence who insist the sandwich must be weighted down before eating.

Mozzarella en Carrozza

(A deep-fried mozzarella sandwich)

12 slices white sandwich bread
¾ pound whole milk mozzarella
cheese
Flour for dredging
2 large eggs
½ cup milk
Salt and freshly ground pepper to taste
Peanut, vegetable or corn oil
for deep frying
Anchovy sauce (see recipe)

1. Place 6 slices of bread on a flat surface. Using a sharp knife, cut the mozzarella cheese into 6 square slices of equal thickness. Or cut the cheese on its side into 12 rectangles. Place 1 square of cheese on each of the 6 slices of bread, or place 2 rectangles of cheese side by side on the bread. Cover with remaining bread slices. Neatly trim off the crusts of the bread. Cut the sandwiches into rectangles, or triangles if you prefer.

2. Dredge the sandwiches top and bottom and on the sides in flour.

3. Beat the eggs with milk, salt and pepper. Carefully dip the sandwiches into this mixture, keeping the sandwiches intact as you turn them. After coating with batter it will help if you skewer each sandwich with 2 toothpicks.

4. Heat the oil for deep frying and carefully drop the sandwiches into it, one at a time. Using a slotted spoon, turn the sandwiches in the oil so that they brown evenly. When golden brown, drain the sandwiches on absorbent toweling. Remove the toothpicks and serve with anchovy sauce spooned over.

Yield: 6 servings.

Anchovy sauce

¾ cup butter
6 tablespoons olive oil
12 anchovies, coarsely chopped

Combine all the ingredients in a saucepan and let stand over low heat, stirring until anchovies dissolve. Serve hot.

Yield: About 1¼ cups.

Watercress Sandwiches

1 bunch watercress
2 to 3 tablespoons mayonnaise
Lemon juice to taste
Salt and freshly ground pepper to taste
8 thin slices sandwich bread

1. Pat the watercress to remove excess moisture. Coarsely chop the watercress using a knife, blender or food processor. Do not chop it too fine, just fine enough to blend with mayonnaise.

2. Add the mayonnaise, blended with lemon juice, salt and pepper, a little at a time, stirring after each addition. The problem with a mayonnaise and watercress filling is generally an excess of mayonnaise. The filling becomes too liquid. Add just enough so that the filling holds together. Two tablespoons should be enough.

3. Spoon equal portions of the filling onto 4 thin slices of sandwich bread. Top with the remaining 4 slices. Neatly trim the crusts of the bread. Cut the sandwiches as desired into finger sandwiches, or into 2 rectangular sandwiches, or into 2 or 4 triangle-shaped sandwiches.

Yield: 4 to 6 servings.

Watercress sandwiches

Paula Peck's Jewish-style Chopped Chicken Livers

½   *pound unrendered, solid fresh chicken fat (see note)*
½   *pound yellow onions, peeled and chopped, about 2 cups*
½   *pound chicken livers*
    Salt to taste
4   *hard-cooked eggs*
    Freshly ground pepper to taste

1. Cut the chicken fat into small cubes and put it in a heavy saucepan. When some of the fat is rendered into a liquid form, add ½ cup of the onions and continue cooking until onion and bits of fat are brown.

2. Strain the liquid and set the browned pieces of rendered fat aside.

3. Add the remaining onions to a heavy saucepan with no other ingredients. Cover and let steam over low heat until they are almost dry and sticking to the pan. Add ⅓ cup of the liquid fat and cook the onions until golden brown. Remove them with a slotted spoon and set aside.

4. Add the chicken livers to the fat in the pan and cook, stirring occasionally, until no blood shows when livers are pierced with a fork. Sprinkle with salt.

5. Grind together in a meat grinder the cooked onions, livers, the pieces of rendered fat and the hard-cooked eggs. Add any pan drippings. After grinding, mix well with a spoon. Taste and correct seasonings. Add 2 or 3 more tablespoons of liquid chicken fat. Pack into a 2-cup terrine. Cover with a little chicken fat. This will keep fresh for about 2 weeks. When ready to use, spread on sliced bread, preferably rye.

Yield: 2 cups chopped liver.

Note: Chicken fat (already rendered and generally with onion flavor) is available in supermarkets. It may be used, of course, in place of rendering your own.

Monte Carlo Sandwiches

(Grilled ham, chicken and cheese)

8   *thin slices white sandwich bread, preferably with a firm texture*

Butter at room temperature
4 thin slices boiled ham
4 thin slices gruyère, or Swiss cheese
4 thin slices cooked breast of chicken
1 egg, lightly beaten
¼ cup milk
Salt and freshly ground pepper to taste

1. Butter each slice of bread on one side. Place 4 slices of bread, buttered side up, on a flat surface. Neatly arrange 1 slice of ham, 1 of cheese and 1 of chicken over the buttered side. Cover each sandwich with another slice of bread, buttered side next to the filling.

2. Neatly trim the crusts of bread.

3. Blend the egg, milk, salt and pepper and add to a flat dish. Dip the sandwiches on both sides in the batter.

4. Heat 2 tablespoons of butter in a large, heavy skillet and add the sandwiches. Cook over fairly low heat until sandwiches are browned on one side, about 5 minutes. Turn the sandwiches and cover the skillet with a lid. Cook about 5 minutes on the other side. Serve hot.

Yield: 4 sandwiches.

Parmesan, Meat and Cheese Hero

1 long, crusty loaf Italian or French bread
¼ cup olive oil
1 clove garlic, crushed

2 tablespoons grated Parmesan cheese
¼ pound or less thinly sliced salami
¼ pound or less thinly sliced prosciutto
¼ pound or less thinly sliced mortadella
¼ pound or less thinly sliced capicola
¼ pound or less thinly sliced provolone, fontina or smeared gorgonzola cheese
6 to 8 Tuscan peppers (pepperoncini)
3 roasted sweet peppers, preferably red (see recipe)
5 or 6 crisp lettuce leaves, optional
1 red, ripe tomato, cored and sliced, optional
Salt and freshly ground pepper to taste
Additional olive oil, optional
2 teaspoons vinegar, optional

1. Preheat the broiler.

2. Slice the bread lengthwise. Combine the oil and crushed garlic. Stir briefly. Brush the split halves of the bread with the oil. Sprinkle each half with Parmesan cheese. Run the bread under the broiler, split-side up, until cheese is golden.

3. Arrange layers of salami, prosciutto, mortadella, capicola, provolone, Tuscan peppers, sweet peppers, lettuce and tomatoes on one of the bread halves. Sprinkle with salt and pepper. Sprinkle, if desired, with more oil and vinegar. Cover with remaining bread half.

Yield: 4 to 6 servings.

Roasted sweet peppers

Place 3 firm, unblemished red or green sweet peppers under the broiler, turning as necessary, until the skin is lightly charred all over. Remove the peppers and place them in a small brown bag. Seal the bag and let stand until peppers are cool. Remove the peppers. Peel away and discard the skin, core and seeds.

Reuben Sandwiches

8   *slices fresh rye bread, or pumpernickel*
8   *teaspoons melted butter*
½   *cup Russian dressing (see recipe)*
½   *pound very lean corned beef cut into the thinnest possible slices*
¼   *pound uncooked drained sauerkraut*
⅓   *pound thinly sliced gruyère, or Swiss cheese*

1. Preheat oven to 400 degrees.
2. Place the bread slices on a flat surface and brush one side of each with the melted butter.

3. Turn the slices over and spread the other sides with Russian dressing. Arrange equal amounts of corned beef on 4 of the slices smeared with Russian dressing. Add equal amounts of sauerkraut over the corned beef. Arrange an equal number of slices of cheese over the sauerkraut. Cover the layered slices with the remaining four slices of bread, Russian dressing side touching the filling.

4. Place the sandwiches on a hot griddle or in a large skillet and cook until browned on one side. Turn and brown briefly on the other. Place the griddle or skillet in the oven and bake briefly, just until the cheese is melted. If the cheese melts normally while on the griddle or skillet, do not use the oven.

Yield: 4 sandwiches.

Russian dressing

½   *cup mayonnaise*
1   *tablespoon chili sauce, or tomato ketchup*
1   *teaspoon finely grated or chopped onion*

The American sandwich, as interpreted in sculpture by Jack Newman

½   *teaspoon horseradish*
¼   *teaspoon Worcestershire
     sauce*
1   *tablespoon finely chopped
     parsley*
1   *tablespoon black or red caviar,
     optional*

Combine all the ingredients in a mixing bowl. Blend well.

Yield: About ½ cup.

Croque Monsieur

(A baked ham and cheese sandwich)

2   *square slices firm-textured
     white bread*
4   *thin slices Swiss cheese
     (Emmenthal with the holes or
     gruyère, which is stronger in
     flavor)*
2   *thin slices baked ham*
1   *or 2 tablespoons butter*

1. Preheat oven to 400 degrees.

2. For one sandwich, place a slice of bread on a flat surface. Top it neatly with two thin slices of cheese trimmed to fit. Cover with the ham, also trimmed to fit. Cover with the remaining bread slice.

3. Melt the butter and generously brush the top of the sandwich with butter. Brush the bottom of a heavy skillet just large enough to hold the sandwich. Add the sandwich, brushed side down. Now, generously brush the unbuttered side with butter.

4. Cook the sandwich on top of the stove until the bottom is nicely browned. Turn the sandwich over and immediately put it in the oven. Bake it just until the filling is piping hot and the cheese has melted. If desired, trim the sides. Cut in half and serve piping hot.

Yield: 1 sandwich.

Irma Rhode's Onion Sandwiches

12   *thin slices sandwich bread,
      preferably with a fairly firm
      texture*
 6   *tablespoons mayonnaise*
12   *wafer-thin onion slices
      Salt and freshly ground pepper to taste*
 1   *cup finely chopped parsley*

1. The measurements listed here are purely arbitrary. Much will depend on the size of the sandwiches and the amount of mayonnaise you wish to spread on each sandwich.

2. Select a cooky cutter measuring from 1½ to 2½ inches in diameter. Cut out rounds from the center of the bread slices.

3. Using a small spatula spread mayonnaise on each of the bread rounds. Place 1 onion slice in the center on half the bread rounds. The diameter of the onion slice should approximate that of the bread round. Sprinkle with salt and pepper. Cover with another bread round, mayonnaise side on top of the onion.

4. Using the spatula, liberally smear the outside rim of the sandwiches with mayonnaise. Roll the rim of each sandwich in parsley to coat the outside rim generously. Continue until all the sandwiches are coated, adding more ingredients as necessary.

Yield: 12 or more sandwiches.

May

A S THE TITLE of this and earlier volumes indicates, this is a collection of favorite recipes and there is, of course, unquestioned pleasure for the author in having immediate reference. Such a thought occurred in perusing the recipes for sorrel—that delicacy that appears in late spring and early autumn. One of the delights of sorrel is that it is one of the few seasonal foods—like home-grown tomatoes and just-picked corn on the cob—left to Americans. We are so accustomed to discovering the likes of asparagus spears and strawberries in mid-December that new, bright green leaves just plucked from the garden are a special treat.

We are also somewhat partial to May in that on those first warm days we can feast out of doors on barbecue.

There are certain foods in this world that know absolutely no season—a category that would include stuffed vegetables. If anyone had ever indexed or otherwise charted my personal affinities by way of food, they would surely have discovered that stuffed onions, peppers, tomatoes and almost anything else that can be adapted to a savory filling rank high on my personal list of things that are choicest.

In a separate item, there is a lengthy discourse on the many ways to prepare and cook fresh artichokes, including stuffed.

And lastly, special mention should be made of the writeup on Guy Pascal, one of Manhattan's finest pastry chefs, who started out in this country as a French import dancing the cancan with a troupe from the Folies Bergère. We printed Guy's recipe for a cheesecake that purportedly was that of the original Lindy's restaurant. The letters that followed involved me in a controversy that will not soon be forgotten.

Stuffed Quartet

WITH PIERRE FRANEY

If anyone were to trace the patterns of our enthusiasms, there would certainly be one in bold and clear outline for stuffed vegetables. Who cares or needs to reason why. Perhaps it is the sheer versatility of stuffing them. Perhaps it is the endless combinations of flavors and textures that can be achieved in the act. Hence this quartet of good things stuffed—onions, sweet peppers, tomatoes and zucchini. These dishes are excellent when served as a main course, perhaps for lunch or supper. Most of them are also equally as good the next day served cold or at room temperature.

Tomates Farcies

(Stuffed tomatoes)

6   *red, ripe, firm tomatoes, about 2½ pounds*
    Salt and freshly ground pepper
2   *tablespoons butter*
1   *cup finely chopped onion*
1   *clove garlic, finely minced*
2   *bay leaves*
½   *teaspoon chopped thyme*
2   *teaspoons chopped fresh basil, or 1 teaspoon dried*
¾   *pound ground pork, or pork with veal*
3   *tablespoons pine nuts, optional*
4   *tablespoons grated Parmesan cheese*
2   *tablespoons finely chopped parsley*
10 *tablespoons bread crumbs*
2   *tablespoons peanut, vegetable or corn oil*

1. Preheat oven to 400 degrees.

2. Cut out and discard the core of each tomato. Using a sharp knife, cut off a thin slice from the bottom. Reserve.

3. Starting at the bottom and using a melon ball cutter, scoop out the center pulp of each tomato, leaving the natural shell of the vegetable. Sprinkle the insides of each tomato with salt and pepper and set aside.

4. Heat the butter in a skillet and add the onion. Finely chop the garlic with one of the bay leaves. Add this to the skillet. Add the tomato pulp and cook about 10 minutes.

5. Spoon half the tomato sauce over the bottom of a baking dish just large enough to hold the tomatoes in one layer.

6. To the remaining sauce add the thyme, basil, ground meat, pine nuts, half the cheese, parsley and 8 tablespoons of the bread crumbs.

7. Stuff the hollowed-out tomatoes with equal portions of the filling.

8. Arrange the tomatoes stuffed-side up over the sauce in the baking dish.

9. Sprinkle with the remaining cheese blended with the remaining crumbs. Sprinkle with oil and place in the oven. Bake 30 to 35 minutes, basting occasionally.

Oignons Farcies

(Stuffed onions)

8 onions, about ½ pound each
   Salt and freshly ground pepper
8 slices bacon, cut into ½-inch cubes
¼ cup finely chopped onion
2 teaspoons finely chopped garlic
¼ pound finely chopped ham

6 tablespoons fine, fresh bread crumbs
1 tablespoon heavy cream
1 egg, lightly beaten
¼ teaspoon freshly grated nutmeg
¼ cup finely chopped parsley
2 tablespoons grated Parmesan cheese
2 tablespoons peanut, vegetable or corn oil
¼ cup chicken broth

1. Preheat oven to 400 degrees.

2. Peel the onions. Cut off a thin slice from the bottom and top of each onion. Using a melon ball cutter, hollow out the center of each onion, leaving a shell about ½-inch thick all around and on the bottom.

3. Drop the onions into boiling water and simmer about 10 minutes. Drain.

4. Sprinkle the inside of each onion with salt and pepper to taste.

5. Meanwhile, cook the bacon in a skillet until rendered of fat. Add the chopped onion and garlic and cook until wilted. Remove from the heat and add the ham, 4 tablespoons crumbs, cream, egg, nutmeg, parsley, salt and pepper to taste. Return to the heat, stirring, about 1 minute, or until heated through. Do not cook. Let the filling cool slightly.

6. Stuff the cavities of the onions with the filling, piling it up over the top. Sprinkle with a blend of remaining bread crumbs and cheese and sprinkle with oil. Arrange the onions on a buttered baking dish and pour the broth around them. Place in the oven and bake 45 minutes, basting occasionally. If necessary, cover loosely with foil to prevent overbrowning.

Yield: 4 servings.

Courgettes Farcies

(Stuffed zucchini)

4   zucchini, about 1½ pounds
3   tablespoons olive oil
½   cup finely chopped onion
1   clove garlic, finely minced
1   hot, red pepper, crushed, or
     ½ teaspoon hot red pepper
     flakes, optional
¼   pound ground pork or a com-
     bination of pork and veal
8   tablespoons bread crumbs
1   egg, lightly beaten
     Salt and freshly ground pep-
     per
4   tablespoons grated Parmesan
     cheese
¼   cup fresh or canned chicken
     broth

1. Preheat oven to 400 degrees.

2. Trim off the ends of the zucchini. Split each zucchini lengthwise
in half. Cut off a thin slice from the
bottom of each half to aid the halves in
sitting flat when stuffed. Drop into
boiling water and let simmer 1 minute. Drain.

3. Using a melon ball cutter,
scrape out the center of each half,
leaving a shell about ¼-inch thick. Set
the shells aside. Chop the pulp.

4. Heat 1 tablespoon of the oil in
a skillet and add the onion and garlic.
Cook until onion is wilted and add the
chopped pulp, hot pepper, pork, 6 tablespoons bread crumbs, egg, salt and
pepper to taste and 2 tablespoons
Parmesan cheese. Cook briefly, stirring and blending thoroughly. Cool
briefly.

5. Add equal portions of the mixture to the cavity of each half. Lightly
oil a baking dish and arrange the

halves on it. Blend remaining 2 tablespoons each of crumbs and cheese and
sprinkle over the top. Sprinkle with
the remaining oil. Add the broth to
the baking dish and bake 30 minutes,
basting occasionally, until piping hot
and cooked.

Yield: 4 servings.

Poivrons Vert Farcies

(Stuffed green peppers)

4   green peppers, about 1½
     pounds
8   sweet or hot Italian sausages
1   cup finely chopped onion
1   clove garlic, finely minced
1   tablespoon curry powder
     Salt and freshly ground pep-
     per
1½ cups cooked rice
1   egg, lightly beaten
¼   cup chicken broth
2   tablespoons fresh bread
     crumbs
2   tablespoons grated Parmesan
     cheese
2   tablespoons olive oil

1. Preheat the oven to 400 degrees.

2. Cut off the stem of each pepper if there is one. Cut the pepper in
half lengthwise or widthwise. Drop
into boiling water for 1 minute. Drain
thoroughly.

3. Remove the meat from the
sausage skins. Put the meat in a skillet
and cook, stirring to break up any
lumps. Add the onion, garlic, curry
powder, salt and pepper to taste.

4. Cook, stirring often, 8 to 10
minutes. Let cool briefly.

5. Scrape the mixture into a mixing bowl and add the rice, egg and broth. Stir to blend. Stuff the pepper halves with equal portions of the mixture and sprinkle with crumbs blended with the cheese. Sprinkle with the oil. Arrange the halves on a baking dish and bake 45 minutes, or until piping hot and cooked.

Yield: 4 servings.

Artichokes: Hearts and Other Parts

Legend has it that Catherine de Medici of Italy was the mother of classic French cooking. Culinary history tells us that when she came to France as a child bride to marry Henry II, the future king, she brought with her an assortment of chefs and cooks from her home in Renaissance Italy.

Not the least of the fascinating facets of that lady's tastes (she is also said to have introduced refined table manners into her husband's domain), her favorite food was hearts of artichokes, which are, along with asparagus, among the most elegant of vegetables.

The name is derived from the Italian, articiciocco and archiciocco. Many of the European names for the globe artichoke are similarly derived: The current Italian name is carciofi; the Spanish, alcachofas; the French, artichauts, and the Polish, karzochy.

In any event, this is the absolute midst of the artichoke season in America, and most of the artichokes that may grace your table probably come from a town in California called Castrovilla. It is a few miles off the Pacific Ocean, south of San Francisco and just north of Monterey. It is especially suited to the growing of artichokes because the farmlands around the town are frequently shrouded in fog, a condition that artichoke plants thrive on.

Unlike most vegetables, artichokes cause an interesting chemical reaction in the mouth when eaten. They have a nutty flavor and cause any subsequent food or drink to taste "sweet" in the mouth. Thus there are certain wine fanciers who declare that wine should never be poured at any point during a meal when artichokes are served. To my own taste, it is a trivial point.

There are basically three ways in which artichokes are cooked. They are cooked whole (with the tips of the leaves trimmed for the sake of elegance) to be served with the likes of a vinaigrette or mayonnaise sauce. They are trimmed and pared all around to leave only the bottom to be stuffed at will and according to any desired recipe. Or the whole is trimmed and hollowed out and made ready for stuffing, perhaps to be used as a main course.

There are hundreds of ways to prepare and dress artichokes. Here are several.

How to Cook Whole Artichokes for Vinaigrette

Cut off the stems of the artichokes, using a sharp knife, to produce a neat, flat base. As the artichokes are cut, rub any cut surfaces with lemon to prevent discoloration. Slice off the top "cone" of the artichoke, about 1 inch from the tip.

Rub cut surfaces with lemon

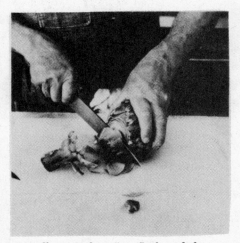

Cut off stem and top "cone" of artichoke

Using a pair of kitchen scissors, cut off the sharp tips of the leaves, about ½ inch down.

Place in a kettle and add cold water to cover and salt to taste. For each 2 quarts of water, add the juice of 1 lemon. Cover and bring to the boil. Cook 45 minutes.

Drain the artichokes. Using a melon ball scoop, hollow out the fuzzy choke in the center. Arrange them bottom-side up on a rack to drain. Let cool. Chill. They are now ready to be served with cold sauces such as vinaigrette or mayonnaise.

How to Prepare Whole Artichokes for Stuffing

Cut off the stems of the artichokes, using a sharp knife, to produce a neat, flat base. As the artichokes are cut, rub any cut surface with lemon to prevent discoloration. Slice off the top "cone" of the artichoke about 1 inch from the tip.

Using a pair of kitchen scissors, cut off the sharp tips of the leaves, about ½ inch down.

Use a melon ball scoop and hollow out the fuzzy choke in the center, taking care to remove all of it. Turn the artichokes upside down and press down to open up the center and facilitate stuffing. Turn right side up and stuff as desired.

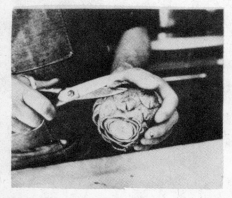

Cut off the sharp tips of the leaves

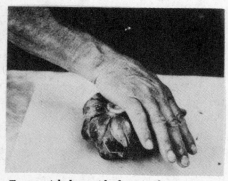

Turn artichoke upside down and press to open up center

Artichauts Farcis

(Stuffed artichokes)

4	large artichokes prepared for stuffing (see instruction)
3	tablespoons olive oil
1½	cups finely chopped onions
½	pound ground pork
2	cloves garlic, finely minced
3	tablespoons finely chopped parsley
1	small bay leaf
	Salt and freshly ground pepper to taste
½	teaspoon dried thyme
1½	cups bread crumbs
	Hot red pepper flakes to taste
2	slices bacon, cut into small pieces
1½	cups chicken broth

1. Prepare the artichokes for stuffing and preheat the oven to 350 degrees.

2. Heat 1 tablespoon oil in a skillet and add 1 cup of onion. Cook, stirring, until wilted. Add the pork and 1 clove of minced garlic. Cook, stirring, until meat changes color. Add the parsley, bay leaf, salt, pepper, thyme, bread crumbs and red pepper flakes. Blend well.

3. Stuff the artichokes throughout, that is to say, in the hollowed-out cavity and between the leaves, pushing the stuffing down toward the bottom.

4. Cook the bacon in a casserole large enough to hold the artichokes in one layer. When rendered of fat, add remaining ½ cup onion and remaining 1 clove minced garlic. Add the artichokes, bottom side down. Dribble remaining oil over the artichokes and pour the chicken broth around them.

Stuff the artichoke in the hollowed-out cavity and between the leaves

Sprinkle with salt and pepper. Bring to the boil and cover closely. Place in the oven and bake 1 hour.

Yield: 4 servings.

How to Prepare Artichoke Bottoms

Cut off the stems of the artichokes, using a sharp knife to produce a neat flat base. As the artichokes are cut, rub any cut surface with lemon to prevent discoloration.

Using a sharp knife, trim all around the sides and base of the artichoke until the base is smooth and white with the green exterior pared away.

Place 1 artichoke at a time on its side on a flat surface. Using the knife, slice off the top of the artichoke, leaving a base about 1½ inches deep. Using a paring knife, trim all around the sides and bottom to remove the green exterior that remains. Do not remove the fuzzy choke at this time. This comes out easily when the artichokes are cooked.

The artichokes are now ready to be cooked in what is called a blanc légume, or vegetable whitener, a blend of water and flour. Enough blanc légume is used to barely cover the artichoke bottoms as they cook.

For each 6 cups of water to be used, use ¼ cup flour.

Place an ordinary kitchen sieve over the kettle in which the artichokes will be cooked. Add the flour. Pour cold water over the flour, rubbing to dissolve the flour in the water. Add salt to taste. Add the artichoke bottoms and bring to the boil. Cover the kettle closely and cook about 25 minutes, or until bottoms are tender. Remove the kettle from the heat. If the artichokes are not to be used immediately, let them rest in the cooking liquid until ready to use. Before using, drain the bottoms and pull or scrape out the fuzzy chokes.

Artichoke bottoms may be reheated in two ways if not used immediately. They may be reheated in the cooking liquid, or they may be drained, the fuzz removed and placed, hollowed-out side down, on a baking dish. They may be brushed with butter and baked briefly until heated through in a preheated 350 degree oven.

Fonds d'Artichauts Archiduc

(Artichoke bottoms stuffed with spinach and mushrooms)

6   *cooked artichoke bottoms (see instructions)*

2   *pounds fresh spinach in bulk,*
     or 2 10-ounce packages
     Salt
1   *tablespoon butter*
¼   *pound mushrooms, thinly*
     sliced
     Freshly ground pepper to taste
¼   *teaspoon freshly grated nut-*
     meg
1½   *cups mornay sauce (see recipe)*
6   *teaspoons grated Parmesan*
     cheese

1. Cook the artichoke bottoms and set aside.

2. Pick over the spinach. Tear off and discard any tough stems and blemished leaves. Rinse the spinach well and drop into boiling salted water to cover. Cook about 3 minutes and drain. Let cool. Squeeze between the palms of the hands to remove excess moisture. Chop the spinach on a flat surface and set aside.

3. Heat the butter in a skillet and add the sliced mushrooms. Sprinkle with salt and pepper. Cook, stirring, until golden brown. Add the spinach and nutmeg and toss to blend and heat through.

4. Drain the artichoke bottoms. Stuff each bottom with equal amounts of the spinach and mushroom filling. Spoon a little mornay sauce over the bottom of a baking dish and arrange the stuffed bottoms on it. Spoon more mornay sauce over the spinach and mushroom filling and sprinkle with equal amounts of grated Parmesan.

5. When ready to cook, preheat the oven to 400 degrees. Bake the stuffed artichoke bottoms until piping hot throughout and bubbling on top. To glaze further, run briefly under the broiler.

Yield: 6 servings.

Mornay sauce

2   *tablespoons butter*
3   *tablespoons flour*
1¼   *cups milk*
     Salt and freshly ground pep-
     per to taste
¼   *teaspoon grated nutmeg*
     A pinch of cayenne pepper
¼   *cup grated gruyère, or Swiss*
     cheese
1   *egg yolk*

1. Melt the butter in a saucepan and add the flour, stirring with a wire whisk. When blended, add the milk, stirring rapidly with the whisk. Add salt, pepper, nutmeg and cayenne.

2. Stir in the cheese and heat until cheese is melted and blended. Remove from the heat and add the yolk, stirring vigorously.

Yield: About 1½ cups.

Artichoke Bottoms and Mushrooms Bordelaise

4   *cooked artichoke bottoms (see*
     instructions)
¼   *pound mushrooms, about 4*
     large
2   *tablespoons butter*
     Salt and freshly ground pep-
     per to taste
2   *tablespoons chopped shallots*
2   *tablespoons finely chopped*
     parsley

1. Drain and hollow out the cooked artichoke bottoms. Place the bottoms, hollowed-out side down, on a flat surface. Cut in half, holding the knife at a slight diagonal. Cut each half into thirds, once more holding the knife at a slight diagonal. Set aside.

2. Slice the mushrooms similarly and set aside.

3. Heat 1 tablespoon of butter in a skillet and add the mushrooms, salt and pepper. Toss and stir until browned. Add the artichokes, remaining 1 tablespoon butter, shallots and parsley. Cook, stirring and tossing the ingredients, until piping hot. Serve as a vegetable course.

Yield: 4 to 6 servings.

Fonds d'Artichauts Provençale

(Artichoke bottoms stuffed with tomatoes)

6 *to 8 cooked artichoke bottoms (see instructions)*
1 *pound red, ripe tomatoes, peeled and chopped, or use an equal amount of imported canned tomatoes*
4 *tablespoons butter Salt and freshly ground pepper to taste*
1 *clove garlic, finely minced*
2 *tablespoons finely chopped parsley*

1. Prepare the artichoke bottoms.

2. Prepare the tomatoes. Heat 1 tablespoon butter in a saucepan and add the tomatoes, salt and pepper. Bring to the boil and simmer about 10 minutes, stirring often from the bottom to prevent sticking.

3. Preheat the oven to 350 degrees.

4. Arrange the hollowed-out bottoms on a baking dish and brush with butter. Bake until piping hot, about 10 minutes.

5. Fill the hot artichoke bottoms with equal portions of boiling tomato mixture.

6. Heat the remaining butter in a small skillet and add the garlic. When foamy but not browned, add the parsley. Pour this mixture over the tomatoes and serve immediately.

Yield: 6 to 8 servings.

Lindy's Cheesecake Controversy

When Lindy's restaurant in Manhattan closed its doors in September 1969, it was the end of a legend in more ways than one. It was fabled for its sturgeon, corned beef and blintzes, but most of all for its cheesecakes, which were as integral a part of Gotham culture as Yankee Stadium, Coney Island, Grant's Tomb and the Staten Island Ferry.

Approximately twenty years ago, shortly before his death, I approached Leo Lindermann, the owner of the establishment, and pleaded with him to let me have the recipe for his cheesecake. I was rewarded with a rather wan and tolerant smile as though I had demanded the Kohinoor diamond.

Presumably the recipe for the cheesecake had disappeared from the face of the earth, but I now have what is purported to be that recipe. It was offered to me by Guy Pascal, the distinguished pastry chef at La Côte Basque restaurant who, tomorrow, will open what promises to be one of the finest pastry shops in Manhattan, the Délices la Côte Basque, 1032 Lexington Avenue (between 73rd and 74th Streets).

How Mr. Pascal came into possession of the recipe is a six-month study in intrigue, subterfuge and deception in and around the sugar bins and flour barrels of a Las Vegas kitchen.

The case of the Purloined Recipe began when the young chef opened a small pastry shop in the kingdom of casinos ten years ago.

"One day," Mr. Pascal said, "an old man came to ask for a job. Among his other credentials he had spent years in New York preparing the cheesecake at Lindy's. At that time I'd never heard of Lindy's cheesecake, and I hired him in spite of the fact. Well, he started to make his dessert and my business started to boom, people were standing in line. I was fascinated at the appeal of the cake. So much so, I offered him money for the recipe. He refused and I offered him more. He still refused.

"He was such a stubborn old man I decided there was only one way I'd ever get that recipe. I would have to, how should I say, borrow it?

"For weeks I didn't mention the cake. When he worked he was pretty furtive in assembling his ingredients. But I kept a strict account of the number of cakes he produced balanced against the amount of cream cheese we purchased. I have very good peripheral vision, and out of the corner of my eye as the weeks passed I figured out the quantity of orange peel he used, how much lemon peel, the number of eggs and so on. And after six months I had it perfected."

Although Guy Pascal is acknowledged to be a master pastry maker, it is almost as if he were pursued by his profession rather than the other way around.

A few days ago he put the dazzling finishing touches on a series of desserts he had prepared—the cheesecake; a four-tiered, sinfully rich fantasy called le délice de la Côte Basque; almond tiles, and a delicate mousselike strawberry dessert called Eugénie.

As he smeared the bottom and sides of le délice with whipped cream, he stated that he was born in the town of Avignon, famed for its bridge.

"My father was a farmer and his one great goal in life was to make me a patissier, to some day open a pastry shop in Avignon. I had other ideas. When I was four years old I was "The Merry Widow" and I knew the one thing I wanted to be was a dancer.

"My father was appalled. My son! A dancer! It would be the scandal of the town! So he apprenticed me at the local pastry shop. As soon as I could I went to work in another pastry shop in Cannes. I'd heard of a ballet instructor there who had danced with Pavlova. My father didn't know it, but I enrolled in her class. Every day at noon I'd tell my boss I had to go for English lessons and I'd head for ballet." Within two or three years he was accomplished in two fields, pastry and the dance.

In Paris he became a pastry cook at the well-known hotel Prince des Galles. There he enrolled in the Serve Perritti School of the Dance. Eventually he became a solo dancer at the Chatelet in Paris and spent a year in the Roland Petit dance company. He danced at the Casino de Vichy and met the choreographer of the Folies Bergère.

"At that time," he says, "I had to admit to myself that I would never be a great star. So when I was asked to go with the Folies Bergère troupe to dance at the Tropicana Hotel in Las Vegas, I accepted. That was in 1961, and I danced the cancan night after night.

"Eventually, I said the hell with it. I decided to go back into pastry making. I hadn't touched it in ten years, but when I asked the chef at the Tropicana if he would take me on, he hastily employed me. I would dance in the show from midnight on and get up at five o'clock to go to the kitchen."

Sometime later, he opened his own pastry shop, where he met the former pastry chef of Lindy's, and that's how he surreptiously and deviously developed the recipe for Lindy's cheesecake. As far as we know, it is the first time the recipe—or a reasonable approximation of it—is being published.

Lindy's Cheesecake?

Butter
½   cup fine cake crumbs, or gra-
     ham cracker crumbs (see note)
2   lemons
1   orange
1½   pounds cream cheese
1   teaspoon vanilla
½   cup heavy cream
¾   cup plus 2 tablespoons sugar
4   large eggs
2   tablespoons sour cream
¼   cup half-and-half

1. Preheat the oven to 375 degrees.

2. Generously butter an 8-by-2-
inch round cake pan. Sprinkle the inside with the crumbs, then shake out
excess crumbs.

3. Grate the lemons and orange.
Set the grated rind aside. Use the 2
lemons and orange for another purpose.

4. Put the cream cheese in the
bowl of an electric mixer. Add the
grated rind and vanilla, beating.
Gradually add the heavy cream and
sugar, beating constantly on moderate
speed. The important thing to avoid
in making this recipe is beating on
very high speed. This would incorpo-
rate air into the cheesecake and make
the cake rise like a soufflé. Add the
eggs, one at a time, beating well after
each addition.

5. Beat in the sour cream and
half-and-half.

6. Pour the mixture into the prepared pan and smooth the surface. Set
the pan in a larger pan and pour boiling water around it. Place in the oven
and bake 1¼ hours until the center
does not quiver when the pan is sha-
ken. Remove from water bath and let

stand on a rack about 10 minutes. Invert and unmold while hot. Let stand until cool.

Yield: 8 to 12 servings.

Note: Crumbs can be made from any day-old cake, such as poundcake or a genoise.

Le Délice de la Côte Basque

(A multi-layered meringue dessert)

4   meringue crusts (see recipe for Le Succès)
Ganache à la suisse (see recipe)
Café crème (see recipe)
Crème chantilly (see recipe)
Broken and random pieces of meringue
3   tablespoons confectioners' sugar

1. Spread one meringue crust with a thick layer of ganache, using it all.

2. Top the ganache with another meringue crust and spread this with a thick layer of coffee-flavored butter cream (café crème). Reserve enough butter cream to coat the top and sides of the délice at the end.

3. Top with a third meringue crust and spread with a layer of whipped cream (crème chantilly), using it all. Top with the final meringue crust.

4. Spread the bottom and sides of the dessert with the reserved butter cream. Crush the broken and random pieces of meringue to make crumbs. Coat the bottom and sides with the

crumbs. Sprinkle the top with confectioner's sugar. Refrigerate until well chilled.

Yield: 10 or more servings.

Guy Pascal spreads meringue with ganache

Le succès
(An almond meringue crust)

1   cup egg whites
½   pound blanched ground almonds (see note)
3   tablespoons cornstarch
2   cups plus ⅓ cup superfine sugar
Butter
Flour

1. Preheat the oven to 275 degrees.

2. Measure out the egg whites and set aside.

3. Combine the ground almonds

Top ganache with meringue

with the cornstarch and 2 cups sugar and blend well. Set aside.

4. Place the egg whites in the bowl of an electric mixer and start beating on medium speed. When they are frothy but still soft, gradually add remaining ⅓ cup of sugar, beating constantly. Start beating on high speed and beat the egg whites until stiff.

5. Remove the bowl from the beater and, using a rubber spatula, fold the ground almond mixture into the meringue.

6. Butter and lightly flour a baking sheet. Shake off excess flour. Place a 9-inch disk such as the removable tin bottom of a quiche pan on the floured baking sheet. Trace out 4 9-inch circles.

7. Outfit a pastry bag with a round tip pastry tube (No. 4) and add

the meringue mixture. Place the tip of the tube in the center of one of the traced-out circles. Push out the meringue in an ever increasing circle to the rim of the traced-out circle. Continue filling in the remaining circles. Squirt out the remaining meringue at random places on the baking sheet. The shape of this doesn't matter. After baking, the random meringues will be crushed for decoration.

8. Place the baking sheet in the oven and bake 25 minutes or longer or until golden and crisp. Take care that the meringues do not become too brown.

Yield: 4 meringue circles plus random-shaped meringues.

Note: Blanched almonds may be ground at home in a blender or food processor. They are also available at some specialty food shops.

Spread with thick layer of cafe creme

Top with a third meringue crust

Ganache à la suisse
(A stiff chocolate cream filling)

½   *pound sweet chocolate*
2   *cups heavy cream*
1   *vanilla bean*

1. Using a heavy knife, cut the chocolate into fairly small cubes. Put the cubes in a large mixing bowl. Set aside.

2. Combine the cream and vanilla bean in a saucepan and bring to the boil. Do not boil. Pour this over the chocolate and stir to dissolve the chocolate pieces.

3. Place in the refrigerator. This filling is a bit tricky to make and its success depends on temperature. If the chocolate cream becomes too cold before whipping, the end product will be grainy. If it is not cold enough, the cream will not whip.

4. Occasionally stir the chocolate cream. When it seems nicely chilled but not cold, start beating with a wire whisk. When the choclate cream becomes almost but not quite like stiffly beaten whipped cream, stop beating. Refrigerate once more. The chocolate cream will continue to harden as it stands.

Yield: About 4 cups.

Top with final meringue crust

Café crème
(Coffee butter cream)

1   *cup egg whites*
1   *pound confectioners' sugar*
1   *pound butter at room temperature*
3   *tablespoons powdered instant coffee, preferably Sanka*
¼   *cup boiling water*

1. Put the egg whites in the bowl of an electric mixer. Add the confectioners' sugar. Using a large wire whisk, start beating the mixture over very low heat or boiling water until it is slightly warmed, creamy and smooth. This mixture must not become hot. The temperature should not exceed 90 degrees. Remember that this temperature is less than body temperature.

2. Transfer the bowl to the mixing machine and beat on high speed until quite cool, snow white and thick.

Spread third meringue with whipped cream

3. While beating, add the butter bit by bit. Beat, using moderate speed. The mixture will look as if it is about to separate. This is normal. Continue beating until the butter and meringue adjust themselves to an identical temperature. It will become smooth.

4. Blend the instant coffee with the boiling water. Fold this into the butter cream and beat thoroughly. Refrigerate.

Yield: Enough pastry cream for a 9-inch délice.

Spread bottom and sides with reserved butter cream

Crème chantilly

1½   *cups heavy cream*
¼   *cup confectioners' sugar*

1. Put the cream in the container of an electric mixer and start beating on high speed.

2. When the cream starts to thicken, gradually add the sugar, beating constantly. Continue until the cream is stiff. Do not overbeat. Refrigerate.

Yield: About 3 cups of whipped cream.

Coat bottom and sides with crumbled meringue

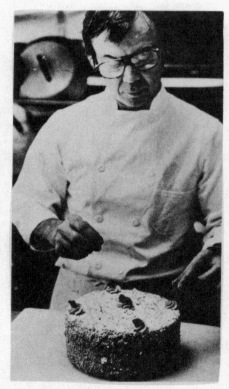

Sprinkle top with confectioners' sugar

Eugénie

1   pint red, ripe strawberries, plus 6 more for garnish
4   tablespoons kirsch or framboise
3   cups heavy cream
5   tablespoons sugar
2   envelopes unflavored gelatin
¼   cup cold water

1. Pick over the berries and hull them. Rinse well and drain. Pat dry.

2. Cut 1 pint of berries into eighths and place in a bowl. Add 1 tablespoon of kirsch and set aside.

3. Lightly butter an 8-cup soufflé dish. Refrigerate.

4. Start beating the cream with a wire whisk or electric beater and, as it starts to stiffen, gradually beat in 3 tablespoons of sugar. Continue beating the cream until stiff.

5. Soften the gelatin and water in a small saucepan and heat, stirring, until the gelatin dissolves. Scrape this into a large mixing bowl and add remaining kirsch and 1 cup of the whipped cream, stirring rapidly with a whisk to blend well. Beat in 2 more tablespoons of sugar and the strawberries and stir.

6. Add the remaining cream and fold it in with a rubber spatula. Spoon into the prepared mold. Refrigerate several hours or until set.

7. When ready to serve, dip the mold into a basin of hot water. Remove, dip again. Remove and dip a third time. Place a round serving dish over the mold, invert the dish and unmold the Eugénie. Garnish with the remaining strawberries, left whole or cut in half.

Yield: 10 to 12 servings.

Tuiles d'Amande

(Almond tiles)

1   cup chopped almonds
½   cup sugar
3   tablespoons flour
1   large egg
1   teaspoon vanilla

1. Preheat the oven to 375 degrees.

2. The texture of the almonds must not be too fine. The coarseness of the pieces should be like that of rice.

3. Place the almonds in a bowl and add the remaining ingredients. Blend well.

4. Grease a baking sheet with butter and sprinkle with flour. Shake off excess flour. Spoon about 1½ teaspoonsful of the mixture onto the prepared sheet. There should be about 32 mounds with about 2 inches of space between each. Flatten each spoonful with the tines of a dampened fork.

5. Place in the oven and bake 8 to 10 minutes or until golden brown. Do not let them become too dark.

6. Immediately remove them and place them top-side down in a small round ring mold. The purpose of this is to give each tile a slightly curved shape. Let cool briefly and turn out onto a flat surface. Let cool and serve.

Yield: 32 tiles.

Visidantine

(An almond tart)

The crust

2	*cups flour*
½	*cup granulated sugar*
2	*eggs*
½	*teaspoon pure vanilla extract*
½	*tablespoon lemon juice*
¼	*pound butter cut into small pieces*

The filling

¼	*pound butter at room temperature*
⅔	*cup sugar*
1⅓	*cups ground, blanched almonds*
3	*large eggs*
1	*tablespoon dark rum*
1	*cup thinly sliced blanched almonds*

The glaze

¼	*cup apricot preserves*

1. There are two preferred methods to make the crust. The easiest is with a food processor. Add the flour and sugar to the container of the food processor and start the motor. Add the eggs, one at a time, blending, and add the vanilla and lemon juice. Add the butter and continue blending until a workable dough forms.

2. Alternatively, spoon the flour onto a marble or formica surface and make a well in the center. Add the sugar to the center of the well and break the eggs at some point where the sugar and flour border each other. Add the vanilla and lemon juice to the eggs. With the fingers, blend the eggs, sugar, lemon and vanilla. Add the butter and start kneading and working the center ingredients while gradually bringing the flour to the center mass and working it in. Knead well, pushing the mixture from you with the heel of the hand, then scraping it back, kneading, scraping back and so on until well worked.

3. Roll the dough in a circle on a lightly floured board. Line a 9-inch quiche tin with a removable bottom with the mixture. Build up the sides slightly. Prick the bottom. Refrigerate. There will be leftover dough, which may be used to make an assortment of cookies.

4. Preheat the oven to 400 degrees.

5. To prepare the filling, cream the butter in the bowl of an electric mixer.

6. Separately, blend the sugar and ground almonds. Add about ⅓ of this mixture and 1 egg to the butter. Beat well. Add another ⅓ of the mixture and 1 more egg and beat well. Add the final ⅓ of almond mixture and the last egg and blend well. Beat in the rum.

7. Spoon and scrape this mixture into the prepared pan and sprinkle with the almonds. Place in the oven and bake 35 minutes. Remove the tart from the ring.

8. Melt the apricot preserves

with a little water over low heat, stirring. Spread this over the top of the tart.

Yield: 6 to 8 servings.

There's no doubt about it, New York is rich with cheesecake addicts. My publication of Chef Pascal's "purloined" recipe for Lindy's cheesecake triggered scores of letters from readers. Some disputed the recipe itself, others questioned technique. Many insisted that the real Lindy's cheesecake had a cooky dough shell and a fruit topping of cherries, strawberries or pineapples. The following is what the majority of readers suggested was the real, definitive, ultimate and final recipe for Lindy's cheesecake.

Lindy's Cheesecake

The dough

1	cup sifted all-purpose flour
¼	cup sugar
1	teaspoon grated lemon rind
	Pinch of vanilla bean pulp
1	egg yolk
½	cup butter

The filling

2½	pounds cream cheese
1¾	cups sugar
3	tablespoons flour
1½	teaspoons grated orange rind
1½	teaspoons grated lemon rind
	Pinch of vanilla bean pulp or
¼	teaspoon vanilla extract
5	eggs
2	egg yolks
¼	cup heavy cream

1. Prepare dough by combining flour, sugar, lemon rind and vanilla. Make a well in center and add egg yolk and butter. Work together quickly with hands until well blended. Wrap in waxed paper and chill thoroughly in refrigerator, about 1 hour.

2. Prepare filling by combining cheese, sugar, flour, grated orange and lemon rind and vanilla. Add eggs and egg yolks, one at a time, stirring lightly after each addition. Stir in cream. Set aside.

3. Preheat oven to 400 degrees. Butter the inside of a 9-inch springform pan. Remove top from pan.

4. Roll out ⅓ of dough ⅛-inch thick and place over bottom of pan. Trim off the dough by running a rolling pin over the sharp edge. Bake for 20 minutes or until a light gold. Cool.

5. Place the top of spring-form over the base. Roll remaining dough ⅛-inch thick and cut to fit the sides of the buttered pan. Fit strips to side of pan, joining ends of strips to line inside completely. Trim dough so it comes only ¾ of the way up the side.

6. Fill form with cheese mixture, bake in a 550-degree oven for 12 to 15 minutes. Reduce temperature to 200 degrees and continue baking 1 hour. Remove from oven and cool completely. If desired, top with strawberry glaze (see recipe).

7. To serve, loosen pastry from side of pan with a spatula. Remove top of spring-form pan. Cut cheesecake into wedges.

Yield: 12 servings.

Strawberry glaze

1 *quart strawberries*
¾ *cup sugar*
¼ *cup cold water*
    Salt
1½ *tablespoons cornstarch*
1 *teaspoon butter*

1. Wash berries. Crush about 1 cup of berries and put in a saucepan. Add sugar, water, a dash of salt and the cornstarch. Boil gently, for 2 minutes, stirring constantly. Stir in 1 teaspoon butter. Cool slightly.

2. Arrange uncooked strawberries on top of the pie, and spoon glaze over them. Chill for several hours.

Guy Pascal with a selection of his pastries

Feasting al Fresco

For the inveterate food enthusiast whose passion is dining out of doors, the arrival of summer has no more to do with the reckoning of "the apparent northward or southward motion of the sun" than the arrival of Capistrano swallows to indicate spring. Fie on calendars and bird watchers! Summer for the al fresco appetite more reasonably dates from the arrival of Memorial Day when the epicurean mind starts flexing itself toward thoughts of charcoal-grilled foods and other delights of feasting in sunlight and shade.

Summer comes with the firing up of barbecue pits and the welcome scent of fat dropped from a choice steak onto the white-hot coals. And a plague on those who say that charcoal grilling is the scourge of fine meats.

It is a question of semantics, but there is—or should be—a fine yet distinct line between what are simply grilled dishes and those that are barbecued. I maintain that grilling has to do with cooking foods on a grill. No sauce necessary. No seasoning for that matter. Just foods cooked on a metal frame or the equivalent thereof.

A barbecue depends on a sauce of a reasonably involved nature even if it is a blend of ketchup, Worcestershire sauce, butter and lemon juice. A sauce for grilled foods is something as simple as melted butter applied after the food is cooked. A barbecue sauce must be dabbed onto the food as it is grilled and afterward. And those rotisserie or spit-cooked chickens one encounters universally are in no way "barbecued," as they are frequently proposed to be. They are purely and simply spit-roasted.

Both barbecued foods and simply grilled dishes require a good deal of sensitivity to be done properly. It is not simply a question of throwing a hunk of beef, a chop or a chicken half on the grill. Techniques vary a good deal, depending on what is being cooked.

One of the first considerations is the grill itself. The metal should be scrubbed after each use and ideally it should be washed and drained and wiped. Foods to be cooked should be brushed or marinated with oil or butter or in a sauce containing one or the other to prevent sticking once applied to the grill.

A charcoal fire should be started well in advance of the time for grilling, and the factors to be considered where the fire is concerned are as follows:

Some foods demand intense heat and quick cooking. Such foods include very thin slices of meat such as a paillard of beef or veal. These are tossed on a very hot grill situated close to the firebed and the food might cook in one minute or less to the side.

Some foods demand moderate heat and are destined to be cooked for a reasonable length of time. These are foods such as a chicken split for broiling or a whole, cleaned, modest-size fish.

Some foods demand slow heat and prolonged cooking, frequently covered at times by the hood of the grill. These are foods such as spareribs and large portions of meat such as a loin of pork or a rump of beef. Long cooking is necessary to make them tender and well done.

Grilling, which includes charcoal grilling, of course, calls for more practical judgment than almost any other form of cookery and a manual can give only a broad outline of the factors involved. Charcoal should be heated until a white ash forms. Generally speaking, the charcoal should be one or two layers. The coals must be checked to make certain that heat is emanating from them at all times.

It is an obvious conjecture, of course, to say that grilled foods (not barbecued dishes—they came later with sophistication) were one of the earliest known forms of cooking, ranking in time just after foods cooked directly over flame or coals. Grilled dishes are universal and one of the earliest recorded is in oriental cookery, a Mongolian grill in which meat and vegetables are cooked on a rounded brazier. Legend has it that the first braziers were Mongol helmets heated over a fire with the food cooked on their rounded crowns.

There is certainly nothing arcane about grilling or barbecuing foods. It is largely a question of common sense.

In the several charcoal-grilled or barbecued dishes outlined here the cooking times are meant as a basic frame of reference.

Charcoal-grilled Duck, French-style

1   whole, cleaned, 4½- to 5-
    pound duck with giblets
½   bay leaf
    Salt and freshly ground pep-
    per to taste
¼   teaspoon dried thyme
1   tablespoon peanut, vegetable
    or corn oil
3   tablespoons butter
1   clove garlic, peeled and
    crushed
2   tablespoons chopped parsley

1. In this method of grilling duck, the breast is cut away in 2 neat, flat pieces without skin or bone. The legs and thighs are left more or less intact with skin on and bones in. The legs and thighs are cooked first because they require the longest cooking, about 30 minutes. The breast meat is grilled just before serving for it cooks quickly like a small, thin steak or scaloppine.

2. Place the duck back-side down on a flat surface. Rub a sharp knife such as boning knife along the breast bone, cutting through the skin and down to the bone. Carefully, run the knife between the skin and the meat,

pulling the skin with the fingers to expose the smooth breast meat. Cut off and discard the skin. Now, carefully, run the knife between the breast meat and the carcass, using the fingers as necessary. Remove the 2 pieces of breast meat.

3. Cut or carve off the 2 thighs, leaving the legs attached. Use the carcass for another purpose such as soup. Place the legs and thighs on a flat surface, skin side down, and carefully cut away the excessive peripheral skin fat that borders the thighs.

4. Sever the bone joint between the legs and thighs. This will facilitate cooking, but do not cut the legs and thighs in two.

5. Chop together the bay leaf, salt, pepper, and thyme, chopping until the bay leaf is quite fine. Rub this mixture on the legs and thighs and over the breast and giblets. Brush all with oil.

6. Arrange the breast pieces, ends touching, in a flat dish. Cover with giblets and neatly arrange the legs and thighs, skin side up, over all. Let stand till ready to cook.

7. Prepare a charcoal grill and have it ready. The coals must be white hot but not too plentiful or the meat will cook too fast. Arrange the bed of coals about 6 inches from the grill that will hold the duck for broiling. Arrange the giblets on a skewer and add them to the grill.

8. Place the legs and thighs, skin side down, on the grill. Grill the legs and thighs, turning as often as necessary, until skin is crisp and flesh is cooked. If necessary, brush the food with a little more oil as it cooks. Grill the giblets until done, turning as often as necessary. About 5 minutes before these foods are done, add the breast

meat and cook, 1 or 2 minutes to a side, until done. Ideally, the breast meat should be served a bit rare.

9. Transfer the pieces to a serving platter. Slice the breast meat on the bias and cut legs and thighs in half where they join.

10. Heat the butter and garlic and pour over the grilled pieces. Sprinkle with chopped parsley and serve immediately.

Yield: 2 to 4 servings.

Barbecued chicken and skewered giblets

Pork and Scallions in Lettuce Leaves

(Adapted from a recipe by
May Wong Trent)

The pork

2 *pounds ground pork*
1 *teaspoon sugar*
 Salt to taste
1 *tablespoon finely chopped garlic*
2 *teaspoons finely chopped fresh ginger*
1 *tablespoon dry sherry or shao hsing wine*

2   *tablespoons light soy sauce*
2   *tablespoons peanut, vegetable*
      or corn oil
6   *long scallions*

The sauce

½   *cup fish sauce (see note)*
⅓   *cup freshly squeezed lime juice*
1   *tablespoon finely chopped gar-*
      lic
2   *teaspoons grated fresh ginger*
½   *to 1 teaspoon hot red pow-*
      dered chilies (see note) or hot
      red pepper

The wrapping and garnishes

12   *large Boston lettuce leaves,*
       well rinsed and patted dry
12   *or more sprigs fresh coriander*
       Fresh mint leaves

1. Prepare a charcoal or other grill for cooking the meat. This should be done before starting to prepare the ingredients.

2. Combine the pork, sugar, salt, garlic, ginger, wine, soy sauce and peanut oil in a bowl. Blend well. Divide the mixture into 12 portions of approximately the same size.

3. Trim the ends of the scallions and pull off any tough or blemished outer leaves.

4. Cut each scallion in half widthwise.

5. Combine all the ingredients for the sauce and blend well. Set aside.

6. Flatten 1 portion of meat at a time between the palms. Arrange 1 scallion half down the center and wrap the meat around, sealing to enclose the scallion. Press the meat firmly about the scallion, but leave the ends of the scallion exposed. Arrange on a rack and refrigerate until ready to cook.

7. Arrange the meat on the grill and grill, turning often, until nicely browned on all sides and thoroughly cooked. Serve hot. To eat, open a lettuce leaf and add a sprig of fresh coriander and a fresh mint leaf. Add the pork and wrap the leaf around the sides, tucking in the bottom to prevent dripping. Serve the sauce on the side as a dip.

Yield: 4 to 8 servings.

Note: Fish sauce and powdered red pepper are widely available in Chinese markets in Chinatown, including the Southeast Asia Food and Trading Company, 68A Mott Street and the Chinese American Trading Company, 91 Mulberry Street. Also at Sunflower, 2445 Broadway (between 90th and 91st Streets).

Neset Eren's Turkish-style Grilled Lamb on Skewers

1   *pound ground lamb*
      Salt and freshly ground pep-
      per to taste
1   *small egg, lightly beaten*

1 *small onion*
  Oil
¾ *cup yogurt*
1 *clove garlic, finely minced*
4 *slices hot buttered toast*
3 *tablespoons hot melted butter*
1 *teaspoon paprika*

1. Prepare a charcoal grill. The grill should be placed about 4 inches above the hot coals.

2. In a mixing bowl combine the lamb, 2 tablespoons salt, pepper and egg. Grate the onion and squeeze it through cheesecloth to make one tablespoon of juice. Add it to the lamb.

3. Divide the mixture into 4 portions and roll each portion out into a sausage shape. It helps if the hands are dampened lightly with water before shaping. Brush the lamb rolls with oil and run one wooden skewer through the center of each roll, lengthwise.

4. Meanwhile, blend the yogurt, garlic, salt and pepper to taste.

5. Grill, turning often, until the lamb is cooked through. Arrange one roll on a slice of toast.

6. Spoon equal amounts of sauce over the lamb rolls and pour melted butter over this. Sprinkle with paprika and serve.

Yield: 4 servings.

Southern Barbecued Spareribs

1 *3½-pound slab of spareribs*
  Salt and freshly ground pepper to taste
  Southern barbecue sauce (see recipe)

1. Prepare a charcoal grill and have it ready. The coals must be white hot but not overly plentiful or the food will cook too fast. Arrange the grill 6 to 8 inches above the coals.

2. Cut the slab of spareribs in half, slicing between the center ribs, or leave it whole. Sprinkle all over with salt and pepper.

3. Arrange the spareribs on the grill and cook on one side about 10 minutes. Turn and cook on the other side about 10 minutes.

4. Start basting with sauce. Cook, turning the meat and basting as necessary until the meat is tender and cooked through, about 2 hours.

5. Give the spareribs a final brushing with the sauce and remove to a serving dish.

Yield: 2 to 4 servings.

Southern barbecue sauce

2 *tablespoons butter*
6 *tablespoons cider vinegar*
¼ *cup water*
1½ *cups tomato ketchup*
2 *tablespoons Worcestershire sauce*
¼ *teaspoon Tabasco sauce, or more to taste*
1 *teaspoon finely chopped garlic*
3 *tablespoons peanut, vegetable or corn oil*
  Salt and freshly ground pepper to taste
¼ *teaspoon red pepper flakes*
½ *bay leaf*
2 *tablespoons sugar*
1 *teaspoon paprika*
1 *lemon*

1. Combine all the ingredients except the lemon in a saucepan. Add the juice of the lemon. Cut the lemon into quarters and add it.

2. Heat thoroughly without boiling. Use to baste chicken, fish, spareribs and so on as they are grilled. This sauce will keep for days, tightly sealed, in the refrigerator.

Yield: About 2¾ cups.

Southern Barbecued Chicken

1 2½-pound chicken
   Salt and freshly ground pepper to taste
1 tablespoon oil or, preferably, softened lard
   Southern barbecue sauce (see recipe)

1. Prepare a charcoal grill and have it ready. The coals must be white hot but not overly plentiful or the food will cook too fast. Arrange the grill 6 to 8 inches above the coals.

2. Split the chicken in half for grilling. Place it skin side up on a flat surface and flatten it lightly with a flat mallet. This will help it lie flat on the grill. Sprinkle with salt and pepper to taste. Sprinkle the chicken with oil or rub with lard.

3. Place the chicken skin-side down on the grill and cook until browned, about 10 minutes. Brush the top with barbecue sauce and turn. Brush the skin side with sauce. Continue grilling, brushing often with sauce. Continue cooking until chicken is thoroughly cooked, 30 minutes or less.

4. Give the chicken a final brushing with the sauce and remove to a serving dish.

Yield: 2 to 4 servings.

Gourmet Grass

WITH PIERRE FRANEY

There is a rule of thumb in the world of food that the more scarce a food may be, the more it is held in high esteem in the minds and appetites of epicureans. This is certainly true in the case of truffles and foie gras and cockscombs and caviar.

One notable exception is the leaf of the sorrel plant—that slightly tart, delicate and multipurpose herb also known as sour grass. If sorrel seems scarce, it is probably because of the public's lack of familiarity with its many virtues and uses. Sorrel prospers and grows like grass throughout the spring, summer and fall. It is also available at the stands of most self-respecting greengrocers. Only a few of its uses are outlined here. One of them, the spectacular cream soup known as germiny; the other, that darling of la nouvelle cuisine, fresh salmon in sorrel sauce.

Potage Germiny

(Cream of sorrel soup)

1   *pound tender, fresh, un-blemished sorrel leaves*
¼   *cup butter*
½   *cup chopped onion*
3   *cups fresh or canned chicken broth*
2   *large egg yolks*
1   *cup heavy cream*
⅛   *teaspoon Tabasco sauce*
    Salt and freshly ground pepper

1. Pick over and remove the tougher parts of the sorrel stems. Rinse the leaves and drain well. Place the leaves on a flat surface and cut them into fine shreds (chiffonade). There should be about 5 cups. Set aside.

2. Heat the butter in a large saucepan and add the onion. Cook, stirring often, until wilted. Add the sorrel and cook until wilted.

3. Add the broth and bring to the boil. Simmer briefly.

4. Beat the yolks and add the cream, stirring to blend. Add the yolk and cream mixture to the soup, stirring rapidly with a wire whisk. Bring just to the boil but do not boil. Add the Tabasco sauce, salt and pepper to taste. Serve piping hot or chill and serve very cold.

Yield: 6 servings.

Saumon à l'Oseille

(Salmon with sorrel sauce)

1¼   pounds fillets of salmon
      (skinned and boned)
7   teaspoons butter
2   tablespoons finely chopped
      shallots
¼   cup dry vermouth
½   cup dry white wine
1   cup fresh fish broth
1   cup heavy cream
1   tablespoon flour
2   tablespoons finely chopped
      fresh sorrel
      Juice of half a lemon

1. Place the salmon fillets on a flat surface and cut on the bias, against the grain, into 8 slices of equal weight.

2. Place the slices between sheets of freezer paper and pound with a flat mallet to make "steaks" about the thickness of veal scallopine.

3. Melt 1 tablespoon (3 teaspoons) butter in a saucepan and add the shallots. Cook briefly and add the vermouth and wine. Cook until reduced by half and add the fish broth. Cook about 5 minutes and strain the liquid, using a fine sieve and pushing the solids with the back of a wooden spoon to extract their juices. Discard the solids.

4. Add the cream to the juices and simmer about 5 minutes.

5. Blend 1 teaspoon of butter with the flour and add this bit by bit to the sauce, stirring. Add the chopped sorrel and lemon juice.

6. Swirl in the remaining tablespoon of butter. Do not boil, but keep hot while cooking the salmon.

7. Use a Teflon pan to cook the salmon. Do not add fat. Add the salmon pieces and cook until delicately golden on one side. Turn and cook on the other. Do not overcook or the salmon will have a dry texture.

8. Spoon equal portions of the sauce in the center of 8 hot plates. Place 1 piece of the cooked salmon in the center of the sauce and serve.

Yield: 8 servings.

Sorrel and Potato Soup

1   pound tender, fresh, un-
      blemished sorrel leaves
1½   pounds potatoes
1   tablespoon butter
1   cup coarsely chopped onion
5   cups chicken broth
1   cup heavy cream
      Salt and freshly ground pep-
      per

1. Pick over and remove the tougher parts of the sorrel stems. Rinse the leaves and drain well. Place the leaves on a flat surface and cut them into fine shreds (chiffonade). There should be about 5 cups. Set aside.

2. Peel the potatoes and drop them into cold water to prevent discoloration. Cut the potatoes into 2-inch cubes. Let stand in cold water to cover.

3. Melt the butter in a skillet and add the onion. Cook, stirring, until wilted. Add the drained potatoes and the chicken broth. Stir in 4 cups of the sorrel and cook 20 minutes.

4. Purée the soup in a food mill or in a food processor. Return to the kettle and simmer briefly. Add the heavy cream, salt and pepper to taste and bring to the boil. Stir in the remaining sorrel and stir. Serve piping hot or chill and serve very cold.

Yield: About 2 quarts.

Crevettes à l'Oseille

(Shrimp with sorrel)

1½	*to 1¾ pounds raw shrimp in the shell*
1	*pound fresh sorrel*
5	*tablespoons butter*
⅓	*cup finely chopped onion*
3	*tablespoons finely chopped shallots*
1	*tablespoon flour*
1	*cup dry white wine*
3	*tablespoons tomato paste*
2	*cups heavy cream*
	Salt and freshly ground pepper
¼	*cup cognac or bourbon*
2	*egg yolks*
	Toast rounds, optional (see note)

1. Peel and devein the shrimp. Rinse well and pat dry. Reserve the shrimp shells.

2. Pick over the sorrel and remove and discard any tough stems. Rinse well and pat dry. On a flat surface, cut the sorrel into fine shreds (chiffonade). Set aside.

3. Heat 2 tablespoons of butter in a small deep skillet and add the shrimp shells, stirring. Cook briefly and add the onion and shallots. Cook about 2 minutes, stirring frequently, and sprinkle with flour, stirring. Add the wine and tomato paste, stirring until well blended. Cook about 5 minutes.

4. Add the cream and cook about 5 minutes over high heat. Strain through a sieve, pushing down to extract as much liquid as possible from the solids.

5. Heat 1 tablespoon of butter in a small saucepan and add the sorrel. Cook, stirring, just until wilted.

6. Heat the remaining butter in a saucepan and add the shrimp. Sprinkle with salt and pepper to taste and cook briefly, stirring, just until the shrimp change color. Add the cognac and ignite it. When the flame dies down, stir in the cream sauce and sorrel. Bring to the boil and simmer about 1 minute.

7. Beat the yolks and add a little of the hot sauce, stirring constantly. Return the mixture to the sauce and stir without boiling. Remove from the heat immediately. Serve on toast rounds.

Yields: 6 to 8 servings.

Note: The best way to make toast rounds is to cut fresh white bread slices with a bread cutter. Brush with butter and bake in a 400-degree oven until toasted.

June

THERE ARE A FEW FOODS in this world that invariably put me in mind of the line from Izaak Walton's *The Compleat Angler:* "We may say of angling as Dr. Boteler said of strawberries: Doubtless God could have made a better berry, but doubtless God never did." I can easily paraphrase that by substituting salmon for strawberries and fish for berry. There is simply nothing that swims in the water more delicate and eminently edible than a choice morsel of salmon. It may be happenstance or not, but salmon was treated twice in the month of June, first as a column unto itself, and secondly as one of numerous suggestions for what is potentially the most cheerful and delectable meal ever contrived for casual relaxed hours—the Sunday brunch.

It was certainly not plotted that way, but another column introduced a series of dishes that would be neatly suited to a splendid midday meal on the seventh day. These are eggs in ramekins topped with such choice good things as fresh tomato sauce or chicken livers or creamed chicken.

Many years ago at a hotel school in Switzerland, I first discovered the miracle known as a beer batter. This is a crisp, puffy, gossamer coating for deep-frying assorted things like shrimp, tangy balls of camembert cheese, fillets of fish and bits of calves' brains.

Beer Batter

WITH PIERRE FRANEY

Although a can of flat beer may be the bane of those who dote on a frosty and lively brew, it is, to a knowledgeable cook, a liquid of considerable merit. The beer makes a fine fermented batter for deep-frying. It yields a crusty, delicate coating to such good things as shrimp, cheese (deep-fried camembert balls are delicious), brains and assorted vegetables.

Beer Batter

¾ cup flour
½ cup beer at room temperature
  Salt to taste
1 teaspoon peanut, vegetable or corn oil
1 egg, separated

1. Place the flour in a bowl and stir in the beer, salt and oil. Stir to blend roughly. There should be a few small lumps. Cover the bowl with plastic wrap and let stand in a warm place about 3 hours.

2. Stir in the egg yolk.

3. When ready to cook, beat the white until stiff and fold it in.

Yield: Enough batter for 1½ pounds of shrimp.

Batter-fried Shrimp

1½ pounds shrimp
  Beer batter (see recipe)
1½ tablespoons cornstarch

1 tablespoon dry sherry wine
2 tablespoons finely chopped parsley
  Salt
  Peanut, vegetable or corn oil for deep frying
  Lemon wedges, optional
  Hot mustard (see recipe), optional
  Chopped chutney, optional
  Marmalade and mustard sauce (see recipe), optional
  Soy and ginger dip (see recipe), optional

1. Peel and devein the shrimp but leave the last tail segment intact. Refrigerate until ready to use.

2. Prepare the beer batter well in advance.

3. Combine the shrimp with the cornstarch, sherry, parsley and salt to taste.

4. When ready to cook, heat the oil. Add a few shrimp at a time to the batter and, using a 2-pronged fork, drop them, one at a time, into the hot oil. Cook, turning as necessary, to brown evenly. Drain on paper towels. Sprinkle with salt.

5. Serve immediately with lemon wedges or any of the desired sauces.

Yield: 4 to 6 servings.

Hot mustard

Combine 6 tablespoons of powdered mustard in a mixing bowl with 3 tablespoons beer or water. Add salt to taste. Let stand 20 minutes to develop flavor.

Yield: About ⅓ cup.

Marmalade and mustard sauce

½ cup orange marmalade
1 teaspoon prepared or homemade hot mustard (see recipe)
1 teaspoon Grand Marnier

Combine all the ingredients and serve.

Yield: About ½ cup.

Soy and ginger dip for shrimp

½ cup soy sauce
2 tablespoons plus 2 teaspoons
   white vinegar
1 tablespoon sugar
⅛ teaspoon cayenne pepper
1 teaspoon grated fresh ginger

Blend all the ingredients until sugar dissolves.

Yield: About ⅔ cup.

Deep-Fried Camembert Balls

Beer batter (see recipe)
½ pound camembert
   Oil for deep-frying

1. Prepare the batter.

2. Cut the camembert, rind and all, into 1-inch pieces and put in a mixing bowl. Using the hands, work the mixture to blend. Shape the mixture into 24 marble-shaped balls. Set aside.

3. Heat the oil for deep-frying.

4. Dip the balls, one at a time, into the beer batter and drop into the hot oil. Cook, turning as necessary with a wooden spoon, until golden brown. Remove each as soon as brown and drain on absorbent paper toweling. Serve immediately.

Yield: 24 balls.

Fish Fillets in Beer Batter

Beer batter (see recipe)
1 pound fish fillets such as sole,
   flounder or fluke
   Juice of ½ lemon
2 tablespoons chopped parsley
2 tablespoons peanut, vegetable
   or corn oil
   Salt and freshly ground pepper
   Oil for deep frying

1. Prepare the batter.

2. Cut the fish fillets into 2-inch

pieces. Place in a bowl and add lemon juice, parsley, 2 tablespoons oil, salt and pepper to taste.

3. Heat the oil for deep-frying. Dip the pieces of fish, one at a time, into the batter and then in the hot fat. Cook, turning and submerging the pieces in the oil, until golden brown all over. Drain on paper toweling.

Yield: 4 to 6 servings.

Brains in Beer Batter

Beer batter (see recipe)
2 sets precooked calves' brains, about 1 pound (see recipe)
Juice of ½ lemon
2 tablespoons chopped parsley
2 tablespoons peanut, vegetable or corn oil
Salt and freshly ground pepper
Oil for deep drying

1. Prepare the batter.

2. Cut the brains into 24 cubes of equal size. Place in a bowl and add lemon juice, parsley, 2 tablespoons oil, salt and pepper to taste.

3. Heat the oil for deep-frying. Dip the pieces of brains, one at a time, in the beer batter and then put in the hot fat. Cook, turning and sub-

merging the pieces in the oil as necessary, until golden brown all over. Drain on absorbent paper toweling.

Yield: 4 to 6 servings.

Precooked calves' brains

2 sets calves' brains (about 1 pound)
12 peppercorns
Salt
2 tablespoons vinegar
1 bay leaf
2 sprigs fresh thyme, or ½ teaspoon dried

1. A calf's brain consists of a pair of lobes. Place in a mixing bowl and add cold water to cover. Let stand several hours, changing the cold water frequently.

2. Drain and pick over the brains to remove the outer membranes, blood and other extraneous matter. Place the brains in a saucepan and add cold water to cover to a depth of about ½ inch above the brains. Add the peppercorns, salt to taste, vinegar, bay leaf and thyme. Bring to the boil and simmer about 3 minutes. Let cool in the cooking liquid. They are now ready to be drained and given a final preparation as for brains in beer batter.

Yield: 2 sets of precooked brains.

Breakaway Brunches

Although the word brunch has a distinctly American ring to it, it is, like smog and chortle, according to H. L. Mencken, of British origin.

"Brunch, designating a combination of breakfast and brunch, eaten about noon, appeared in England about 1900," Mencken wrote, "but it was thirty years later before it began to make any headway on this side of the water." The author added the following footnote, "On April 10, 1941, the Fifth Avenue Hotel in New York was advertising a 'Sunday strollers' brunch, $1 per person, served from 11 A.M. to 3 P.M.' in *The Villager,* page 8."

Patterns of dining in Western culture are as mindlessly entrenched in our mores and style of living as is the use of knives and forks (which is remindful of the Chinese gastronome who, when asked why the Chinese use chopsticks, replied casually, "We do not choose to butcher at table.") We take our three meals a day at more or less regular and established intervals. Which explains why meals taken out of that humdrum and predictable routine seem stimulating and appetite-whetting: Dinner at 11 in the evening in Spain; cress sandwiches, crumpets with marmalade and tea on a late afternoon in England; and, for back-packing, rod and reel jocks, fried trout cooked over an open fire at sun-up beside a mountain stream.

High on that list of breakaway routines are late breakfasts or brunches served at home or in the home of friends on weekends, preferably Sunday at midday or thereafter.

There may be no other meal when amateur (or even professional) menu-planners can let their imaginations run so free. Thought runs counter to the hot-and-cold-cereal-bacon-and-eggs-and-toast syndrome. Unless, of course, that bacon and those eggs are cooked and served in an unaccustomed fashion.

The crisp bacon atop grilled calf's liver, for example; the eggs scrambled with cream, perhaps, and a touch of fresh chopped tarragon added. Or served on toast with anchovies in the form of Scotch woodcock; or in a happy liaison with broiled kippers and grilled tomatoes.

It is difficult to define precisely which dishes are eminently suited to a fine brunch and which are not. The food should definitely be on the light side—no porterhouse steaks, although grilled lamb chops are ideal. Almost all specialty cuts—liver, kidneys, sweetbreads and so on—in almost any preparation, grilled, creamed and so on, are excellent. Broiled tomatoes go with a variety of main courses.

Preprandial drinks may be spiritous or not. Fruit juices should be freshly squeezed, and may then be served with vodka (the orange juice for a screwdriver; the grapefruit with a dash of salt for a salty dog). Plain spiced tomato juice over ice (salt, pepper, fresh lemon or lime juice plus generous dashes of Worcestershire and Tabasco sauce) or a bloody Mary (same ingredients plus vodka) is in order.

Any or a combination of breads are suitable for an elegant brunch: croissants, brioches, buttered toast, English muffins, biscuits, hot homemade rolls. Needless to say, homemade breads would be flattering and complimentary to guests. An assortment of marmalades, jams, jellies and preserves are also fitting.

The choice of beverage is highly subjective. The ultimate drink would be dry champagne, although there are some foods that go best with other beverages. Grilled kippered herrings are infinitely compatible with hot tea. Both coffee and tea should be offered guests who have an adventurous appetite (you'd be surprised at how many Americans haven't the foggiest notion of the elegance of the many teas available to them).

Generally speaking, a fine champagne is, as noted, an ideal beverage for brunch. Other than that I prefer still white wines to red. A dry white wine is excellent, but I prefer for the occasion the somewhat more fruity wines of Alsace, the Rhine, the Mosel and Austria.

The end of a brunch might include an assortment of fine cheeses such as brie, camembert, gorgonzola and so on and then a fine burgundy would not be at all amiss.

In any event, in menu planning, let your imagination run riot. Enjoy!

Mock Eggs Benedict

(Eggs and ham on toast with cheese sauce)

3 tablespoons butter
2 tablespoons flour
1 cup milk, or use half milk and half cream
Salt and freshly ground pepper to taste
Tabasco sauce to taste
½ teaspoon Worcestershire sauce
⅛ teaspoon nutmeg
¼ pound grated cheese, such as cheddar, swiss or gruyère
¼ cup white vinegar
4 eggs
4 slices cooked ham
4 slices hot buttered toast
Paprika

1. Melt 2 tablespoons butter in a saucepan and add the flour, stirring with a wire whisk.

2. When blended, add the milk, stirring rapidly with the whisk. Season with salt, pepper, Tabasco sauce, Worcestershire and nutmeg. Remove from the heat and add the cheese, stirring until melted.

3. In a skillet bring enough water to the boil to cover the eggs when added. Add the vinegar and salt to taste. Carefully break the eggs into the water, one at a time, and cook gently until the white is set and the

yolk remains runny. Carefully remove and drain on paper toweling.

4. Meanwhile, heat the ham in remaining 1 tablespoon of butter, turning once.

5. Arrange the toast on 4 hot plates. Cover each slice with a slice of ham and add a poached egg to each serving. Bring the sauce to the boil and spoon it over. Sprinkle each serving gingerly with paprika and serve hot.

Yield: 4 servings.

3. Grease a baking dish large enough to hold the tomato halves with 1 tablespoon of oil. Arrange the halves over it, cut-side up.

4. Sprinkle each half with about ½ teaspoon of chopped rosemary, salt and pepper. Sprinkle about 1 teaspoon oil over each half and place them under the broiler. Broil about 5 minutes.

Yield: 8 to 10 servings.

Grilled Tomatoes with Rosemary

5   *large red, ripe tomatoes*
1   *tablespoon plus 10 teaspoons peanut, vegetable or corn oil*
5   *teaspoons chopped fresh or dried rosemary*
    Salt and freshly ground pepper to taste

1. Preheat the broiler.

2. Core the tomatoes and slice them in half.

Scotch Woodcock

4   *slices buttered toast*
16 *egg yolks*
1   *cup heavy cream*
    Salt and freshly ground pepper
2   *tablespoons cold butter*
    Tabasco sauce to taste
4   *teaspoons anchovy paste*
8   *flat fillets of anchovy*
    Buttered asparagus spears (see recipe), optional

1. Prepare the toast and keep it warm.

2. Bring water to the boil in a saucepan large enough to hold the saucepan in which the eggs will be cooked.

3. Combine the yolks and cream in a mixing bowl and beat lightly to blend. Add salt and pepper to taste.

4. Pour the mixture into a heavy saucepan and set the saucepan in the boiling water. Cook, stirring constantly, taking care to scrape around the bottom of the saucepan to make certain the egg mixture does not stick. Continue cooking until the egg mixture has the texture of soft scrambled eggs. Do not overcook. The moment the eggs are done, add the cold butter and stir. This should stop the cooking action. Add Tabasco sauce.

5. Smear one side of each piece of toast with 1 teaspoon of anchovy paste. Heap equal amounts of the hot egg mixture onto the toast and garnish each serving with 2 crossed anchovies. Serve, if desired, with buttered asparagus spears.

Yield: 4 servings.

Buttered asparagus spears

Trim or cut off the tough bottoms of each stalk of asparagus. If desired, scrape the sides of the spears with a swivel-bladed potato peeler, leaving about 2 inches of the asparagus tips untouched. Place the asparagus spears in a skillet and add cold water to cover and salt to taste. Bring to the boil and simmer about 2 minutes. Do not overcook. The asparagus should be somewhat crisp when served. Drain and serve with melted butter poured over.

A Smoked Fish and Bagel Brunch

1½	*pounds smoked salmon or lox*
1	*pound smoked sturgeon*
1	*whole smoked whitefish fillet*
¾	*pound pickled salmon in cream sauce*
2	*matjes herring fillets in natural sauce, cut into bite-size pieces*
2	*matjes herring in wine sauce, cut into bite-size pieces*
4	*pickled herring fillets in cream sauce, cut into bite-size pieces*
½	*pound caviar, optional*
10	*bagels*
5	*bialys*
1	*pound cream cheese*
¼	*pound black olives packed in brine*
½	*cup drained capers*
1	*large Bermuda or Spanish onion, about ¾ pound, peeled and cut into about 15 slices*
	Dill sprigs or parsley to garnish platters
	Lemon halves or wedges for garnish
	A peppermill
	Sour cream for caviar, optional
	Chopped hard-cooked eggs for caviar, optional
	Chopped onion for caviar, optional

1. Combine the various components for the brunch on platters, in sauce boats and so on as necessary. Garnish with lemon wedges, dill and so on.

2. Serve with a peppermill on the side.

3. If desired, make sandwiches as follows: 1 slice of toasted, buttered

bagel smeared with cream cheese, an onion slice, sturgeon and/or salmon, capers, a few drops of lemon juice and a grind of black pepper. Caviar is best eaten separately. It makes the sandwich too rich.

Yield: 10 servings.

Note: Excellent salmon, sturgeon and so on can be purchased at Murray's Sturgeon Shop, 2429 Broadway (near 90th Street), Zabar's, 2245 Broadway (between 80th and 81st Streets), as well as other delicatessens in New York.

Toasted bagels

The usual way to prepare a bagel for toasting is to slice it in half. It is more manageable and to some minds preferable to slice it into thirds and to toast all 3 pieces on both sides. Butter before or after toasting.

Grits and Chili Casserole

3¾   cups water
    Salt to taste
¾   cup regular (not instant) grits
¾   pound cheddar cheese, grated, about 3½ cups
¼   to ½ cup chopped canned jalapeno or other chilies
4   eggs, beaten
1   teaspoon finely minced garlic

1. Bring the water to the boil and add salt to taste. Gradually add the grits, stirring often, and cook until grits are done, about 30 minutes.

2. Meanwhile, preheat the oven to 350 degrees.

3. Pour and scrape the grits into a mixing bowl and add all but ½ cup of the cheese and all the remaining ingredients. Blend well. Scrape the mixture into a buttered 2-quart soufflé dish or other casserole. Sprinkle remaining cheese on top. Bake about ½ hour or until piping hot and bubbling in the center.

Yield: 4 to 8 servings.

Broiled kippered herring, scrambled eggs and grilled tomato

Broiled Kippered Herring

2 kippered herring, available in cans and packaged in plastic
2 tablespoons butter
2 lemon wedges or halves
   Parsley for garnish

1. Preheat the broiler to medium heat.

2. Place the herring skin-side down on a baking dish and dot each with 1 tablespoon of butter.

3. Place the herring under the broiler and let cook long enough to become piping hot throughout. Do not overcook. When lightly browned, remove.

4. Place 1 herring on a plate and garnish with lemon wedges and parsley. Serve, if desired, with scrambled eggs, grilled tomato halves and pickled walnuts, available in jars in supermarkets and food specialty shops.

Yield: 2 servings.

Basic Scrambled Eggs

2 eggs
2 tablespoons heavy cream
1 teaspoon butter
   Salt to taste

1. Beat the eggs with the cream until blended.

2. Heat the butter in a heavy saucepan placed over gentle heat or in a basin of boiling water. Cook the eggs, stirring all around the bottom and sides of the saucepan until they are at the desired degree of firmness. As the eggs start to firm up, add salt. Use a plastic spatula or wooden spoon to stir.

Yield: 1 serving.

Scrambled eggs with herbs

When the eggs and cream are beaten, add 1 tablespoon of chopped herbs such as parsley, tarragon, chives or chervil, or 1 tablespoon of the herbs mixed together.

Sausages and Fried Apples

6   *breakfast sausage links*
1   *large apple, about 6 ounces*
2   *tablespoons butter*
2   *teaspoons sugar*
⅛   *teaspoon cinnamon*

1. Place the sausages in a skillet and cook over moderate heat, turning as often as necessary until nicely browned and cooked through.

2. Meanwhile, peel the apple and core it. Quarter the apple, then cut it into 12 wedges of equal size.

3. Heat the butter in a skillet large enough to hold the apples in one layer. Add the apples and sprinkle with sugar and cinnamon. Cook, stirring and tossing gently, over high heat, about 3 minutes.

4. Reduce the heat and continue cooking the apple wedges about 5 minutes longer, or until the wedges are nicely browned and starting to caramelize.

Smoked fish

5. Drain the sausages on absorbent toweling and serve with the fried apples. Garnish, if desired, with hot cherry peppers, chow chow, pepper hash and so on.

Yield: 2 servings.

Mushrooms with Sesame Seeds on Toast

¾   *pound mushrooms*
1   *tablespoon sesame seeds*
4   *tablespoons butter*
    Salt and freshly ground pepper to taste
½   *pound cooked ham, thinly sliced*
4   *slices buttered toast*
½   *teaspoon Worcestershire sauce Juice of half a lemon*

1. Wash the mushrooms and pat dry. Trim off the stems.

2. Scatter the sesame seeds on a sheet of aluminum foil and brown briefly under the broiler or in a hot oven. Take care they do not burn.

3. Heat 1 tablespoon of butter in a skillet and add the mushroom caps. Sprinkle with salt and pepper. Cook, turning once, until golden brown and tender.

4. Meanwhile, heat another tablespoon of butter and cook the ham gently until heated through.

5. Arrange 1 slice of toast on each of 4 plates. Cover the toast with an equal amount of ham. Cover the ham with an equal proportion of mushroom caps, stem side down.

6. To the skillet in which the

mushrooms cooked, add the remaining butter, Worcestershire sauce and lemon juice and bring to the boil. Add the sesame seeds and spoon equal amounts of this over the mushrooms. A good accompaniment for this dish is grilled tomatoes.

Yield: 4 servings.

The Egg and Us

WITH PIERRE FRANEY

There are a few dishes—often elegant—that enjoy a certain celebrity in fine restaurants and then seem to fall into regrettable desuetude (how nice to use that word again). We thought of this one recent Sunday morning in the course of preparing eggs en cocotte for a party of six in our home. They are easy to prepare, just as stylish as an omelet or a soufflé and marvelously tasteful. The method of preparing eggs en cocotte, or eggs in ramekins, is basically the same. There is usually a well-seasoned base of some sort—chicken livers in madeira sauce, a tomato sauce, or perhaps creamed chicken. The eggs are baked for about ten minutes until the white has become firm while the yolk remains liquid, or "runny" if you will. Care must be taken that they are not overcooked because the eggs continue to cook from retained heat of the ramekins when they are removed from the oven. It is customary to serve two baked eggs to each guest, although one would serve as an appetizer.

Les Oeufs en Cocotte aux Tomates

(Eggs in ramekins with tomato sauce)

5	tablespoons (approximately) butter
⅔	cup finely chopped onion
1	cup drained canned tomatoes, preferably imported Italian plum tomatoes (it may take about 2 cups to yield 1 cup drained)
1	teaspoon finely chopped rosemary
	Salt and freshly ground pepper
	Tabasco sauce
12	eggs
	Chopped parsley for garnish

1. Preheat oven to 400 degrees.

2. Heat 2 tablespoons butter in a saucepan and add the onions. Cook, stirring, until onions are wilted, about 2 minutes.

3. Add the tomatoes, rosemary, salt and pepper to taste. Simmer about 8 minutes and add a dash of Tabasco. Swirl in 2 tablespoons of butter and season to taste with salt and pepper.

4. Lightly grease with remaining butter 12 ramekins or "cocottes" (see note). These should be about 1½ inches deep and 2 inches in diameter. Sprinkle the bottoms lightly with salt and pepper.

5. Spoon about 2 tablespoons of the tomato sauce in the bottom of each ramekin, but reserve a small portion to use as a garnish.

6. Break 1 egg into each ramekin and sprinkle lightly with salt and pepper. Arrange the ramekins in a baking dish and pour boiling water around them. This will keep them from baking too rapidly. Bake 10 to 12 minutes. When cooked, the whites should be firm and the yolks liquid or just starting to firm. Do not overcook.

7. Spoon a little of the remaining tomato sauce on top of each serving. Sprinkle each serving with chopped parsley. Serve 2 eggs to each guest along with French bread or buttered toast. The traditional method of serving dishes in ramekins is to cover a small plate with a napkin, then place the ramekin on the napkin. Provide each guest with a salad fork and a small spoon.

Yield: 6 servings.

Note: In a pinch, you could use small Pyrex glass cups.

Les Oeufs en Cocotte aux Foies de Volailles

(Eggs in ramekins with chicken livers)

½ *pound chicken livers (4 to 6) Salt and freshly ground pepper*

3 *tablespoons peanut, vegetable or corn oil*

3 *to 4 tablespoons butter*

3 *tablespoons finely chopped shallots*

4 *tablespoons madeira or marsala wine*

⅔ *cup brown sauce, or canned brown beef gravy*

12 *eggs*

1. Preheat oven to 400 degrees.

2. Cut the chicken livers in half, then cut the halves into ¾-inch cubes. Sprinkle with salt and pepper to taste.

3. Heat the oil in a small skillet and when it is quite hot, add the chicken livers, stirring and tossing over high heat, about 1 minute. They must not become dry. Drain in a sieve.

4. To a small saucepan add 2 teaspoons of butter. Add the shallots and cook about 30 seconds, stirring. Add the wine and brown sauce. Simmer about 2 minutes and add the chicken livers. Swirl in 2 tablespoons of butter and add salt and pepper to taste.

5. Lightly grease with remaining butter 12 ramekins or "cocottes" (see note). These should be about 1½ inches deep and 2 inches in diameter. Sprinkle the bottoms with salt and pepper.

6. Spoon about 2 tablespoons of

the chicken liver mixture in the bottom of each ramekin, but reserve a small portion to use as garnish. Keep it warm.

7. Break 1 egg into each ramekin and sprinkle lightly with salt and pepper. Arrange the ramekins in a baking dish and pour boiling water around them. This will keep them from baking too rapidly. Bake 10 to 12 minutes. When cooked, the whites should be firm and the yolks liquid or just starting to firm. Do not overcook.

8. Spoon a little of the remaining chicken liver mixture on top of each serving. Serve 2 to each guest along with French bread or buttered toast. The traditional method of serving dishes in ramekins is to cover a small plate with a napkin, then place the ramekin on the napkin. Provide each guest with a salad fork and a small spoon.

Yield: 6 servings.

Note: In a pinch, you could use small Pyrex glass cups.

Les Oeufs en Cocotte a la Reine

(Eggs in ramekins with creamed chicken)

½   chicken breast with skin and bones left intact
1   carrot, scraped and sliced
1   rib celery with leaves, sliced
1   small onion, peeled and left whole
    Fresh or canned chicken broth, or water
    Salt and freshly ground pepper

4   tablespoons (approximately) butter
2   tablespoons flour
    Cayenne pepper to taste
¾   cup heavy cream
⅛   teaspoon grated nutmeg, or to taste
12 eggs

1. Place the chicken breast in a small saucepan and add the carrot, celery, onion, chicken broth to cover, salt and pepper to taste. Bring to the boil and simmer partly covered about 20 minutes. Let the chicken cool in the broth.

2. Preheat oven to 400 degrees.

3. Remove the chicken and reserve the broth. Remove and discard the skin and bones. Cut the chicken meat into ½-inch or slightly smaller cubes. Reserve.

4. Melt 2 tablespoons of butter in a saucepan and stir in the flour. Add 1 cup of the reserved chicken broth, stirring rapidly with a wire whisk. Cook, stirring, until thickened and smooth. Add the cayenne pepper.

5. Heat 1 tablespoon of butter in a skillet and add the cubed chicken, salt and pepper to taste. Cook, stirring gently, about 1 minute. Add the sauce and stir gently, just enough to blend. Add ¼ cup heavy cream and nutmeg and bring just to the boil. Keep warm.

6. Lightly grease with the remaining butter 12 ramekins or "cocottes" (see note). These should be about 1½ inches deep and 2 inches in diameter. Sprinkle the bottoms lightly with salt and pepper.

7. Spoon about 2 tablespoons of the chicken sauce in the bottom of each ramekin.

8. Break 1 egg into each ramekin and spoon about 2 teaspoons of heavy cream on top of each egg. Sprinkle with salt and pepper to taste.

9. Arrange the ramekins in a baking dish and pour boiling water around them. This will keep them from baking too rapidly. Bake 10 to 12 minutes. When cooked, the whites should be firm and the yolks liquid or just starting to firm. Do not overcook.

10. Serve 2 to a guest along with French bread or buttered toast. The traditional method of serving dishes in ramekins is to cover a small plate with a napkin, then place the ramekin on the napkin. Provide each guest with a salad fork and a small spoon.

Yield: 6 servings.

Note: In a pinch, you could use small Pyrex glass cups.

A Salmon Celebration

In gastronomic lore, there's an imaginary land called Cockaigne where "the houses are built of sugar and cake, the streets are paved with pastry," and, among other things, "the shops supply their wares for free." The birds fall out of the sky, spit-roasted or oven-ready, and fish spring out of rivers and streams into the nets of fishermen.

It is said that in the earliest days when white men arrived on this continent, the rivers of New England and New York were so abundantly filled with salmon it was like a reflection of Cockaigne's territory. So much so that after the Declaration of Independence was signed those two hundred years ago it became the custom of New England, principally around Boston and in the Connecticut area, to serve steamed salmon with green peas and new potatoes as the holiday meal. There was strawberry shortcake for dessert. Although doubtless there are families that will observe that happy custom next Monday, the salmon that graces those holiday tables will almost surely come from far afield, from Canada or the West Coast. July, nonetheless, remains the finest month for contemplating the uses and virtues of salmon, luxury though it may be.

Salmon, it would seem, has always been a prized fish. There is said to be an etching of a salmon on a cave wall in Southern France that dates to more than twelve thousand years ago. To Pliny is attributed the observation that in southwestern Gaul "the river salmon is preferred to all the fish that swim in the sea." Perhaps for genuine salmon fanciers, the ultimate time to have lived was in an era described by Sir Walter Scott: "Salmon," he wrote, was in that age "caught in such plenty . . . instead of being accounted a delicacy, it was generally supplied to feed the servants who are said sometimes to have [protested] that they should not be required to eat a food so luscious and surfeiting . . . above five times a week."

Remember the legend of Jonah and the whale? There is a painting in the Smithsonian Institution, executed by an American Indian of the Northwest a century or so ago. So awed was the artist by the salmon that it shows Jonah in the stomach of an enormous salmon.

The delectable nature of salmon is not to be denied. What on earth would the New York diet be without nova and lox? One of those most curious traditional dishes in America, to my mind at least, is the lomi-lomi of Hawaii. Salmon, I have been told, does not exist in the Pacific waters within a thousand miles of Hawaii and yet lomi-lomi, made with salted king salmon, is one of the national dishes. The origins of the dish date from the time of the trading vessels, which anchored in the islands en route from the United States or Europe to the Orient. The vessels, of course, carried stores of salted foods that would not spoil easily. They traded salt salmon to the Hawaiian natives for fresh fruit. The Hawaiians soaked the salmon, worked it with their fingers to the desired texture and served it with tomatoes and scallions.

In America today, the kinds of salmon available commercially are, generally speaking, four. There are Atlantic salmon; Pacific Chinook or king salmon; Pacific silver or Coho salmon, and what is called "fall" salmon, which arrives in autumn. According to John von Glahn of the Fishery Council and our favorite authority on such matters, the vast majority of the fresh salmon consumed on the East Coast arrives from the Pacific by air freight. Predominant is the king salmon. Nearly 850,000 pounds are sold each year. Fifty-eight thousand pounds of silver salmon satisfy the appetites of gastronomes. Twenty-three thousand pounds of Atlantic salmon arrive by truck from Canadian waters. In addition to which, 1,137,000 pounds of frozen salmon are directed to those who smoke fish commercially, supermarkets and fish markets, and for canning purposes.

Salmon is, of course, one of the most versatile of fish. It is the basis for many an elegant dish from salmon mousse to a simple poached salmon with mayonnaise sauce and cucumbers. We have recently made and sampled an uncommon version of gravlax, the traditional Scandinavian cured salmon and dill dish. This one is seasoned not only with dill but with rosemary and sage and other herbs as well as pernod and cognac. It is different and good.

Salmon cutlets made with chopped fresh salmon and known as Pojarski are choice. There is a fine Danish sauce for poached hot salmon and a recipe for grilled salmon steaks mirabeau, which is to say with anchovy butter and olives.

Poached salmon garnished with cherry tomatoes and tarragon

Poached Salmon

The court bouillon

24   *cups water*
1   *bottle dry white wine*
1½   *cups coarsely chopped carrots*
1½   *cups coarsely chopped celery*
3   *cups chopped onion*
4   *cloves garlic, unpeeled but cut in half*
1   *hot red pepper*
10   *dill sprigs*
6   *sprigs fresh parsley*
     Salt to taste
1   *bay leaf*
1½   *cups coarsely chopped leeks*

The salmon

1   *whole, cleaned salmon, up to 7½ pounds, or use 1 large section of salmon such as the tail section or center cut, about 3½ pounds*

The garnishes

Tarragon sprigs
Cherry tomatoes, halved
Boston lettuce
Hard-cooked eggs, quartered
Small tomatoes, quartered
Lemon wedges
Mayonnaise sauces and cucumber salad with dill (see recipes)

1. Combine all the ingredients for the court bouillon in a fish cooker or a kettle large enough to hold the fish. Bring to the boil and simmer, covered, about 20 minutes. Let cool.

2. Wrap the whole salmon or salmon piece in cheesecloth or a clean towel and tie neatly with string. Lower it into the fish cooker or kettle and cover. Bring to the boil and simmer gently exactly 20 minutes. The cooking time will be the same for a whole salmon or a large center section. Let stand briefly and serve hot or let it cool completely until ready to use if it is to be served at room temperature.

3. Remove the salmon and untie it. Remove the cheesecloth or towel. Place the salmon carefully on a flat surface and pull and scrape away the skin. Scrape away the thin dark brown flesh that coats the main pink flesh.

4. Decorate and garnish the salmon as desired. As a suggestion, drop large tarragon sprigs in boiling water and drain immediately. Chill instantly in ice water. Pat dry. Garnish surface of salmon with halved cherry tomatoes and tarragon leaves. Arrange around the salmon small Boston lettuce cups filled with quartered hard-cooked eggs wedged neatly between quartered small tomatoes. Serve with lemon wedges and mayonnaise sauces such as cucumber mayonnaise, mustard mayonnaise, anchovy mayonnaise or sauce verte and cucumber salad with dill.

Yield: 12 to 24 servings, depending on size of salmon and whether served as an appetizer, buffet item or main course.

Sauce verte
(Mayonnaise with green herbs)

2   *cups mayonnaise, preferably homemade*
½   *cup coarsely chopped watercress*
1   *tablespoon chopped parsley*
1   *tablespoon loosely packed tarragon leaves*
1   *tablespoon chopped chives*

1. Spoon the mayonnaise into a mixing bowl.

2. Blend the watercress, parsley, tarragon and chives in the container of a food processor or blender. Or simply chop almost to a purée. Add to the mayonnaise and blend well.

Yield: About 2 cups.

Sauce danoise
(Cream sauce with anchovy butter)

6   *tablespoons butter at room temperature*
8   *anchovies, chopped (about 1½ tablespoons chopped)*
2½ *tablespoons flour*
1   *cup water*
½   *cup heavy cream*
    Salt to taste (use very little inasmuch as anchovy butter, which is salty, will be added later)
    Freshly ground pepper to taste
⅛   *teaspoon cayenne pepper or to taste*
    Juice of half a lemon
1   *egg yolk*

1. Combine 4 tablespoons of butter with the chopped anchovies and blend well. Put through a sieve and set aside.

2. Melt remaining 2 tablespoons of butter in a saucepan and add the flour, stirring with a wire whisk. Add the water and cream, stirring vigorously with the whisk, until thickened and smooth. Add salt, pepper and cayenne. This may be made in advance.

3. When ready to serve, bring the sauce to the boil and add the lemon juice and egg yolk, stirring rapidly with the whisk. Bring the sauce

just to the boil, but do not boil, or the egg may curdle. Remove the saucepan from the heat and immediately stir in the anchovy and butter mixture. Do not reheat, or the sauce may separate. Serve with hot poached salmon.

Yield: About 2 cups.

Cucumber salad with dill

2   *to 4 large cucumbers*
7   *tablespoons white wine vinegar*
½   *cup plus 1 teaspoon sugar*
4   *teaspoons salt*
2   *tablespoons chopped fresh dill*

1. If the cucumbers are new and unwaxed, there is no need to peel them. Otherwise, peel them. Cut into thin slices and put in a mixing bowl. There should be 6 cups. Add 6 tablespoons vinegar, ½ cup sugar, 3 teaspoons salt and the dill. Cover and refrigerate 1 hour or longer.

2. Drain. Add the remaining 1 tablespoon vinegar, 1 teaspoon salt and 1 teaspoon sugar.

Yield: 12 or more servings.

Aline Landais' Gravlax
(Salt-cured salmon with herbs)

2   *fillets of salmon, about 2½ pounds total weight*
4   *teaspoons salt, preferably sea salt*
1   *teaspoon finely crushed fennel seeds*
¼   *teaspoon ground cloves*

½　teaspoon ground pepper
¼　teaspoon saltpeter, available
　　in drug stores
1　teaspoon anise-flavored
　　liqueur, such as pernod or
　　ricard
2　teaspoons cognac
1　teaspoon white wine vinegar
¼　cup freshly squeezed lime juice
6　sprigs fresh thyme, or 1 tea-
　　spoon dried
2　sprigs fresh sage, or 1 tea-
　　spoon dried
2　sprigs fresh rosemary, or ½
　　teaspoon crushed dried leaves
4　sprigs fresh dill, rinsed and
　　patted dry
　　Mustard and dill sauce (see
　　recipe)

1. Peel the salmon on the flesh side and if there are any bones, remove them with a pair of pliers.

2. Lay out a long length of heavy-duty aluminum foil.

3. Place the salmon fillets, skin-side down, on the foil.

4. Blend the salt, crushed fennel, cloves and pepper. Sprinkle over the fillets. Blend the saltpeter with the liqueur and cognac and sprinkle this over. Sprinkle the fillets with vinegar and lime juice.

5. Arrange the herbs evenly over one of the fillets. Cover with the other fillet, skin-side up, sandwich-fashion. Neatly bring up the ends of the foil and enclose the salmon tightly and securely so that the salmon will not leak when it gives up liquid. Arrange the package in a dish and place a weight on it up to 7 pounds. Refrigerate for at least 2 and up to 5 days. Turn the package once a day. Unwrap, remove and discard the herbs. Serve sliced on the bias like smoked salmon. Serve with mustard and dill sauce.

Yield: 16 or more servings.

Mustard and dill sauce

¾　cup imported mustard such as
　　Dijon or Düsseldorf
2　teaspoons dry mustard
6　tablespoons sugar
¼　cup white wine vinegar
½　cup plus 3 tablespoons peanut,
　　vegetable or corn oil
½　cup chopped fresh dill
　　Salt and freshly ground pep-
　　per to taste

1. Put the imported mustard, dry mustard and sugar into a mixing bowl and blend with a wire whisk.

2. Add the vinegar, stirring with the whisk. Gradually add the oil, stirring rapidly with the whisk. Add the dill, salt and pepper.

Yield: About 1½ cups.

Cotelettes de Saumon Pojarski

(Salmon cutlets with brown butter
sauce)

1¼　pounds skinless, boneless fil-
　　lets of fresh salmon
1½　cups (approximately) fine fresh
　　bread crumbs
1　cup heavy cream
　　Salt and freshly ground pep-
　　per to taste
¼　teaspoon nutmeg, more or less
　　to taste
　　Pinch of cayenne
4　tablespoons peanut, vegetable
　　or corn oil
8　tablespoons butter

1. Use the fine blade of a meat grinder and grind the salmon, putting it through once. The salmon cannot be put in a blender. It could be chopped very fine, using a sharp knife and a flat surface.

2. Put the salmon in a mixing bowl and add ½ cup bread crumbs and ⅓ cup heavy cream, stirring briskly with a wooden spoon. Add salt, pepper and nutmeg. Add cayenne and continue beating rapidly with the spoon.

3. Beat in the remaining ⅔ cup of heavy cream.

4. Lay out a length of wax paper. Divide the mixture into 6 equal portions. Shape each portion first into an oval like a small football, then place each portion on the wax paper and shape each piece to look like a pork chop with bone. The "chop" should be about ¾-inch thick. Arrange the "chops" on a jelly roll pan or other utensil and refrigerate until ready to cook.

5. Coat cutlets on all sides with remaining bread crumbs. Use 2 skillets. Heat 2 tablespoons of oil and 2 tablespoons of butter in each skillet and, when it is hot, add the salmon chops. Cook on one side about 4 minutes, until golden brown and turn. Cook 3 to 4 minutes longer until golden brown on the second side. Transfer salmon to a warm platter.

6. Add the remaining 4 tablespoons of butter to one of the skillets and cook, shaking the skillet, until the butter starts to brown, no longer. Do not let the butter burn. Pour the hot butter over the salmon.

Yield: 6 servings.

Saumon Grillé Mirabeau

(Grilled salmon steaks with anchovy butter and olives)

The salmon

6 *1-inch-thick slices fresh salmon, with bone in*
Oil
Salt and freshly ground pepper to taste

The anchovy butter

8 *flat fillets of anchovy, chopped (about 1 ½ tablespoons)*
8 *tablespoons butter at room temperature*

The garnish

6 *lemon slices, seeds removed*
6 *flat fillets of anchovy*
6 *jumbo pitted green olives*
6 *tiny sprigs fresh parsley*

1. Prepare a fire of charcoal or wood for grilling the fish. Or preheat the broiler to high.

2. Place the steaks in a flat dish such as a jelly roll pan and brush lightly with oil on all sides. Sprinkle with salt and pepper. Set aside.

3. Put the chopped anchovies in a small mixing bowl and add the butter. Blend well. Put the mixture through a fine sieve. Spoon it into a small serving bowl. Let stand at room temperature unless it is exceedingly hot, in which case keep it in a cool spot.

4. Prepare the lemon slices and set them aside.

5. Wrap 1 fillet of anchovy around the middle of each olive like a belt. The olives should be bottom up.

Make a small hole in the bottom of each olive and stick the stem of 1 small sprig of parsley in each olive.

6. Grill the salmon 4 or 5 minutes to a side until cooked but not dry. Turn and cook 4 or 5 minutes longer. To test for doneness, insert the point of a knife somewhat firmly into the center of each small salmon bone. If the knife can be withdrawn removing the center bone, the fish is done.

7. To serve, place the fish steaks on a hot platter. Place 1 anchovy-wrapped olive in each piece where the bone was removed. Garnish with 1 lemon slice. Serve hot with anchovy butter on the side for guests to help themselves.

Yield: 6 servings.

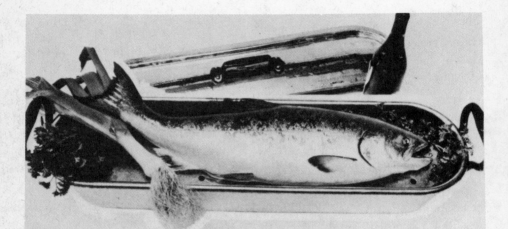

An eight-pound salmon in a traditional fish poacher

July

THIS WAS A MONTH of great nostalgia. It brought home my first acquaintanceship with foods that were not as American as corn on the cob, fried chicken and pecan pie. The year was 1942 and I was stationed as a third-class petty officer aboard the U.S.S. *Augusta*. The occasion was the invasion of North Africa. I vividly recall stepping out on deck on the morning of November 8 to let my eyes gaze on foreign soil. All around the harbor of Casablanca were ships that had been sunk or were sinking and there was the sound of gunfire. In the distance, through binoculars, I saw figures walking and I felt an undeniable urge to be ashore. There had been no official intention of my staying in Casablanca, but my timid request to remain with the admiral in charge of the amphibious forces was granted and, a day or so later after the cease-fire, I found myself in a place of pure enchantment. I fell in love with Morocco and, naturally, with Moroccan cooking. I had the good fortune to be invited into several Moroccan homes and, although rations were scarce, my hosts managed to gather together the makings of a mutton couscous, spicy salads and that marvel among main courses, b'steeya. B'steeya, which we recreated in July for a feast in my home, is a splendid pigeon pie that includes, oddly enough, confectioners' sugar and cinnamon as flavorings and garnish.

July was also a month of reminiscenses of childhood—the corn on the cob that came from my father's garden, barbecued dishes that frequently included skewered foods cooked on an enormous open pit that resembled a trench (sometimes whole pigs and baby goats were cooked for hours over that vast expanse of burning wood reduced to charcoal). And then there were picnics, consisting mostly of things like cold fried chicken and deviled eggs. I must say the picnic fare outlined in this chapter is a bit more sophisticated and international in scope, dishes about which I could scarcely have dreamed in my youth—eggs in tapenade, cold shrimp with dill and cognac, and rillettes of pork.

Moorish Delight

WITH PIERRE FRANEY

One of the great main courses of this world is a buttery, fragile-crusted pigeon pie that comes out of Morocco. It is a curious dish but infinitely gratifying. Curious because it contains, in addition to shredded cooked flesh of pigeons (Cornish game hens make an admirable substitute), ground almonds, confectioners' sugar and cinnamon. It is called b'steeya or pastilla. We first sampled it and became enamored of it about thirty years ago in Morocco and, in the ensuing period, on a brief visit to Casablanca. Our most recent tasting was at the much admired Moroccan restaurant, the Dar Maghreb, in Beverly Hills. The dish would seem, on reading the recipe, to be complicated in its preparation. Actually it isn't, and is well worth the effort. The dish is admirably complemented by two Moroccan salads, recipes for which we obtained from Mrs. Ralph Elmaleh, a friend and native of Agadir, who now lives in Cedarhurst, Long Island. They are spectacularly good—a spicy orange salad and a spicy tomato salad. Even without the b'steeya they are much recommended. For a buffet item, perhaps.

B'steeya or Pastilla

(Moroccan pigeon or poultry pie)

The squab or game hens

5   squab or, more economically, 4 Cornish game hens
    Salt and freshly ground pepper
2   tablespoons butter
2   cups chopped onions
1   large clove garlic, unpeeled but crushed
1½ teaspoons ground turmeric
½   teaspoon stem saffron
5   small slices fresh ginger, or ½ teaspoon ground ginger
1   teaspoon crushed coriander seeds

1   small hot dried red pepper
6   sprigs fresh parsley
12 peppercorns, crushed
2   cinnamon sticks, each about 2 inches long
4   cups water

The almond, cinnamon and sugar filling

1   cup blanched almonds
2   tablespoons peanut, vegetable or corn oil
1½ tablespoons confectioners' sugar
½   teaspoon ground cinnamon

The egg mixture

8   large eggs
¼   cup lemon juice
2   tablespoons butter

The final assembly

18 *to 24 squares (see note) phyllo pastry, available in shops that specialize in Greek pastries, as well as in the refrigerator or freezer sections of many other shops that specialize in foreign foods*

1 *cup clarified butter (see instructions)*

The garnish

3 *tablespoons confectioners' sugar*

1. Rub the squab or game hens inside and out with salt and pepper to taste. Heat the butter in a large casserole or Dutch oven and brown the squab lightly on all sides, turning as necessary. Do not burn the butter. Scatter the onions around the birds and cook until wilted. Add the garlic, turmeric, saffron, ginger, coriander, hot red pepper, parsley, peppercorns, cinnamon sticks and water. Bring to the boil. Simmer, covered, 45 minutes to 1 hour. When ready, the birds should be quite tender.

2. Remove the birds to a platter and let cool. Let the cooking liquid reduce over high heat to about half the volume. Let this cool.

3. As the birds cook, brown the almonds in a skillet containing the oil. Cook, shaking the skillet and stirring, until the nuts are evenly browned. Drain on absorbent toweling and let cool. Chop or blend them coarsely with a rolling pin. Blend them with the sugar and cinnamon and set aside.

4. Remove the flesh from the birds. Discard the skin and bones. Shred the flesh and set aside.

5. Put the eggs in a mixing bowl and add the lemon juice and about ¾ cup of the reduced liquid. Discard the remaining liquid. Beat the eggs with a whisk until thoroughly blended.

6. Heat about 2 tablespoons butter in a large skillet and add the egg mixture. Stir with a rubber spatula, scraping the bottom and sides as for making scrambled eggs. Continue cooking until eggs are fairly firm but not dry. Some of the liquid may separate. Ignore it. Remove from the heat and let cool.

7. Preheat oven to 475 degrees. Generously butter a 10-by-10-inch or slightly larger cake pan.

8. Lay out the 18 squares of phyllo pastry on a flat surface. At this point it is best to work as a team of two with one person brushing clarified butter on the pastry, the other transferring the leaves as they are prepared. Work quickly.

9. Brush the top pastry copiously with melted butter. Transfer it quickly to the buttered pan. It should be situated symmetrically. Press the center down gently inside the pan. Butter another sheet and repeat. Continue until a total of 10 generously buttered pastry layers are piled on top of each other.

10. Add a light layer of the shredded squab or game hens to the pastry-lined pan. Add the scrambled egg mixture, leaving the liquid, if any, in the skillet. Add the remaining squab, smoothing it over to the edges of the pastry. Sprinkle all but ¼ cup of the almond mixture over the squab. Dribble a little butter on top.

11. Butter 4 more sheets of pastry and cover the top of the "pie" as before. Bring up the edges and corners of the pastry, folding them inward to enclose the filling. Butter 4

more sheets of pastry and arrange these buttered side up. Quickly and with great care, tuck and fold these under the entire pie, lifting the pie up with the fingers so that, when ready, it nestles neatly inside the cake pan.

12. Place the pie in the oven and bake 20 minutes, brushing the top occasionally with more butter. When nicely browned on top, cover loosely with foil and continue baking about 20 minutes longer.

13. Or, preferably, when the pie has baked the first 20 minutes and is nicely browned, place a rimmed but otherwise flat pan, like a pizza pan, over the pie. Hold it over a basin to catch any dripping. Invert quickly, turning the pie out. Now, invert a similar rimmed but otherwise flat pan over the pie and turn it over once more. This way the pie has its original crust side up. Return it to the oven. Cover loosely with a sheet of aluminum foil and continue baking until the sides are nicely browned, about 20 minutes.

14. Immediately sprinkle the top of the pie with confectioners' sugar and the remaining ¼ cup of the almond mixture.

15. Serve the pie hot. Traditionally, this pie is eaten with the fingers in Morocco. The thumb, index and middle fingers are used. It may be served in wedges, however, Western style.

Yield: 6 servings.

Note: To make this pie, use a minimum of 18 pastry sheets. A few additional sheets of pastry will not matter. Note, too, that there will probably be leftover butter, which can be reserved for another use.

A note about working with phyllo or filo pastry. Reasonable caution must be taken when working with phyllo pastry to prevent its drying out. This is easily prevented, however, by keeping the sheets covered with a damp cloth as you work. Do not be afraid of tearing the pastry, however. It can be repaired with another sheet.

Clarified butter

Place ¾ pound of butter (the quantity is arbitrary) in a 1-quart measuring cup and let it stand on an asbestos pad over very low heat, or place it in a 200-degree oven until melted. Do not disturb the liquid. Let cool, then refrigerate. The clarified butter will harden between two soft, somewhat liquid or foamy layers. Scrape off the top layer. Invert the cup so the clarified butter comes out in one solid piece (you may have to encourage this with a fork or knife). Wipe off the clarified butter with paper toweling. This butter will keep for weeks in the refrigerator. Melt the butter before each use.

Spicy Orange Salad Moroccan-style

3   large, seedless oranges
⅛   teaspoon cayenne pepper
1   teaspoon paprika
½   teaspoon garlic
3   tablespoons olive oil
1   tablespoon vinegar
     Salt and freshly ground pep-
     per
⅓   cup freshly chopped parsley
12   pitted black olives, preferably
     imported Greek or Italian
     olives

1. Peel the oranges, paring away all the exterior white pulp. Cut the oranges into eighths. Cut each segment into 1-inch pieces. Set aside.

2. Place the cayenne, paprika, garlic, olive oil, vinegar, salt and pepper to taste in a salad bowl and blend well with a wire whisk. Add the oranges, parsley and olives. Toss gently to blend and serve cold or at room temperature.

Yield: 4 servings.

Spicy Tomato Salad Moroccan-style

3   or 4 large red, ripe tomatoes
3   or 4 tender ribs of celery with a
     few leaves
½   cup chopped parsley
⅓   cup drained capers
1   to 3 long, hot green peppers
3   to 5 bottled hot cherry pep-
     pers, or pickled jalapenos
½   lemon in brine, optional
     Salt
¼   teaspoon cayenne
1   teaspoon paprika
¼   cup olive oil

1. Core the tomatoes and cut them into 1½-inch cubes. Put them in a salad bowl.

2. Trim the celery and chop it coarsely. Add to the tomatoes.

3. Add the parsley and capers.

4. Trim the green peppers and chop them. Chop the cherry peppers and cut the lemon into ½-inch pieces. Add this to the salad bowl.

5. Blend the salt to taste, cayenne, paprika and olive oil and pour over the salad. Toss to blend well.

Yield: 4 to 8 servings.

A Time to Be Corny

It is not a freshly coined thought, the observation that there is almost no food out of season—given a purse that's large enough and a few hours notice—that can't be whisked to the kitchen and thence to the dinner table.

If you have an old-fashioned turn of mind, there can be cause to resent the reality of that circumstance. There is something infinitely desirable about having things arrive according to a natural pattern, things that staunchly preserve their own season, their own time.

We have a small personal catalog of such things and await their arrival throughout the year with almost childish delight and unabashed pleasure. That list includes the first shad (which also implies 'shad roe); the first asparagus; strawberries and fraises des bois; the sweet green peas of early summer, and the fresh salmon of July. As often as not we will arrange a timetable to arrive in Europe, particularly France, in October to sample new foie gras, the first oysters, ortolans from the Landes region and wild game.

We mention this because of a hunger that occurs, a hunger that can be happily assuaged starting the first two weeks of this month and lasting almost throughout the summer, depending on the vagaries of weather and other conditions of nature. That hunger is for fresh corn. Those who deplore the produce of this country must be wholly unfamiliar with the bounty of the fertile fields of eastern Long Island, which produce the sweetest corn anywhere in this country (and, therefore, the world).

Corn is not, of course, the most sophisticated food on earth, nor does it have such pretensions. Fresh corn is the basis for such comforting, home-spun, delicious and down-to-earth fare as corn pudding, corn chowder and just plain corn on the cob.

There are few, very few, uses of fresh corn in classic French cooking. One of these is supreme de volaille Washington, named for George, of course. It consists of chicken breasts in a cream sauce lightly flavored with bourbon whisky. The chicken doesn't necessarily include corn, but the essential garnish does, corn fritters. This dish, by the way, is sometimes confused with supremes de volaille Maryland (breaded chicken breasts), but they are not the same. The Maryland dish (also classic French) is served with crêpes made with corn meal rather than the fritters, which contain fresh corn kernels.

It was inevitable that corn would become a descriptive word in the English language, thus "pure corn" and "corny." Like onions, however, one suspects if corn weren't quite so abundant, if it did not flourish in proper soil, if it were scarce like diamonds, it would doubtless have an admirable snob appeal like truffles and foie gras.

Corn in its broadest sense refers to any kind of grain including oats and wheat. The Early English colonists gave the name corn to the grain that we cherish in this season now beginning. This is the grain they found on arrival in North America. The Indians taught them how to cook it, how to eat it and how to transform it into scores of products including corn meal and hominy. Today, when the word corn is used in any recipe in the English-speaking world, it invariably means Indian corn, infrequently called maize and known in France as maïs.

There are hundreds of hybrids of corn, but basically corn falls into two categories. The indentata, which is high in starch and is used to produce, among other things, corn starch; and the saccharata, which is table corn or sweet corn.

There follows a sampling of favorite corn dishes including a soufflé, pudding, soup, chowder, bread, relish and salad.

How to Cook Corn on the Cob

Put enough water in a kettle to cover the shucked corn and bring the water to the boil. Add the corn and cover. When the water returns to the boil, remove the kettle from the heat. Let the corn stand in the water 5 to 10 minutes and serve immediately without further cooking.

The corn may stand in the water for as long as 20 minutes without damage to its flavor and quality.

Corn and Salmon Soufflé

4   ears raw corn
1   cup cooked, skinless, boneless salmon, fresh or canned
3   tablespoons butter
3   tablespoons flour
1   cup milk
    Salt and freshly ground pepper to taste
1   cup grated gruyère, muenster, Swiss or cheddar cheese
1   tablespoon cornstarch
2   tablespoons water
6   eggs, separated
¼   teaspoon grated nutmeg
⅛   teaspoon cayenne pepper

1. Preheat the oven to 375 degrees. Generously butter 2 1-quart soufflé dishes or 1 8-cup soufflé dish. Refrigerate or place briefly in the freezer.

2. Cut and scrape the kernels from the cob. There should be about 1 cup. Set aside.

3. Flake the salmon coarsely. Set aside.

Corn and salmon souffle

Corn and Crab Meat Chowder

3   *ears cooked corn (see recipe)*
5   *tablespoons butter*
5   *tablespoons flour*
2   *cups chicken broth*
2½ *cups milk*
¼   *cup finely chopped onion*
¾   *cup picked over, fresh or frozen crab meat (about 6 ounces)*
    Salt and freshly ground pepper to taste
⅛   *teaspoon cayenne pepper*
½   *cup heavy cream*

4. Melt the 3 tablespoons butter in a saucepan and add the flour, stirring with a wire whisk. When blended, add the milk, stirring rapidly with the whisk. When blended and smooth, add salt and pepper. Add the corn and cook, stirring frequently, about 3 minutes. Remove from heat and add ¾ cup cheese.

5. Blend the cornstarch and water and add it. Cook briefly, stirring with the whisk.

6. Add the egg yolks, stirring them in briskly with the whisk. Add salt, pepper, nutmeg and cayenne. Heat briefly but do not boil. Remove from the heat and let cool briefly.

7. Beat the whites until stiff and fold them in.

8. Fill the soufflé dishes half full with the mixture. Make layers with the salmon. Cover with the remaining mixture. Sprinkle with remaining cheese and bake 25 to 35 minutes, or until well risen and nicely browned on top.

Yield: 4 to 8 servings.

1. Scrape the corn off the cob. There should be about 1½ cups.

2. Melt 4 tablespoons of butter in a saucepan, stirring with a wire whisk. When melted, add the flour, stirring until blended.

3. Add the broth and milk, stirring rapidly with the whisk. Cook, stirring frequently, about 10 minutes.

4. Meanwhile, melt the remaining butter in another saucepan and add the onion. Cook until wilted. Add the crab meat, corn, salt, pepper and cayenne. Cook briefly and add to the sauce. Add the cream and bring to the boil. Simmer gently about 5 minutes.

Yield: 4 to 6 servings.

Corn and Pimentos Vinaigrette

4   *ears cooked corn (see recipe)*
½   *cup pimentos cut into ¼-inch cubes*
½   *cup finely chopped onions*

½   teaspoon minced garlic
¼   cup finely chopped parsley
1   teaspoon imported mustard,
    such as Dijon or Düsseldorf
1   tablespoon red wine vinegar
    Juice of half a lemon
5   tablespoons olive oil
    Salt and freshly ground pep-
    per

1. Cut and scrape the kernels of corn from the cob. There should be about 2 cups. Put in a mixing bowl.

2. Add the pimentos, onion, garlic and parsley.

3. Blend the remaining ingredients with a wire whisk. Pour over the corn mixture and toss to blend.

Yield: 4 to 6 servings.

Corn, Zucchini and Cheese Pudding

4   ears raw corn
1   tablespoon butter
½   cup finely chopped onion
1   teaspoon garlic
3   zucchini, about 1 pound,
    trimmed and cut into ¼-inch-
    thick rounds
2   egg yolks
1   large egg
½   cup milk

½   cup heavy cream
    Salt and freshly ground pep-
    per to taste
⅛   teaspoon nutmeg
¼   pound grated muenster or
    cheddar cheese, about 1 cup

1. Preheat the oven to 375 degrees.

2. Using a knife or another tool (special gadgets for scraping corn off the cob are sold in certain houseware outlets), scrape the corn off the cob. There should be about 2 cups. Set aside.

3. Melt the butter in a skillet and add the onion and garlic. Cook until wilted and add the zucchini. Cook, shaking the skillet until zucchini is slightly wilted. Remove from the heat.

4. Blend the yolks, whole egg, milk, cream, salt, pepper and nutmeg. Add the corn and cheese and stir. Pour this over the zucchini and stir to blend.

5. Pour the mixture into a 4½- to 5-cup baking dish (an oval baking dish measuring about 1½-by 7-by 11½-inches is suitable). Set the dish in a shallow pan and pour about ½ inch of boiling water around it. Place in the oven and bake about 25 minutes, or until custard is set in the center.

Yield: 4 to 6 servings.

Picnic Particulars

"And we meet, with champagne and a chicken, at last." Those words were written by Lady Mary Wortley Montagu in England in 1749.

Now I have never read the works of Lady Mary Wortley Montagu. But I like that line and I have my own visions of the lady and her lover sitting in some ant-free, leafy, sun-dappled glade, munching on that cold roast bird between sips of a bottle of well-chilled brut.

That's because I am romantic by nature and I like marvelous trivia and that's what picnics are all about.

Until recently I've had the origin of the name picnic all wrong. I have always presumed that anything casual and trivial where food was concerned was uniquely American. It isn't true. It began with the French.

According to my redoubtable *Dictionnaire Etymologique de la Langue Francaise,* by O. Bloch and W. von Wartburg, the word *piquenique* came into the language in the late seventeenth century, notably in 1694. It comes from *picorer,* meaning to pick, peck or scratch around for food, and *nique,* which, in the old days, meant something with little value, a trifle. Picnic, the work adds, crossed the Channel into England in 1748 or thereabouts.

According to Theodora Fitzgibbon's generally excellent book, *The Food of the Western World,* picnics were tremendously popular and elaborate affairs in nineteenth-century England. In that age, a "Picnic Society" was formed in London, the members of which supped at the Pantheon in Oxford Street and drew lots as to what part of the meal each should supply.

Of course, there are no set rules as to what does and what does not qualify an outdoor meal as a picnic. One food chronicler has recently defined a picnic as "any outing consisting of a sandwich, a blanket, two ants and a six-pack."

We have assisted (as the French say) at such an outing.

We have also participated in picnics that involved aspic, pâtés, terrines, whole poached fish, great mayonnaise garnishes, admirably chilled white burgundies and ladies sporting parasols to guard against the sun. Crystal and china by Baccarat, silver by Christofle. Then there was that heat-crazed day when people threw stuffed eggs and bathed their heads in beer and a boat sank, and . . .

Besides the basic or principal dishes—sandwiches, cold roast chicken, whatever—much thought should be given to incidentals. There is nothing worse than wanting to bite into a hard-cooked egg, only to discover no one remembered the salt and pepper. Or how do you open that bottle of montrachet, carefully chilled in that rivulet, when there isn't a corkscrew or a neighbor for miles around? What about kitchen knives to slice the onion or a clam knife to open those littlenecks freshly retrieved from the cold and salty bay nearby? And what about lemons? Limes? Pickles? Horseradish, anyone? Tabasco? Worcestershire?

A careful and thoughtful picnic planner will always produce napkins, be they two-ply paper or double damask linen; and glasses, be they stemmed plastic or Waterford. Beer can openers, sardine can openers, buckets of ice. Knives, forks, plates, serving pieces, kitchen towels, both cotton and paper, charcoal and charcoal lighter, in addition to the grill to facilitate the proceedings. And lots of large, plastic bags for trash. A post-picnic cleanup is essential. This is but a small checklist for would-be revelers in sun and shade.

Now's the season for picnics, now and the weeks that follow. Stuff the eggs, fill the sandwiches and chill the wine. And if you are hungry for an idea or two, a few suggestions follow:

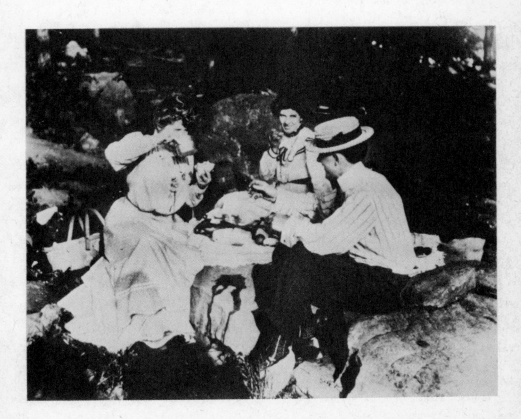

Steak Tartare

¼   pound top sirloin, or top
      round
4   egg yolks
½   cup finely chopped onion
4   teaspoons chopped parsley
6   flat anchovies, split in half
      lengthwise
¼   cup capers
8   teaspoons finely chopped
      chives
4   lemon halves
4   teaspoons cognac
2   teaspoons Worcestershire
      sauce
4   teaspoons imported mustard,
      such as Dijon or Düsseldorf
      Tabasco sauce to taste
      Buttered toast

1. The fresher the beef, the redder it will remain. After the meat is ground, it is best to serve it as expeditiously as possible. If the butcher grinds it, have him grind it twice. Or grind it at home using a meat grinder or a food processor. Take care not to overgrind the meat and make it mushy if a food processor is used.

2. Place 4 mounds of meat of equal weight in the center of 4 chilled plates. Make an indentation in the center of each mound and add 1 yolk. Or embed half a clean egg shell in the center of each mound and add the yolk to that.

3. Surround the meat with equal portions of onion, parsley, anchovy halves, capers, chopped chives and lemon half. Serve the cognac, Worcestershire sauce, mustard and Tabasco sauce in bottles or separate containers on the side. All the quantities to be added to the meat are, of course, arbitrary and optional.

4. Blend the ingredients together as desired. Serve with buttered toast.

Yield: 4 servings.

Shrimp with Dill and Cognac Sauce

1½ pounds boiled shrimp (see recipe)
¾   cup mayonnaise, preferably
      freshly made
1   tablespoon tomato paste
1   tablespoon finely chopped dill
2   teaspoons cognac
1   tablespoon finely chopped
      chives, optional
      Tabasco sauce to taste
      Dill sprigs for garnish

1. Peel and devein the shrimp. There should be about 2 cups.

2. Blend the mayonnaise, tomato paste, dill, cognac, chives and Tabasco. Stir to blend. Pour this over the shrimp and mix thoroughly. Garnish with dill sprigs and serve.

Yield: 4 servings.

Boiled shrimp

1½ pounds fresh shrimp
8   whole allspice
1   hot red pepper
1   clove garlic, crushed
      Salt to taste
1   bay leaf
10   peppercorns
      Tail ends of 12 dill sprigs,
      optional

Combine all the ingredients in a saucepan and bring to the boil. Simmer about 30 seconds. Remove the saucepan from the heat and let the shrimp cool in the cooking liquid. Drain well and peel, or cover, refrigerate and peel just before using.

Yield: 4 servings.

Jean Troisgros' Sweet Pepper and Roquefort Canapé

3 *not too large sweet peppers, preferably red, or 6 to 8 long green Italian peppers*
2 *3-ounce packages cream cheese*
¼ *cup packed roquefort, stilton or gorgonzola cheese*
1 *tablespoon grated onion*
3 *tablespoons butter*
   Salt to taste
   Buttered toast

1. Slice off the core ends of the peppers. Cut off another thin slice from the bottom of each pepper.

2. Using a food processor or blender, blend the cream cheese, roquefort, grated onion, butter and salt. Blend thoroughly.

3. Stuff the peppers with the mixture, packing them full, using a spatula. Refrigerate until the filling becomes firm. Neatly slice into ½-inch rounds and serve with buttered toast.

Yield: 4 to 6 servings.

Tapenade

1 *2-ounce can anchovies, undrained*
3 *tablespoons drained capers*
   Juice of 1 lemon
1 *tablespoon imported mustard, such as Dijon or Düsseldorf*
3 *dried figs, stems removed*
¾ *to 1 cup olive oil*
2 *tablespoons cold water*
¼ *cup finely chopped, stoned black olives, preferably Greek or Italian olives packed in brine*

1. Empty the anchovies and the oil in which they were packed into the container of an electric blender or food processor, preferably the latter.

2. Add the capers, lemon juice, mustard and figs and start blending. Gradually add the olive oil while blending. Add ¾ cup and, if desired, continue adding more oil. The tapenade should have the consistency of a thin mayonnaise. Add the cold water. Serve in a bowl, sprinkled with chopped olives, as a dip. This is also an excellent sauce for hard-cooked eggs.

Yield: About 1½ cups.

Eggs in tapenade

Eggs in tapenade

1½ cups tapenade (see recipe)
8 to 10 hard-cooked eggs
8 to 10 capers
   Parsley for garnish, optional

1. Spoon the tapenade over the bottom of a serving dish.

2. Cut the eggs in half and arrange them cut-side up or down. Garnish with capers and, if desired, parsley sprigs.

Yield: 8 or more servings.

Mock Head Cheese

("Head" cheese made with pork knuckles)

2½ pounds pork knuckles, 4 pieces
1½ pounds pigs' feet
12 cups water
2 small carrots
1 rib celery, quartered
1 onion stuck with 2 cloves
2 whole allspice
1 bay leaf
   Salt to taste
6 crushed peppercorns
2 cloves garlic, unpeeled but lightly flattened
2 sprigs fresh thyme, or ½ teaspoon dried
1 pound cooked ham steak
1 hot red pepper
2 tablespoons white wine vinegar
⅛ teaspoon ground nutmeg
¼ cup chopped parsley

1. Put the knuckles and pigs' feet in a small kettle and add water to cover. Bring to the boil and simmer about 1 minute. Drain well.

2. Return the knuckles and pigs' feet to a clean kettle and add the 12 cups of water, carrots, celery, onion, allspice, bay leaf, salt, peppercorns, garlic and thyme.

3. Bring to the boil and simmer 3 hours, skimming the surface as necessary. Remove from the heat and let cool.

4. Remove the knuckles and pigs' feet. Remove and reserve all meat and skin. There should be about 4 cups. Discard the bones. Strain the liquid. There should be about 3½ cups.

5. Combine the meat, skin and liquid. Cut the ham into ½-inch cubes and add it. Add the red pepper, vinegar, nutmeg and salt and bring to the boil. Cook down about ½ hour and remove from the heat. Stir in the chopped parsley.

6. Pour the mixture into a 9½-by-5¼-by-2-inch loaf pan and let stand until cool. Refrigerate overnight. Unmold and slice.

Yield: 8 to 12 servings.

Rillettes de Porc

(Pork spread)

1¾ pounds fresh, unsmoked, boneless bacon (see note)
   Salt and freshly ground pepper to taste
2¼ pounds lean shoulder of pork
1 medium-size onion stuck with 3 cloves
1 large whole garlic clove
1 cup dry white wine

1. Cut the bacon into 1-inch cubes. Place the bacon in a kettle and sprinkle with salt and pepper. Cook, stirring frequently, about 10 minutes to render the fat. Cut the pork shoulder into 1-inch cubes and add it.

2. Add the onion and garlic and cover closely. Cook 30 minutes and add the wine, salt and pepper.

3. Cook 3 hours and remove the onion. Do not remove the garlic nor pour off the fat, of which there will be a large quantity.

4. There are three ways of finishing the dish: with a large, heavy whisk, a wooden spoon, or an electric beater. Or perhaps use a combination of the three. Beat the meat and fat together with the whisk or wooden spoon until cool. Then spoon the mixture into the bowl of an electric beater and beat slowly at first then gradually with more speed. The more you beat the ingredients the whiter they become. Beat until the meat is at room temperature.

5. Spoon the mixture into crocks and cover tightly. Properly refrigerated, rillettes will keep for a long while. Serve cold with French bread.

Yield: 12 to 24 servings.

Note: Fresh, unsmoked, boneless bacon is available in pork stores in metropolitan areas. One source in Manhattan is Carmine Castaldo's meat shop at 85 Mulberry Street. The bacon may also be ordered from first-rate butchers.

Backyard Brochettes

WITH PIERRE FRANEY

Cooking on skewers is conceivably the oldest form of cookery on earth. It most assuredly preceded a grill of any sort. And it is easy to surmise that our earliest ancestors had better sense than to get their fingers too close to those newly discovered flames.

We have what amounts to a lickerish tooth for dining out of doors. It is whetted by the merest mention of a cookout (or something like it).

As the summer flourishes, we concoct more and more grilled foods of the season—various dishes on skewers with a couple of sauces on the side. There are, among other palate pleasers, chicken pork and chicken livers served with a special mushroom-and-turmeric rice on the side.

Brochette de Volaille à l'Origan

(Oregano chicken brochette)

3 *chicken breasts, split in half and boned, but preferably with the skin left on*
1 *teaspoon oregano*
   Salt and freshly ground pepper
2 *tablespoons lime juice*
2 *tablespoons peanut, vegetable or corn oil*
2 *tablespoons finely chopped parsley*
   Mexican tomato and chili sauce (see recipe), or melted butter
   Mushroom rice with turmeric (see recipe)

1. There will, of course, be 6 chicken breast halves. Cut each half crosswise into 4 pieces. This will yield 24 cubes.

2. Place the chicken in a dish and add the remaining ingredients except the Mexican tomato and chili sauce and mushroom rice. Turn the cubes occasionally so that they are well seasoned. Let stand until ready to cook.

3. Arrange the pieces on 4 to 6 skewers. If wooden skewers are used, it is best if they are soaked for an hour or so in water. Cover the tips with foil to prevent burning.

4. Prepare a charcoal fire in a grill. When the coals and grill are properly hot, brush the grill lightly with oil. Arrange the skewered chicken on the grill and cook, turning as necessary, until done, 20 minutes or longer. Serve with Mexican tomato and chili sauce or melted butter poured over. Serve, if desired, with mushroom rice with turmeric.

Yield: 4 to 6 servings.

Mexican tomato and chili sauce

1 *or 2 large red, ripe tomatoes*
2 *canned serrano chilies, avail-*
    able in tins where Mexican
    products are sold
1 *tablespoon finely chopped*
    fresh coriander leaves or pars-
    ley
    Salt and freshly ground pep-
    per
2 *ice cubes*

1. Do not peel the tomato, but cut away and discard the core. Cut the tomato into fine dice and put in a mixing bowl. There should be about 1 cup.

2. Cut away the stem of the chilies. Chop the chilies and add them with seeds to the tomato. Add the remaining ingredients and stir until the ice cubes melt. Serve cold.

Yield: About 1 cup.

Mushroom rice with turmeric

¾ *pound mushrooms*
4 *tablespoons butter*
½ *cup finely chopped onion*
1 *clove garlic, finely minced*
½ *teaspoon ground turmeric*
1 *cup rice*
1 *bay leaf*
1¼ *cups chicken broth*
    Salt and freshly ground pep-
    per

1. Preheat oven to 400 degrees.

2. Remove the stems from the mushrooms. Cut the mushroom caps into ½-inch cubes. There should be about 2 cups.

3. Heat half the butter in a saucepan with a tight-fitting lid and add the onion and garlic. Cook about 2 minutes and add the mushrooms. Cook about 5 minutes, stirring. Sprinkle with turmeric and add the rice and bay leaf. Stir until the rice is coated and add the chicken broth, salt and pepper to taste. Cover closely and bring to the boil on top of the stove.

4. Bake exactly 20 minutes. Remove the cover and discard the bay leaf. Using a 2-pronged fork, stir in the remaining butter while fluffing the rice. If the rice is not to be served immediately, keep covered in a warm place.

Yield: 4 to 6 servings.

Brochette de Foies de Volaille

(Chicken livers en brochette)

¾ *pound chicken livers*
¼ *cup soy sauce*
4 *teaspoons mirin (see note), or*
    sweet sherry wine
1 *tablespoon sugar*
1 *clove garlic, finely minced*
⅛ *teaspoon monosodium glu-*
    tamate, optional
⅛ *teaspoon hot red pepper flakes*
10 *or more bacon strips*

1. Pick over the chicken livers and trim them to remove veins and connecting tissues. Cut the livers in half. Place them in a mixing bowl. Add the soy sauce, mirin, sugar, garlic, monosodium glutamate and pepper flakes. Let stand until ready to cook.

2. Cut the bacon in half crosswise. Wrap 1 chicken liver half in half a bacon strip and arrange on 4 to 6 skewers. If wooden skewers are used, it is best if they are soaked for an hour or so in cold water. Cover the tips with foil to prevent burning.

3. Prepare a charcoal fire in a grill. When the coals and grill are properly hot, brush the grill lightly with oil. Arrange the skewered chicken livers on the grill and cook, turning as necessary, 10 minutes or longer, according to the desired degree of doneness.

Yield: 4 to 6 servings.

Note: Mirin is a sweet sake used in many Japanese recipes. It is widely available in wine and spirit shops in metropolitan areas in America.

Brochette de Porc au Romarin

(Rosemary pork en brochette)

1¼ pounds lean shoulder or loin of pork
2 tablespoons peanut, vegetable or corn oil
1 tablespoon red wine vinegar
1 teaspoon chopped rosemary
  Salt and freshly ground pepper
1 clove garlic, finely minced
  Devil sauce (see recipe)
  Mushroom rice with turmeric (see recipe)

1. Cut the pork into 1-inch cubes and place them in a mixing bowl. Add all the remaining ingredients except the devil sauce and mushroom rice and stir occasionally until well seasoned.

2. Arrange the cubed pork on 4 to 6 skewers. If wooden skewers are used, it is best if they are soaked for

an hour or so in cold water. Cover the tips with foil to prevent burning.

3. Prepare a charcoal fire in a grill. When the coals and grill are properly hot, brush the grill lightly with oil. Arrange the skewered pork on the grill and cook, turning as necessary, until done, 30 minutes or longer. Serve with devil sauce or Mexican tomato and chili sauce and mushroom rice with turmeric.

Yield: 4 to 6 servings.

Sauce diable
(Devil sauce)

⅓ cup commercially prepared Escoffier sauce diable (see note)
1 teaspoon imported mustard, such as Dijon or Düsseldorf
2 tablespoons heavy cream
1 teaspoon Worcestershire sauce
  Salt and freshly ground pepper

Combine all the ingredients in a saucepan and bring to the boil, stirring. Serve hot.

Yield: About ½ cup.

Note: Escoffier sauce diable, imported from London, is available in fine food specialty shops.

Coquilles St. Jacques et Crevettes en Brochette

(Scallops and shrimp on skewers)

20 scallops, about ¾ pound
20 shrimp, about ¾ pound
  Salt and freshly ground pepper

2   tablespoons peanut, vegetable
     or corn oil
     Tabasco sauce to taste
1   teaspoon dried rosemary
2   tablespoons lemon juice
1   clove garlic, finely minced
1   slice lemon
½   cup fine, fresh bread crumbs
     Melted butter for basting
     Lemon wedges

1. Place the scallops and shrimp in a mixing bowl and add salt and pepper to taste, oil and Tabasco sauce. Chop the rosemary and add it. Add the lemon juice, garlic and lemon slice. Blend well and refrigerate at least ½ hour.

2. Arrange the scallops and shrimp alternately on 4 skewers. Dredge in bread crumbs.

3. To grill, brush the hot, fired grill with oil and add the skewers. Brush occasionally with melted butter. Turn after 2 minutes and continue to turn frequently while grilling a total of about 12 minutes.

4. To broil, place the skewers on a baking dish and broil 6 inches more or less from the source of heat. Broil about 5 minutes and turn. Brush frequently with melted butter. Broil 10 to 12 minutes. Serve with lemon wedges.

Yield: 4 servings.

August

WHAT A FINE MONTH August was! There was a survey of the restaurants and food in Rome. A re-creation of a well-established but recent addition to the national repertoire of dining—a full-fledged salad bar. And what on earth could be more American than an outing on Chesapeake Bay in pursuit of the Lucullan bounty, the blue crab that flourishes as nowhere else in the waters of the Chesapeake. A feast of crabs is reason enough for, as the guidebooks say, making a detour to Baltimore.

One of the best remembered things of all that month, however, was a spectacular outing aboard a luxury cutter, a fifty-five-foot sailing vessel, with Bob and Ann Bolderson. It was a day of incredible beauty—a brilliant sun, a cool wind—and, on top of everything else, the wonderfully creative dishes out of a small galley prepared by the handsome woman named Ann.

Roman Repasts

After spending almost a week dining in Rome, I am as full of mixed emotions as I am of mixed metaphors. At almost every meal 1) waiting for the next shoe to drop or 2) waiting for a cloud to pass. Believe me, there's an easy explanation for that.

Rarely on this trip have we found a meal of uniform excellence. If the beginnings—the prosciutto and salami and pasta—were something to bring forth bravos, the main dishes would range from something to frown about to something to accept quietly and with good will. And vice versa. If the pasta or risotto was ill-prepared, the main course would almost invariably show the kitchen in a form of brilliance.

The most disappointing thing on this trip has been those fallen idols, restaurants like Piperno's and Dal Bolognese, for which one held a special affection and which have now fallen low in my esteem. The standards are not what they were and somehow it's like losing an old friend.

In many cases there isn't the sense of national pride in regional foods once found throughout Italy. The first day in Rome I asked a waiter where an especially juicy, sweet melon came from. He shrugged indifferently, as if to say, why do you care, and answered: "Who knows? Belgium probably." I'd almost have preferred it if he'd lied and said Sicily.

Let me hasten to add that Rome remains, despite its much written-about problems, very much a pleasant place in which to dine. The Via Veneto is a fine place to while away an hour or so after a meal of whatever nature. Dress for dining is as casual as you're likely to find in any Western capital in the world. Only in one or two places—the fashionable El Toula is one of them—are jacket and tie or a stylish dress for women expected. Relatively speaking, the cost of dining in Rome, as in the rest of Italy, is low. An excellent dinner for two with one or two bottles of Italian wine can be had for $20, and that is in some of the more expensive places.

If we were to single out the most agreeable meal we sampled in Rome, it would be a two-hour lunch taken at a relatively small and relatively unknown regional restaurant called the Colline Emiliane, on Via Avignonesi, not far distant from the Via Veneto. It is a family-style place totally without pretense, with the owner as principal chef and his wife as pasta maker. The pasta, incidentally, was the best we've sampled anywhere in the Eternal City.

The meal began with a superb, abundant serving of a delicacy known as culatello. It comes from Zibello, a small Italian town not far from Parma, a region that is generally conceded to produce the finest prosciutto in the world. Whereas the traditional prosciutto is cured from a whole fresh ham, culatello is made from the knuckle of fresh ham.

The ham as appetizer was followed by a notable array of pastas, each of which seemed more seductive than the last: fine fettucini with a bolognese ragu; tortellini with a light tomato and cream sauce; maccheronini with dried mushrooms; tagliarini with another cream and tomato sauce containing bits of dried mushrooms.

The culatello and pasta would have been sufficient reason to dine at the Colline Emiliane, but the main courses came off admirably as well: a fine braciola di maiale, boneless rolled pork cutlets stuffed with cheese and ham, breaded and sautéed, and a veal cutlet Bolognese style.

The meal ended with plump, juicy cherries and other assorted fruits, plus a delectable budino al cioccolato—a chocolate pudding baked along the lines of a crème caramel.

The kitchen of Passeto's in Rome

Braciola di Maiale Ripiena
(Stuffed pork cutlet)

8   *lean, boneless pork cutlets taken from the loin, about 1½ pounds trimmed weight*
    Salt and freshly ground pepper to taste
¼   *pound thinly sliced prosciutto*
¼   *pound fontina cheese (see note)*
⅓   *cup flour*
2   *eggs*
2   *tablespoons water*

1½   *cups bread crumbs*
    Oil for deep frying
    Lemon wedges

1. The pork cutlets should be trimmed of all fat. Place them, one at a time, on a flat surface and pound them with a flat mallet or the back of a heavy skillet.

2. Sprinkle one side with salt and pepper.

3. Finely chop the prosciutto. Cut the cheese into ¼-inch cubes. Blend the prosciutto and cheese. Divide the mixture into 8 equal portions and shape each into a ball.

4. Place 1 ball of prosciutto and cheese in the center of each flattened piece of pork. Fold up the bottom of each pork cutlet to partly enclose the filling. Bring the two outside edges over, envelope-fashion. Finally, fold over the top to totally enclose the filling. Press down the seams to seal.

5. Dredge each package in flour. Beat the eggs with water and drop the packages in this. Finally, dredge all over with bread crumbs.

6. Add oil to a depth of about 1 inch in a large, heavy skillet. When hot, add the packages and cook until brown, turning as necessary until cooked through, about 6 minutes. Drain on paper toweling. Serve with lemon wedges.

Yield: 4 to 8 servings.

Note: Gruyère cheese can be substituted for fontina.

Budino al Cioccolato

(A chocolate crème caramel)

The caramel base

½   cup sugar
2   tablespoons water
    Juice of ½ lemon

The chocolate custard

2   cups milk
4   ounces (squares) semi-sweet
    chocolate

4   eggs
4   egg yolks
½   cup sugar

1. Preheat oven to 350 degrees.

2. Select 8 ½-cup metal or oven-proof custard molds.

3. Combine the ½ cup of sugar, water and lemon juice in a saucepan and bring to the boil. Let cook, bubbling, until the syrup becomes a light or dark amber color. Take care not to let the syrup burn or it will be bitter. The moment the syrup is ready, pour equal amounts of it quickly into the 8 molds. Swirl the syrup around so that it covers the bottom of each mold. Let cool at room temperature.

4. Heat the milk with the chocolate, stirring often until chocolate is dissolved.

5. Beat the eggs, egg yolks and ½ cup sugar until thickened and smooth. Pour the milk mixture into the egg mixture and blend well. Strain the custard and skim off and discard surface foam.

6. Ladle the custard into the 8 prepared molds. Arrange the molds in a baking dish and pour boiling water around them. Place the dish in the oven and bake until the custard is set in the center, about 30 minutes.

7. Remove the custard molds and let cool. Unmold when ready to serve.

Yield: 8 servings.

Our involvement with Passetto's goes back many years. Our introduction to the restaurant came about one Christmas day when we dined there alone and found it perfection in almost every detail. The chief pleasure of the meal was the zuppa di vongole, a masterpiece, a work of art by some Michelangelo in the kitchen. The clams were about the size of a dime and there were literally hundreds of them piled high in the soup bowl, enrobed in a tantalizing, delectable, rich natural broth lightly flavored with fresh tomatoes, a trace of hot peppers and a smidgin of garlic.

On this recent visit, the reality of that soup, except for one perhaps trifling detail, matched our memory. The clams were approximately twice the size of our recollection, but they were tender and sweet as ever and the soup in which they were served was sublime.

The remainder of the meal was no better and no worse than you're likely to find in a dozen other Roman trattorias of lesser reputation and esteem.

Zuppa di Vongole
(Clam soup)

¼ cup olive oil
1 cup finely chopped onion
⅓ cup finely chopped celery
1 tablespoon finely chopped garlic
1 long hot, dried red pepper
1 cup dry white wine
2 cups fresh, chopped, peeled red ripe tomatoes
2 tablespoons chopped parsley
Salt and freshly ground pepper to taste
24 littleneck clams, the smaller the better
Croutons (see note)

1. Heat the oil in a heavy kettle large enough to hold the clams. Add the onion and cook until wilted. Add the celery, garlic and hot pepper and cook briefly.

2. Add the wine, tomatoes and parsley and bring to the boil. Add salt and pepper and cover. Cook 10 minutes.

3. Add the clams. Cover closely and cook until clams are fully opened, 5 to 10 minutes. Cook as briefly as possible and serve immediately or the clams will toughen. Discard the hot red pepper. Serve with croutons.

Yield: 4 servings.

Note: To prepare the croutons, cut French or Italian bread into 12 thin slices. Arrange on a baking sheet and broil on both sides until golden. If desired, brush with olive oil and garlic before serving.

It almost goes without saying that the American public is not inordinately devoted to dishes made with the innards of animals. A bit of sautéed liver now and then; sweetbreads braised with peas occasionally; grilled kidneys with mustard sauce once in a while. But they do not find tripe and other "specialty cuts" particularly transcending and appetite-whetting. We are passionately fond of such fare and, for others who salivate at the thought of tripe à la mode de caen and brains with black butter, we cordially recommend Agustarella al Testaccio, a tiny restaurant that some consider to have the most authentic Roman cooking in town. We dined with great gusto on the chef's trippa alla Romana, a soaringly good version made with a light tomato sauce and the characteristic herb for the dish, fresh mint. There was rigatoni with calves stomach, a delicate meat with a texture not unlike tripe, and coda di bue alla vaccinara or oxtail stew with vegetables.

Agustarella's, on Via Giovanni Bianca, is a crowded, brightly lit place with families including children. It is great fun but not for all tastes.

Trippa alla Romana

(Tripe with fresh mint)

4   *pounds honeycomb tripe*
2   *ounces salt pork*
1   *cup finely chopped onion*
2   *cloves garlic, finely minced*
½   *cup finely chopped celery*
1   *cup finely chopped carrot*
1   *cup dry white wine*
1½ *cups fresh tomato sauce*
3   *cups chicken broth*
    Salt and freshly ground pepper to taste
1   *or 2 tablespoons finely chopped fresh mint*
    Grated Parmesan cheese

1. Wash the tripe well and put it in a kettle. Add boiling water to cover and bring to the boil. Simmer about 5 minutes and drain. Let cool.

2. Using a large knife, cut the tripe into ½-inch shreds or cut it into 1-inch cubes. There should be about 8 cups of cut tripe.

3. Cut the salt pork into small rectangles and put the pieces in a saucepan. Add cold water to cover and bring to the boil. Drain. Add the pork to a heavy kettle large enough to hold the tripe.

4. When the pork starts to give up its fat, add the onion and garlic. Cook until onion is wilted. Add the celery and carrot and cook briefly. Add the tripe, wine, tomato sauce, broth, salt and pepper. Bring to the boil. Cover closely and cook about 5 hours, or until tripe is tender. Uncover the casserole for the last 15 minutes to let the sauce cook down somewhat. Stir in the mint and serve with grated Parmesan cheese on the side.

Yield: 10 to 12 servings.

Rome's El Toula is said to be the current favorite of the world's fancy folk, and one of their small brochures states there are eight El Toula branch establishments that bear the name throughout Europe. Although we approach warily restaurants that are part of a chain, we had a thoroughly pleasant outing in the original restaurant in Rome—courteous service, some of the most interesting and best food we sampled during our stay and, if you will pardon our name-dropping, Kirk Douglas and wife at the next table.

El Toula is an elegant place—vaulted ceilings, vast archways dividing the rooms, and neatly turned-out and accommodating captains, waiters, wine steward and so on. It is, incidentally, one of the few places in Rome where you might feel uncomfortable in dress that may seem too casual. Jackets for men, cocktail dresses for women are very much in order.

One meal began with soffiatelli con fonduta ai formaggi, which translates as savory cream puffs stuffed with fonduta cheese and baked with a melting cheese fondue on top; tagliolini verde or reed-slender green noodles tossed with a celestial blend of cream and prosciutto and freshly grated cheese; plus rigatoni with an excellent fresh tomato sauce, the pasta spoiled in that it was not properly drained, some of the tiny bits of ribbed pasta swimming in hot water. Main courses included squab grilled to perfection and served with an admirably textured, pungent but expertly seasoned sauce of crushed green peppercorns.

We spotted an unusual salad at the next table and were told it was composed of cold corn kernels, rounds of heart of palm, romaine lettuce, thin slices of Parmesan cheese and a delicate sauce vinaigrette. We sampled it. Uncommon, adventurous and good.

Piccione Novello al Pepe Verde

(Squabs with green peppercorns)

4   squabs, dressed and ready to cook
     Salt to taste
3   tablespoons drained, packed-in-liquid green peppercorns, available at shops that specialize in fine imported foods
1   tablespoon peanut, vegetable or corn oil
1   tablespoon finely chopped shallots
2   tablespoons cognac
¼   cup brown sauce, or canned brown beef gravy
¼   cup heavy cream

1. Preheat oven to 400 degrees.

2. Sprinkle the squabs inside and out with salt. Rub inside and out with 1 tablespoon of the green peppercorns, crushed. Truss the squab, if desired, with string.

3. Heat the oil in a small, shallow, heavy roasting pan. Brown the squabs on all sides, about 3 minutes. Arrange the squabs on their backs and place in the oven. Bake 20 to 30 minutes, basting often. Twenty minutes cooking time will produce a relatively rare squab, 30 minutes, relatively well done.

4. Remove the squabs and set aside. Skim off most of the fat from the roasting pan. Add the shallots to the pan, stirring. Add 1 tablespoon of peppercorns and the cognac. Add the brown sauce and cook, stirring, about 3 minutes. Add the cream.

5. Add the remaining 1 tablespoon of peppercorns to a saucepan. Strain the sauce into the saucepan through a fine sieve, preferably the French sieve known as a chinois. Push with the back of a wooden spoon to extract the juices from the peppercorns. Bring to a boil.

6. Untruss the squabs and serve hot with the sauce.

Yield: 4 servings.

Insalata El Toula

(Corn and heart of palm salad)

3 ears cooked corn on the cob
2 teaspoons red wine vinegar
2 tablespoons olive oil
  Salt and freshly ground pepper to taste
6 to 8 crisp, unblemished heart of romaine salad leaves
5 to 6 hearts of palm, available in cans
2 ounces Parmesan cheese cut into wafer-thin slices

1. Using a sharp knife, cut the corn kernels from the cob. Do not scrape the cob after cutting. There should be about 1 cup of corn. Put it in a mixing bowl.

2. Add the vinegar, oil, salt and pepper. Cut the romaine into bite-size pieces. There should be about 2 cups, loosely packed. Add this to the bowl.

3. Cut the palm hearts into ½-inch rounds. There should be about 1 cup. Add this to the bowl. Add the cheese, toss and, if desired, add a touch more vinegar or oil according to taste.

Yield: 4 servings.

Speaking of fallen idols, when we were in Milan earlier we revisited Savini, where there is so much to admire it is all the more deplorable to consider its shortcomings. The location is ideal, of course, situated as it is in that spectacular, irresistibly gaudy Galleria Vittorio Emanuele. The decor belongs to the golden age of restaurants—crystal chandeliers, wood paneling, high ceilings. The food, generally, is above average. But the haughtiness, the smug, holier-than-thou attitude of the service staff is stifling. There were several well-made dishes and some insipid ones. But the absolutely triumphant dish of the day was the costata di bue Savini—pure joy. It was prepared with a whole rib roast of beef that had not been roasted, but boiled to a precise point of rareness, sliced and served hot with an elegantly conceived salsa verde.

Costata di Bue

(Boiled ribs of beef)

1 9½-pound ready-to-cook rib roast of beef (4-rib roast)
4 large carrots, trimmed and scraped
2 turnips, about 1½ pounds, trimmed and peeled
8 to 12 "new" red potatoes
1 pound zucchini
½ pound green beans
  Beef broth to cover (see recipe)
  Salt to taste
  Salsa verde (see recipe)
  Coarse salt for garnish

1. Place the beef in a large kettle and add cold water to cover. Bring to a boil and simmer about 2 minutes. Drain thoroughly and run briefly under cold water. Let stand at room temperature until ready to cook.

2. Meanwhile, quarter the carrots lengthwise and cut them into 2-inch lengths. Set aside.

3. Cut the turnips into eighths. Set aside.

4. Peel the potatoes and add cold water to cover. Set aside.

5. Trim the ends of the zucchini. Cut them into convenient serving pieces.

6. Trim the green beans and cut them into 2-inch lengths.

7. Place the ribs of beef in a kettle and add beef broth to cover. If necessary, add water to make certain the beef is covered. Add salt to taste. Bring to the boil and simmer 1 hour.

8. Add the carrots and potatoes and cook 15 minutes.

9. Add the zucchini, turnips and green beans and cook 15 minutes longer.

10. Remove the meat and cover with foil. Let it rest 15 minutes.

11. Stand the rib roast on one end and carve like roast beef. Serve with the cooked vegetables on the side. Serve with salsa verde and coarse salt such as kosher salt on the side.

Yield: 8 to 10 servings.

Salsa verde
(Green sauce)

- 3 *tablespoons coarsely chopped chives*
- 1 *cup coarsely chopped, loosely packed parsley*
- ¼ *cup coarsely chopped onion*
- 6 *small cornichons, or 3 tablespoons coarsely chopped sour or dill pickles*
- 2 *tablespoons drained capers*
- 3 *anchovy fillets*
- 1 *clove garlic, coarsely chopped*

- 24 *small cocktail onions, drained*
- ¼ *cup red wine vinegar*
- 1¼ *cups olive oil*
  Salt and freshly ground pepper to taste

Combine all the ingredients in the container of a food processor or electric blender and blend. Do not overblend. This sauce must retain a coarse consistency. Serve with boiled meats, poultry, fish and so on.

Yield: About 2 cups.

Beef broth

- 5 *pounds meaty neckbones of beef*
- 32 *cups (4 quarts) water*
- 1 *large carrot, trimmed and scraped*
- 1 *turnip, trimmed and peeled*
- 1 *large onion, peeled and stuck with two cloves*
- 1 *large rib celery, cut in half*
- 1 *clove garlic, left whole*
- 1 *bay leaf*
- 2 *sprigs fresh thyme, or ½ teaspoon dried*
  Salt to taste
- 24 *peppercorns, crushed*

1. Place the bones in a kettle and add cold water to cover. Bring to the boil and simmer about 2 minutes. Rinse well under cold water.

2. Return the bones to a clean kettle and add the 4 quarts of water and remaining ingredients. Simmer 3 hours. Strain. Discard the solids.

Yield: 3 or more quarts of broth.

Dining at the Salad Bar

Within the past twenty years there has come onto the American scene—quietly and with little fanfare—a substantial, innovative and permanent contribution to the nation's gastronomy. It is altogether indigenous and in no sense a fashionable import along the lines of quiche Lorraine, beef Wellington, fondue bourguignonne, or sushi and sukiyaki. It is rarely, if ever, to be found in extant encyclopedias or dictionaries of food, and yet it is very much in evidence in public dining places across the land. It is much admired in the Midwest and even the sophisticates of the east and west coasts take pleasure in it.

It is something known as a salad bar and at its best it is laudable. It is rarely seen in private homes, but the thought occurs that it could be a marvelous device for home entertaining.

If you don't travel a good deal (it is a standard fixture in most hotel and motel dining rooms, in steak houses and seafood places), you may not be conversant with the components of the salad bar. In its most ambitious form, it may consist of a giant-size and fairly elaborate salad bowl filled with a variety of greens, including romaine, chicory and escarole, plus additional bowls of spinach with mushrooms, watercress and/or Belgian endive and other fancy edible greenery. The ultimate salad bar includes as many as twenty side dishes to be added to the compose-it-yourself salad, including a variety of dressings, relishes, pickles, cottage cheese and whatever else the unleashed imagination finds suitable. Of course, in its most pedestrian form, the salad bar may consist of nothing more than an enormous bowl of torn or cut iceberg lettuce centered on a table and surrounded by fewer than a basic dozen side dishes.

I have heard salads categorized and attacked as unsophisticated, inane and sophomoric. I think they're enormous fun, which reminds me of that classic putdown French chefs use. If one of their number has a tendency to put too many ingredients into a dish, one more pinch of this, one more touch of that, they refer to him as a "vrai pharmacien," or real pharmacist.

When it comes to salad bars, I delight in my expertise, pharmacy-style. A touch of gorgonzola salad dressing on my special blend of romaine and chicory; a bit of anchovy and a sprinkling of grated Parmesan on the spinach and mushrooms; cottage cheese on the side and bacon bits and toasted croutons over all. I will even add a dab of Russian dressing if it is well made, garnish the whole with raw onion rings and sliced green peppers and a few radishes and a short while later I am ready for seconds. I have been known to take a bite or two of three-bean salad. There is one traditional item on the standard bar that I will not indulge in. The multiflavored gelatin salad!

Pharmacien, indeed! But after all, what goes on my plate at a salad bar is for no other mouth nor appetite.

It is noted here that three of the salad dressings found at a typical salad bar are French, Italian and Russian, all the names in standard and accepted usage, all misnomers.

Frenchmen who seriously care about their stomachs are puzzled at what Americans blithely choose to call French dressing, some of the stuff that resembles milky pink axle grease. A Frenchman's basic sauce salade is nothing more than a good grade of oil and vinegar, judiciously blended and seasoned with salt and pepper. A respectable Roman would scoff at what we label Italian dressing, the dominant perfume of which is garlic and oregano. The only thing Russian about Russian dressing is rarely used in this day and age, and that is pure caviar pearls, which occurred in the original recipe and thus the reason for the name.

This is one suggestion for a "complete" salad bar. Other side dishes may be added according to your own talent, devices and imagination.

A Salad Bar

Salad greens

Romaine lettuce, Boston lettuce, chicory and escarole, torn or cut into bite-size pieces. Serve one or all in a large bowl
Crisp, clean spinach leaves with sliced mushrooms in another bowl
Watercress and/or Belgian endive in another bowl

Salad dressings

French
Italian
Russian
Blue cheese, roquefort or gorgonzola
Oil and vinegar
Salt and freshly ground pepper

Cold salads

Macaroni and mayonnaise salad
Cottage cheese
Beets with onion rings
Cucumber salad
Three-bean salad

Pickles and relishes

Spiced crab apples
Corn relish
Watermelon rind pickles
Pepperoncini

Oddments

Toasted croutons
Bacon bits
Radish roses
Black olives
Green stuffed olives
Cherry tomatoes
Raw cucumber slices or strips
Grated Parmesan cheese

Anchovy fillets, either rolled or flat
Drained chick peas
Green pepper rings
Celery sticks
Shredded, sliced boiled ham
Shredded, sliced gruyère or Swiss cheese

Russian dressing

1	cup fresh mayonnaise
1	tablespoon grated onion
3	tablespoons tomato ketchup
¼	cup or more red lumpfish caviar
1	tablespoon finely chopped parsley
½	teaspoon Worchester sauce
	Lemon juice to taste
	Salt and freshly ground pepper to taste

Put the mayonnaise in a mixing bowl. Add the remaining ingredients and stir to blend.

Yield: About 1½ cups.

"Italian" dressing

¼	cup wine vinegar
1	cup olive oil
1	tablespoon finely chopped onion
1	teaspoon finely chopped garlic
½	teaspoon crushed, dried oregano
1	tablespoon finely chopped fresh basil, or 1 teaspoon dried
	Salt and freshly ground pepper to taste

1. Put the vinegar in a mixing

bowl and gradually add the olive oil, beating rapidly with a whisk.

2. Add the remaining ingredients and beat well to blend.

Yield: About 1¾ cups.

Gorgonzola or blue cheese salad dressing

1   *cup fresh mayonnaise*
½   *cup sour cream*
¼   *pound coarsely chopped or crumbled gorgonzola or blue cheese*
1   *teaspoon wine vinegar*
1   *clove garlic, finely chopped Salt and freshly ground pepper to taste*
2   *to four tablespoons water, optional*

1. Put the mayonnaise in a mixing bowl. Add the sour cream, cheese, vinegar, garlic, salt and pepper and blend with a rubber spatula.

2. If the dressing is too thick, add a little water to the desired consistency.

Yield: About 2 cups.

Green beans vinaigrette with dill

¾   *pound fresh green beans, the younger the better Salt and freshly ground pepper to taste*
½   *teaspoon finely chopped garlic*
1   *tablespoon wine vinegar*
3   *tablespoons peanut, vegetable or corn oil*
2   *tablespoons finely chopped dill*

1. Trim off and discard the ends of the beans. Cut the beans into 1½-

inch lengths. There should be about 2 cups. Put in a saucepan with cold water to cover and salt to taste. Bring to the boil and cook about 5 minutes, or until crisp and tender. Do not overcook. The beans must retain some "bite." Drain immediately and run under cold water to stop the cooking action. Drain well.

2. Put the beans in a mixing bowl and add the remaining ingredients. Adjust seasonings to taste.

Yield: About 2 cups.

Cucumber salad

2   *to 3 cucumbers, about 1 pound*
1   *tablespoon salt Freshly ground pepper to taste*
3   *tablespoons sugar*
⅓   *cup white vinegar*
3   *tablespoons finely chopped fresh dill*

1. Trim off the ends of the cucumbers. If the cucumbers are young and fresh there is no need to peel them. Otherwise peel them.

2. Cut the cucumbers into thin slices. There should be about 4 cups. Put them in a mixing bowl. Add salt, pepper, sugar and vinegar and blend until sugar is dissolved. Taste the marinade. Add more salt, sugar or vinegar according to taste.

3. Just before serving add the dill and stir to blend.

Yield: About 4 cups.

Mushrooms for a salad bar

Choose ½ pound fresh, snow-white, unblemished mushrooms.

Rinse and drain thoroughly. Cut the mushrooms into thin slices, about ⅛-inch thick. Sprinkle with a little salt and the juice of ½ lemon to prevent discoloration. Toss and serve within a short period of time.

Pickled beets and onions

- 1 pound raw beets, trimmed
  Salt and freshly ground pepper to taste
- 2 teaspoons sugar
- 2½ tablespoons wine vinegar
- 1 red onion, about ½ pound

1. Place the beets in a saucepan and add cold water to cover. Add salt to taste and bring to the boil. Partly cover and simmer until beets are tender throughout. The cooking time will vary from 15 to 45 minutes or longer, depending on size and age of beets. Let cool in the cooking liquid.

2. Remove the beets and slip off the skins under cold running water. Slice the beets. There should be about 2 cups. Place them in a mixing bowl.

3. Add about 1 teaspoon of salt, pepper to taste, sugar and vinegar and stir until sugar is dissolved. Taste the marinade and add more salt, sugar or vinegar to taste.

4. Peel and slice the red onion. Add it to the mixing bowl and stir until beets and onions are well intermingled.

Yield: 3 to 4 cups.

Herbed cottage cheese salad

- 3 cups curd-style cottage cheese
- ½ cup mayonnaise

- ¾ cup finely chopped scallions
- 2 tablespoons finely chopped onions
- ¼ cup chopped chives
- ¼ cup finely chopped parsley
- 1 cup finely diced cucumber
- 1 tablespoon chopped fresh basil, optional
- ½ cup coarsely chopped radish
  Lemon juice to taste
  Salt and freshly ground pepper to taste

1. Place the cottage cheese in a mixing bowl. Add the mayonnaise and blend.

2. Add the remaining ingredients and blend well.

Yield: About 4 cups.

Three-bean salad

- 1 16-ounce can cut wax beans
- 1 16-ounce can cut green beans
- 1 16-ounce can kidney beans
- ¼ cup sugar
- ½ cup cider vinegar
  Salt and freshly ground pepper to taste
- ¼ cup peanut, vegetable or corn oil
- ¼ cup finely chopped onion
- 2 tablespoons finely chopped parsley

1. Empty the beans and drain well. Place the beans in a mixing bowl. Add the sugar and vinegar and toss until sugar is dissolved. All all the remaining ingredients.

2. Toss well and chill until ready to serve.

Yield: About 6 cups.

Crab: Bounty from the Deep

Within the next ten days this small, sun-baked town—it is said to be built on millions of tons of shucked oyster shells—will set the stage for one of the oldest seafood festivals in America. Crisfield, Maryland, celebrated as the cradle of the nation's blue crab industry, will crown Miss Crustacean, sponsor a crab-picking contest (won last year by a woman who picked nearly five pounds of crab meat in fifteen minutes), a crab-cooking contest and a crab-crawling contest.

The Grand Marshall of the Crisfield Crab Parade this year will be James Michener, the author, whose willingness to participate was, by his own estimate, based on his unabashed enthusiasm for crab meat. It is, indeed, one of the world's foremost seafood delicacies, ranking in some minds above lobster, shrimp, squid, conch, octopus and the toheroa of New Zealand. Even—to some palates—caviar.

In his acknowledgment, Mr. Michener stated, "Although I know absolutely nothing about crabbing; nor about crabbers, nor about crabs themselves, I shall accept your invitation to be Grand Marshall of your National Hard Crab Derby parade on Saturday, September 3, at high noon.

"I accept this honor because, although I may be deficient in knowledge of crabs and crabbing, I am one of the world's great authorities on the consumption of crabs, and if everyone ate as much as I, all crab men would be millionaires.

"Crab imperial, crab salad, crab soup and crab cakes are my specialties, with an added expertise in crab Norfolk. My wife makes one of the best crab salads, Japanese style, in the business and shares my enthusiasm."

On arrival in Crisfield one brilliant-clear day recently we might have known even less about "crabs and crabbing" than the author, had we not previously equipped ourselves with William W. Warner's *Beautiful Swimmers*, an account of *Watermen, Crabs and the Chesapeake Bay*, which was awarded the 1977 Pulitzer Prize for general nonfiction.

It was through that book in a roundabout way that we had made the acquaintance of a rugged, soft-spoken, weather-marked waterman named Alex Kellam, who told us that he would be 69 years old in October, that he was a native of nearby Smith Island and that he was "born with a crab net in my hand."

A waterman is, he explained, "any man here who makes his living off the water."

Mr. Kellam had quit school at 14 and went on his father's shipjack, the *Ruby G. Ford*, "a foc's'le and sail boat. That was in the days of the sailing boats, before the motor age."

Instead of a sail boat, the fisherman welcomed us aboard a sizable motor boat outfitted with a metal-and-net crab scrape, a piece of equipment with two metal triangles joined together at one end that is dragged over one side of the small boat to trap the crabs and, for better or worse, other sea creatures. Fifteen minutes out he threw the scrape overboard and within five minutes hauled it back aboard again. He emptied the contents, which included four hard-shell crabs, three oysters, four trash fish (fish not commonly used for eating) and a batch of seaweed. One of the crabs was a jimmy crab, the large male of the species and one of the most assiduous paramounts of the sea.

Back went the scrape into the shallows, and this time it was retrieved with an even larger haul. After half an hour, the bushel basket aboard was nearly half full. Mr. Kellam veered the boat around the harbor to a buoy marker. In this he was demonstrating another method of crab trapping. He hauled aboard a crab pot in which two crabs were trapped—in the process of mating.

Mr. Kellam pointed out that most visitors who come to Crisfield are of the persuasion that soft-shell crabs and hard-shell crabs derive from different stock. After he had taken aboard about three dozen hard-shell crabs (they must measure five and one-half inches from one tip of the top hard-shell to the other to be legal), he took us to visit the "floats" or pens of a neighboring crab man. The floats are fairly large, shallow, rectangular wooden boxes filled with constantly running bay water where "peelers" are dumped just before they pass from the hard-shell stage to the coveted and highly marketable soft-shell stage. Peelers, called green crabs, are those crabs within a day or two of shedding or "peeling" off their hard shell. The average crab—both male and female—moult or shed three times a year.

Within a half hour period, we saw three pairs go from the hard to the soft-shell stage, one of the most curious of nature's phenomenons. All of a sudden the body of a hard-shell crab will start to expand and slowly, like a small, oddly shaped balloon, a bulbous dark form starts to emerge from the rear opening of the crab. There is an apparently painful pushing and puffing and panting as the new body casts off its old shell. And the moment the soft-shell crab emerges from its former outer prison it is half an inch or so larger than its former self.

Shortly thereafter we were led to a crab-packing plant where they were in the process of picking the meat from the body and claws of hard-shell crabs by the thousand and where the soft-shell crabs were being frozen and shipped, uncooked, all over the country.

The hard-shell crabs are cooked in steam, cooled, cracked and the delicate snow-white meat removed for packing in one-pound tins. The choicest crab meat is lump and backfin. Essentially they are the same—both are taken from identical "chambers" of the crab's body. Lump crab meat is simply the choice or select large pieces; backfin are broken or small pieces of the lump.

The claw meat is extracted and packaged with or without the claw tips. The fourth category of crab meat used in cooking is the "regular," which are bits and pieces of body or claw meat. It has a shredded appearance and is generally used for stuffed crab dishes. One of the principal reasons for the elevated price of crab meat is that it is almost without exception picked or extracted by hand. There are machines to extract the bits and pieces of crab meat once the shells have been picked over, but this is of the least quality.

The soft-shell crab, in that the entire body including the main portion and the claws are edible, are much easier to prepare and package for market. The soft "apron" of the crab is cut off, the tips of the top soft "shell" are lifted up and the lungs on either side are easily removed and discarded; then the mouth and eyes are cut away with scissors. That's all there is to it. They are then shipped frozen all over the country. The reason for the elevated cost of soft-shell crabs is the personal care that must be given them while they are in captivity. They must be carefully tended and removed from the floats or pens within minutes after they shed their shell.

Crab meat from hard-shell crabs and the delicate, wholly edible soft-shell crabs are among the most elegantly blessed foods on earth. When asked which do you prefer, we are once more reminded of the anecdote related by Frederick S. Wildman in his *A Wine Tour of France*. It has to do with the age-old argument of which is the finer wine, burgundy or bordeaux.

"Which is the winner? The classic Bordeaux or the grand vin de Bourgogne? It would be virtually impossible to decide. One can only agree with the jurist of the ancien régime who, when asked by a marquise at supper one evening which he preferred, answered, 'Madame, in this sort of trial I get so much pleasure examining the evidence that I postpone giving my verdict from week to week.'"

Broiled Maryland Crab Cakes

1 pound crab meat, preferably lump or backfin
1 cup mayonnaise
1 egg white
½ teaspoon Old Bay Sea Food Seasoning (see note), optional
3 to 4 tablespoons very fine cracker crumbs
½ cup fine bread crumbs or cracker crumbs
1 tablespoon butter
1 cup hot melted butter

1. Preheat the broiler to moderate.

2. Handle the crab meat as little as possible to avoid breaking up the large, firm lumps. Remove any pieces of shell or cartilage, however.

3. Blend the mayonnaise, egg white, seafood seasoning and cracker crumbs in a mixing bowl.

4. Add the crab and fold gently to blend without breaking up the lumps of meat.

5. Using slightly moistened fingers, divide the mixture into 8 equal portions. Shape each portion into a patty.

6. Coat the patties all over with bread crumbs or cracker crumbs, pressing to make the crumbs adhere. Refrigerate until ready to use.

7. Heat 1 tablespoon butter in a skillet large enough to hold the crab cakes. Turn them in the butter to coat top and bottom. Place under the broiler and broil about 4 inches from the flame. Broil, turning once, until nicely browned and cooked through, about 5 minutes. Serve 2 crab cakes with equal portions of melted butter.

Yield: 4 servings.

Note: A 1-pound can of Old Bay Seafood Seasoning can be obtained by sending a $2 check or money order payable to Baltimore Spice Company, attention Pierre Smith, Post Office Box 5858, Baltimore, Md. 21208.

Deep-Fried Crab Cakes

Follow the instructions for broiled Maryland crab cakes. Instead of broiling them, drop them into hot fat to cover and cook until golden brown. Drain on absorbent paper towels.

Deep-fried Soft-shell Crabs

4   soft-shell crabs
    Salt and freshly ground pepper to taste
1   egg
3   tablespoons water
½   cup flour
1½ cups bread crumbs
    Fat for deep-frying
    Lemon wedges
    Tartar sauce (see recipe)

1. Sprinkle the crabs on all sides with salt and pepper.

2. Break the egg into a flat dish and add the water, salt and pepper to taste. Beat to blend well.

3. In a separate flat dish place the flour, salt and pepper to taste. Blend.

4. Place the bread crumbs in a third flat dish.

5. Dip the crabs first in egg, then in flour and finally in crumbs, turning and patting so that the crumbs adhere.

6. Heat the fat for deep-frying and add the crabs. Cook, turning as necessary, until crisp and golden brown. Drain on absorbent toweling. Serve hot with lemon wedges and tartar sauce.

Yield: 4 servings.

Tartar sauce

1   cup mayonnaise, preferably homemade
4   tablespoons chopped sour pickles, preferably imported cornichons

1 tablespoon chopped drained capers
1 tablespoon finely chopped onion
1 tablespoon chopped parsley

Combine all the ingredients in a mixing bowl and serve.

Yield: About 1¼ cups.

Soft-shell Crabs Meunière

4 soft-shell crabs
¼ cup milk
Salt and freshly ground pepper to taste
½ cup flour
½ cup peanut, vegetable or corn oil
Juice of half a lemon
4 thin slices from a peeled lemon, seeds removed
2 tablespoons chopped parsley
3 tablespoons butter

1. Put the crabs in a shallow dish in one layer and add the milk, salt and pepper. Turn the crabs in the milk.

2. Season the flour with salt and pepper.

3. Heat the oil in a heavy skillet large enough to hold the crabs in one layer.

4. Dip the crabs immediately from the milk into the flour, turning to coat well.

5. Heat the oil until quite hot and add the crabs, belly-side up. Cook 4 to 5 minutes (more or less depending on the size of the crabs) and turn.

Cook until golden on both sides and cooked through. Transfer the crabs to a warm serving platter and sprinkle with lemon juice. Garnish neatly with lemon slices and sprinkle with parsley.

6. Wipe out the skillet with a clean cloth and add the butter. When melted and bubbling, pour the butter over the crabs. Serve with boiled potatoes.

Yield: 4 servings.

How to Steam Hard-shell Crabs

Place any suitable number of hard-shell blue crabs in a basin or sink and run cold water over them to cover. Add ¼ cup salt (or more, depending on the number of crabs) and let stand at least 1 hour. This will rid the crabs of their sediment. Drain the crabs and rinse under more cold water.

Transfer the crabs to the top of a bamboo, stainless steel or other steamer and steam, closely covered, for 20 minutes. Serve hot or cold.

Virginia Lee's Ginger and Vinegar Sauce for Steamed Crabs

¼ cup red wine vinegar
¼ cup chopped fresh ginger
¼ cup sugar
8 teaspoons soy sauce

Combine all the ingredients in a small mixing bowl and stir to dissolve the sugar. Serve with hot or cold steamed crabs.

Yield: About 4 servings.

Crab Imperial

1½	cups crab meat, preferably lump or backfin
1	teaspoon butter
1	cup chopped green pepper
1	cup mayonnaise, preferably freshly made
¼	cup heavy cream
½	teaspoon Old Bay Sea Food Seasoning (see note), optional

1. Preheat oven to 425 degrees.

2. Handle the crab meat as little as possible to avoid breaking up the large, firm lumps. Remove any pieces of shell or cartilage, however.

3. Heat the butter in a small skillet and add the green pepper. Cook, stirring and shaking the skillet until pepper is crisp but slightly wilted. Set aside.

4. Put the mayonnaise in a mixing bowl. Beat the cream until almost stiff. Fold this into the mayonnaise. Add seafood seasoning, crab meat and green pepper and gently fold and stir until well blended.

5. Arrange the crab mixture in 8 individual ramekins or, preferably, crab shells.

6. Place in the oven and bake 15 minutes or until bubbling hot throughout and nicely browned.

Yield: 4 to 8 servings, depending on whether this is served as a first or main course.

Note: Old Bay Seafood Seasoning can be obtained by sending a $2 check or money order payable to Baltimore Spice Company, attention Pierre Smith, Post Office Box 5858, Baltimore, Md. 21208.

Maryland Crab Soup

6	large live crabs
10	cups water
	Salt and freshly ground pepper to taste
1	cup dry white wine
1	bay leaf
1	hot, dried red pepper, optional
2	ears corn, shucked
2	tablespoons butter
1¼	cups chopped onion
1	teaspoon garlic
1	cup chopped green peppers
1½	cups chopped celery
1	cup diced carrots
3	cups peeled, cored and chopped fresh or canned tomatoes
2	cups string beans cut into 1-inch lengths
1	teaspoon Worcestershire sauce
	Tabasco sauce to taste
½	cup sweet or dry sherry wine

1. Rinse the crabs under cold running water. Place in a kettle and add the water, salt, pepper, wine, bay leaf and hot pepper and bring to the boil. Cover and cook about 15 minutes. Drain and strain the broth. There should be about 10 cups. Set the crabs aside to cool.

2. As the crabs cook, drop the

ears of corn into boiling water. Cover and cook about 10 minutes. Drain and let cool.

3. Heat the butter in a kettle and add the onion and garlic. Cook briefly, stirring until onion is wilted. Add the green pepper, celery and carrots. Cook about 10 minutes and add the crab broth and tomatoes. Cook 15 minutes and add the beans. Cook 1 hour.

4. Scrape the corn kernels from the cob. There should be about 1½ cups. Add this to the soup.

5. Remove the meat from the claws and body of the crabs. There should be about 2 cups. Add this to the soup. Add Worcestershire sauce and Tabasco. Add the sherry and bring just to the boil. Serve hot in hot soup bowls.

Yield: 8 or more servings.

Alex Kellam displays crabs he caught in Chesapeake Bay

Peelers are dumped in floats before passing to hard-shell stage

Pull off large claws and set aside

Lift up flap on bottom side of crab

Tear off and discard flap

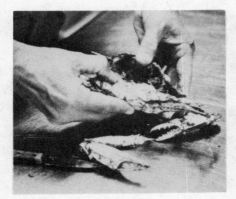

Pull off hard shell

Cut off whisker-like protuberances

To either side of opened crab are spongy lungs. Cut off and discard.

Break the crab in half

Crack each claw at the pincer end and extract
meat by pulling on pincer

With luck, you can pull off one of small claws
or feelers with crab meat attached

Cut crab down center to expose chambers; pry
into chambers to extract meat

Galley Specialties

Years ago, someone wrote to limn the praises of Ann Bolderson's galley caprices while riding at anchor or riding the waves aboard the *Nymph Errant II*, a charter boat that plies the waters of the Bahamas and Caribbean during the season. And sometimes between seasons as well.

"She's pretty as your grandmother's cameo," he wrote, "and cooks with taste, intelligence and uncommon sensitivity."

One recent afternoon and three years after receiving that communique I arrived aboard the Boldersons' luxury cutter shortly after they had returned from the Bahamas. While the boat was made fast to the dock, we surveyed Ann Bolderson's kitchen domain aboard the fifty-five-foot sailing vessel.

It was about the size but slightly more compact than a double telephone booth. A galley entrance about two feet wide, a work area less than six feet square that contains a refrigerator, freezer, wall oven, two small sinks and a small four-burner gas stove. One large coffee pot, an electric blender and a small chopping surface. Limited under-counter storage space and that's that.

It is certainly not the galley of the *QEII* nor the late and lamented S. S. *France*, and yet the food on which we dined that first evening—cocktail turnovers with apéritifs, rare roast beef (complemented by a slightly cool bottle of Chateau Pontet-Canet), oven-roasted potatoes and neatly puffed popovers followed by a gossamer chocola e mousse lightly laced with Grand Marnier and coffee—reconfirmed the notion that it's not the size of the kitchen that counts, it's the stature and flexibility of the cook.

Over that bottle of Bordeaux, the Boldersons told us how they got into the charter boat field in the first place.

"We came down here more than twenty years ago," Bob Bolderson said. "We owned a small, eighteen-foot cat boat at the time and I had just sold my business in Rhode Island." Mr. Bolderson, a handsome, lean, mild-mannered man of 55, still has distinct traces of a Yankee accent—he is skipper of a "chah-tuh" boat and he enjoys "bahley" soup.

"When we got to Fort Lauderdale, we were flat broke, but we fell in love with the place. I opened a Volkswagen franchise, but most of our friends were boating people and they introduced us to the idea of island chartering. In 1963 we got into it with a thirty-eight-footer and finally built this boat in 1972."

Like many people, I presumed that life aboard a chartered boat was one endless cruise wherein one simply sailed hours on end from one island to another. Far from it.

"It depends on the whims of whoever charters the boat," Mr. Bolderson explained. "The people who come aboard rarely want to stay underway for more then four hours a day. Sometimes one hour or less. There's too much to do—skin diving, swimming, snorkeling and spearing, walking the beaches, shelling. And there's lots of food in those waters—lobsters, conch, groupers, red snapper, Spanish mackerel, yellow tail."

On a normal day the boat is anchored at four in the afternoon and that's when Ann—after helping to secure the boat—goes down to the galley to start the evening meal. And prepare for the above deck's cocktail hour.

As we dipped into and admired Mrs. Bolderson's chocolate mousse, we asked about her early training as a cook.

"I'd rarely cooked a day in my life until I married Bob," she said. "I simply couldn't see cooking for myself. I had worked briefly in a small restaurant in Cape Cod and had compared a lot of recipes when I tasted something I liked.

"But I began in earnest when we found ourselves on a boat. When we got into the charter business, I decided that in all those old sea stories I read, whenever there was a mutiny it had to do with food—either poor or nonexistent rations. I decided the best way to keep people happy was to feed them well."

Although the *Nymph Errant*'s kitchen may be diminutive, the provisioning is prodigious. She has a painstakingly detailed list of things to be kept on deck at all times undersail. They are broken down into cereals, canned and packaged goods, frozen foods, perishables, seasonings such as herbs and spices, plus such things as paper goods, cosmetics and first aid. Food, never visible to the naked eye, is stored everywhere, under the banquettes in the main salon, in the bilges, in deck bins and so on. The boat is equipped with a water-maker, incidentally, that produces seventy-two gallons a day, plus a washer and dryer.

There is a good deal of elegance in dining aboard including the use of linen napkins. Underway, when no laundries are available ashore, the napkins are placed in the washer-dryer. They are "ironed" by placing them neatly folded under the cushions of an upholstered sofa.

The only crew aboard the *Nymph Errant* are Ann and Bob Bolderson. They take turns at almost everything. She hoists the rigging, handles the lines and places the fenders alongside when another boat approaches. He does no cooking, but he washes the dishes after each evening meal, scrubs the galley deck and cleans the stove. She is expert at varnishing the boat's wooden structures.

The second day out we were treated to Ann's lobster salad made with Florida lobster, also known as Bahamian crawfish or spiny lobster. The boat had anchored several miles out and the captain had dived overboard. A short while later, in mask and with snorkel, he clambered back aboard with a couple of the spiny creatures. The lobsters have a sweet, nutty flavor and the salad, lightly tarragon flavored, was excellent. It was preceded by a chilled gazpacho and accompanied by one of the best homemade banana breads I have ever sampled. That plus a bottle of chilled brut champagne.

Foresight, as much as anything else, the skipper's wife told us, is essential to running an efficient galley. "You must keep in mind before you leave shore that you won't find a grocery store on most islands. Therefore, you plan in advance. We buy the finest meats and keep them frozen for the duration of a charter—lamb chops, roast beef, legs of lamb and so on." She adds that they have very little waste aboard.

"The roast beef may be turned into more cocktail turnovers or go into soup. And underway I'm almost constantly faced with a surplus of cooked lobster. When we dive and the guests see the lobsters waving in the breeze, fresh from under a coral reef, they yell, 'Oh, I could eat three of those.' They devour the first voraciously, pace themselves through the seond and leave the third. So the next day we have lobster salad, lobster on toast, lobster bisque or whatever else comes to mind."

The *Nymph Errant II* is stocked with surprisingly few "convenience" foods. Most of the bread is made aboard, although Mrs. Bolderson does resort to pie mix for cocktail turnovers, pastry dough and so on. She rarely uses a dough containing yeast. "Has to be watched too closely and who knows? I might have to go out and skin dive or look for shells or take the jib down." They do bring aboard special breads such as rye or whole wheat and bagels. She grows her own bean sprouts in a colored glass container in the kitchen, which has, by the way, one small porthole.

Breakfasts aboard are fairly elaborate: French toast or pancakes or waffles with sausages and, perhaps, amaretto butter made with the sweet liqueur and honey. Sometimes there are Swedish pancakes with lingonberries and sour cream. And omelets, generally mushroom or cheese.

The *Nymph Errant II*, as we have stated, is distinctly a luxury charter, but I'm certain you won't find better accommodations—and certainly better food—anywhere in these waters. The cost per week for the boat is $2,300 for up to six people. There is an additional charge of $10 a person per day for food. The cost of liquor is additional according to what is consumed. The wines are complimentary.

For information, contact Captain Bob and Ann Bolderson, *Nymph Errant II*, 348 N.W. 46th Street, Fort Lauderdale, Fla., 33309.

Cocktail Turnovers

The pastry

1   *package piecrust mix, or use homemade pie pastry made with 2 cups flour*
1   *teaspoon finely chopped chives*
½   *teaspoon dried dill weed*

The filling

3   *tablespoons butter*
3   *tablespoons flour*
⅓   *cup chicken broth*
⅓   *cup dry white wine*
1   *cup finely chopped cooked chicken or turkey*
½   *cup finely chopped mushrooms*
¼   *cup grated Parmesan cheese*

2 tablespoons finely chopped
  parsley
½ tablespoon lemon juice
½ teaspoon Worcestershire sauce
⅛ teaspoon ground mace or nutmeg
  Salt and freshly ground pepper to taste

The baking

1 egg, beaten

1. Prepare the pastry, adding the chives and dill to the mixture. Wrap it in plastic wrap and chill until ready to use.

2. Melt the butter in a saucepan and add the flour, stirring with a wire whisk.

3. Add the broth and wine, stirring rapidly with the whisk. Cook until the mixture is thickened and smooth. Add the chopped chicken, mushrooms, cheese, parsley, lemon juice, Worcestershire, mace, salt and pepper. Set aside. Let cool to room temperature.

4. Preheat the oven to 450 degrees.

5. Roll out the pastry to about a ⅛-inch thickness. Cut the pastry into 3-inch rounds. There should be 28 to 30 rounds.

6. Add equal amounts of filling to the center of each round. Moisten the outer edge of each round with a little beaten egg and fold edges over to make a semi-circle. Press edges together with the tines of a fork. Prick the tops with the fork. Chill in refrigerator.

7. Brush the tops of the turnovers with beaten egg and arrange them on a greased baking sheet. Bake 15 to 20 minutes.

Yield: 28 to 30 turnovers.

Gazpacho

2 large, red, ripe tomatoes,
  cored, peeled and quartered
1 green pepper, cored, seeded
  and quartered
1 medium-sized onion, peeled
  and quartered
1 small clove garlic, optional
1 2-ounce jar pimentos
1 cucumber, peeled and cut into
  cubes
3 cups tomato juice
⅓ cup red wine vinegar
¼ cup olive oil
¾ cup fresh or canned chicken
  broth
  Tabasco sauce to taste
  Salt and freshly ground pepper to taste
  Bread croutons (see recipe)

1. Put the tomatoes, pepper, onion, garlic, pimento and cucumber in the container of a food processor or electric blender. Blend. Add tomato juice and blend again.

2. Pour the mixture into a bowl and add the vinegar, oil, broth, Tabasco, salt and pepper. Blend well and cover. Refrigerate several hours before serving.

3. Serve well-chilled, sprinkled with bread croutons.

Yield: 8 to 12 servings.

Croutons

2 cups bread cut into ½-inch
  cubes
⅓ cup peanut, vegetable or corn
  oil
2 tablespoons butter

1. Prepare the bread cubes and set them aside.

2. Heat the oil and butter in a large skillet and, when quite hot but not smoking, add the bread cubes and cook, tossing and stirring, until cubes are nicely browned.

3. Drain immediately on paper toweling and let cool.

Yield: About 1½ cups.

Pork Chops Stuffed with Roquefort Cheese

6   thick loin pork chops, about ¾ pound each, with pockets for stuffing
    Salt and freshly ground pepper to taste
3   tablespoons butter
2   tablespoons finely chopped onion
⅔   cup chopped mushrooms
½   cup crumbled roquefort or other blue cheese
¾   cup fine dry bread crumbs

1. Preheat the oven to 325 degrees.

2. Sprinkle the chops inside and out with salt and pepper. Set aside.

3. Melt the butter in a small skillet and add the onion and mushrooms. Cook, stirring often, about 5 minutes.

4. Remove from the heat and add the blue cheese, bread crumbs and salt to taste. Add salt sparingly. The cheese is salty.

5. Stuff the chops with equal amounts of the mixture. Secure the openings with toothpicks. Arrange the chops in a baking dish and bake about 45 minutes. Turn the chops.

6. Increase the oven heat to 375 degrees and continue baking about 15 minutes longer.

Yield: 6 servings.

Lobster Salad Nymph Errant

6   cups cooked, cubed lobster meat
⅔   cup finely chopped red onion
⅔   cup chopped celery heart
½   cup chopped green peppers
¼   cup drained capers
¼   cup chopped fresh parsley
1   tablespoon chopped fresh tarragon, or 1 teaspoon dried and crumbled
1½   cups mayonnaise, preferably homemade
1   tablespoon light rum
¼   teaspoon monosodium glutamate, optional
     Lime juice to taste
     Salt and freshly ground pepper to taste
     Lettuce leaves
     Hard-cooked eggs, quartered tomatoes, cucumber sticks for garnish

1. Put the lobster meat in a bowl.

2. Add the onion, celery, green peppers, capers, parsley, tarragon, mayonnaise, rum, monosodium glutamate, lime juice, salt and pepper. Blend well.

3. Make a bed of lettuce on each of 8 individual salad plates. Spoon the lobster salad in the center and garnish with eggs, tomatoes and cucumber sticks.

Yield: 8 servings.

Chicken Parmesan

2   broiling or frying chickens, cut
    into serving pieces
½   cup olive oil
1   teaspoon dried, crumbled
    oregano
    Salt and freshly ground pep-
    per to taste
1   teaspoon finely chopped garlic
6   tablespoons grated Parmesan
    cheese
1   cup dry white wine
1   pound noodles cooked to the
    desired tenderness and
    drained

1. Combine the chicken, oil, oregano, salt, pepper, garlic and 4 tablespoons of grated cheese in a baking pan. The pan must be large enough to hold the chicken pieces in one layer in a not too crowded fashion. Blend well and let stand covered until ready to cook.

2. Preheat oven to 350 degrees.

3. Separate the pieces of chicken in the pan, arranging them skin-side up. Leave the marinade in the pan. Sprinkle the chicken with wine. Sprinkle with remaining cheese and place in the oven.

4. Bake 1 hour, or until chicken is tender. If desired, run the chicken under the broiler for a second or so to crisp the skin. Spoon some of the pan drippings over the chicken. Pour the remaining drippings over the drained noodles and toss. Serve the chicken with the noodles.

Yield: 4 to 6 servings.

Banana Bread

⅔   cup sugar
⅓   cup peanut, vegetable or corn
    oil
2   eggs, lightly beaten
1¾ cups flour
2   teaspoons baking powder
¼   teaspoon baking soda
½   teaspoon salt
⅓   teaspoon grated nutmeg
3   ripe, not too firm, un-
    blemished bananas
⅔   cup coarsely broken walnuts

1. Preheat oven to 350 degrees.

2. Put the sugar and oil in the container of an electric mixer. Beat thoroughly to blend. Add eggs and beat well.

3. Sift together the flour, baking powder, soda, salt and nutmeg. Add this and beat well.

4. Mash the bananas to a pulp. Beat them into the batter. Fold in the walnuts.

5. Grease a standard loaf pan (9¼-by-5¼-by-2¾-inches) and pour in the batter. Bake 1 hour.

Yield: 1 banana loaf.

Note: This bread does not slice well while warm. It is best to bake and let cool, then refrigerate before slicing. It freezes well wrapped closely in aluminum foil. It may then be heated in the foil and served.

Chocolate Cake

1   cup boiling water
4   ounces (4 squares) semisweet
    chocolate

½   *cup butter*
2   *cups sugar*
2   *eggs, separated*
2   *cups flour*
1   *teaspoon salt*
½   *teaspoon baking powder*
1   *teaspoon baking soda*
½   *cup buttermilk*
1   *teaspoon pure vanilla extract*

1. When the water comes to the boil in a saucepan, remove it from the heat. Add the chocolate and stir until chocolate dissolves. Let cool.

2. Preheat oven to 350 degrees. Butter the bottom and sides of a baking dish measuring about 13½-by-9½-by-2½-inches. Cover the bottom with a rectangle of waxed paper cut to fit. Butter the waxed paper. Set the pan aside.

3. Combine the butter and sugar in the bowl of an electric mixer. Cream together and add the egg yolks. Continue beating.

4. Sift together the flour, salt, baking powder and baking soda and add this to the creamed mixture. Beat in the melted chocolate, buttermilk and vanilla.

5. Beat the whites until stiff and fold them into the batter. Pour the batter into the prepared baking dish.

6. Place in the oven and bake about 45 minutes.

Yield: 1 rectangular cake.

Amaretto Butter

(For pancakes, waffles, etc.)

½   *pound butter*
¼   *cup amaretto liqueur*
¼   *cup honey*
¼   *teaspoon grated orange rind*

Put the butter in the bowl of an electric mixer and start beating. Gradually add the amaretto and honey until well blended. Beat in the orange rind and serve or chill.

Yield: About 1½ cups.

Ann Bolderson prepares lobster caught by her husband

September

I F YOU HAVE a natural curiosity about cooking and if food happens to be your working forte, it is extraordinary how some of the great "mysteries" of cooking become unraveled as time goes by. It may take days, it may take months, it may take years to discover certain "secrets" hitherto forbidden you through innocence, ignorance, a conspiracy of chefs or, perhaps, a combination of these things. More than twenty years ago, when I first joined the *New York Times*, I traveled to Rio de Janeiro in search of Brazilian cooking and I recall the food on which I dined in intimate detail. There was a feijoada, the black bean and salt meat dish that is the national dish of the country; there were shrimp bahiana, local shrimp cooked in dende oil and spices; and then there was a churrasco à gaucha, that marvelous and elaborate ritual in which fresh meats are dipped in a saltwater bath before cooking over a charcoal pit. The exact preparation, particularly as it would apply to cooking on home territory, had totally escaped my ken. In September, to my great joy, my old Brazilian friend Dorothea Elman came out to my home and, with all the dexterity and authority of a cowboy, proceeded to skewer foods on long spears and to plunge them into the banks of a fiery pit. There were traditional sauces and salads, farofa and Brazilian beer. The meal had been preceded by glasses of caipirinha, a potent Brazilian concoction made of rum. It was an unforgettable feast and an unforgettable day.

The range of food that September was international. There was moussaka, that estimable speciality of the Greek kitchen as prepared by Steve Johnides, a friend of mine who owns a Greek restaurant called The Old Stove Pub. There was a report with recipes from the lovely Italian villa of the Angelo Bettojas. There was an elegant dinner, Mexican-style, cooked by Margarita de Rosenzweig-Diaz, wife of the then Mexican ambassador to the United States. And finally, a history of duck breeding in the area of America most celebrated for its duck, Long Island, home sweet home.

Gaucho-Style Barbecue

There are many kinds of feasts on this earth based on rituals of either a formal or a highly casual nature. They exist in almost every culture and numerous ones come to mind. In China there are the elaborate "fire pots," or Mongolian hot pots wherein foods, fish, meat, vegetables, and so on are cooked at the table by guests who stand around a communal grill. There are the simple and traditional raclettes or fondues of Switzerland whereby guests share melted cheese from a single simmering earthenware pot. And in America there is the enormously convivial, colorful—and, if properly done, backbreaking—ritual known as a clambake.

One of the grandest ritual feats in the world is of agrarian origin and comes from Brazil (actually there are two great Brazilian feasts, the other being a feijoada completa). This is the churrasco à gaucha, the traditional feast of South Brazil, specifically from the state of Rio Grande do Sul, the center of the nation's cattle country.

I was recently involved in a highly sophisticated version of the churrasco à gaucha, all of it assembled under the expert guidance of a redoubtable, enthusiastic cook, an old friend and a native of Rio de Janeiro, Dorothea Elman. She is the wife of Lee Elman, an investment banker.

"Although the churrasco had basically humble origins—in the beginning it was nothing more than a cattleman's lunch or dinner made of freshly killed beef cooked over an open fire—the meal is tremendously popular in Rio and Sao Paolo," Mrs. Elman explained.

"The best churrascaria or restaurant that specializes in the dish in Rio is, incidentally, Churrascaria Jardin in Copacabana." There, she added, you would find a variation of the meal she was to prepare during the day, to be cooked and consumed late in the afternoon at long tables situated next to a charcoal pit where the assorted meats—beef ribs, chicken, pork, lamb and sausages—would be grilled over hot ashes.

The time in which the meats would be grilled would be sufficient to unleash the hounds of hunger, the enraged appetite only partly assuaged by morsels of spicy Brazilian sausages that would be wrapped in foil and buried in the hot coals. This is taken with a seemingly innocent, superficially innocuous and irresistible but potent Brazilian elixir known as caipirinha, made with the clear distillate of sugar cane, lime and sugar over ice.

The meats, still amber and still sizzling, would be removed from the long skewers, cut, sliced or carved, and served with seductively seasoned salad of mixed vegetables—bits of broccoli, cauliflower, green beans, zucchini, green peas, carrots and so on blended in a tangy mayonnaise. That plus a platter of buttery farofa, a splendid dry cereal dish cooked with banana. And to bind the meal together, to give it an exceptional and uncommon fillip, a spicy onion sauce, made of oil and vinegar, chopped parsley and coriander.

Before noon the pit had been dug. A neat rectangular hole, four feet long, three feet wide and fourteen inches deep. Ten logs would be burned and forty pounds of charcoal heaped onto that. Gaucho knives, not essential to the ceremony but appropriate, had been shipped by air from Brazil. Long iron skewers had been obtained from Gaylord's restaurant in Manhattan (the restaurant uses them for oven cooking; they may be purchased there for $8.95 apiece).

"The skewers," Mrs. Elman remarked, "are a convenience. In the South, the cattlemen are more apt to use neatly whittled long, thin branches to skewer the foods."

Before the meal began, long tables had been covered with sheets of heavy brown wrapping paper, as in Brazil.

Forks and knives were provided plus linen napkins, although the churrasqueira (that's the feminine form for the person who cooks the meal; the masculine is churrasqueiro) explained that these were civilized conceits; the gauchos use their fingers.

Mrs. Elman told us that she had arranged the feast as a preliminary to celebrating the National Day of Brazil, which is today.

Mrs. Elman went about her business of preparing food and cooking it with a cool, assured dedication and determination that was awesome to behold. The meats were threaded or impaled on parallel skewers and, when the coals in the pit were properly ashen, she shoved the metal bottoms into the earth with a powerful, educated thrust, taking care that the foods on the rods were neatly centered directly over the heat. The skewers were inserted into the earth at a fifteen-degree angle, centering the foods twelve to fourteen inches from the heat.

As the meats were seared on one side, the skewers were turned so that the other side would roast. The moment the meats were turned, Mrs. Elman would dip a neatly tied and sizable bundle of leaves together to use as a basting "mop." She would swish the mop inside a vessel containing a basting brine made of water, garlic and salt, then onto the meats.

"You wait until the meats are seared on one side," she said, "before basting with the brine. After that you must brush them often. And if flames start in the pit and under the meat, you must extinguish them at all times with a dash of brine from the mop."

As the meats were ready for eating, the skewers were removed, the tips wiped off with a clean damp rag. The meats were removed, transferred to a cutting board and sliced or carved and served piping hot.

"There's one thing to remember," Mrs. Elman advised. "If you plan to cook at one of these, don't ever plan to sit with the guests until the end of the meal. That's why the table should be close to the pit. So you can cook and talk at the same time."

Dorothea Elman brushes meats with brine

As Linguicas

(The Portugese sausages)

3 linguicas (Portuguese sausages), about 1 pound (see note)

1. Cut each length of linguica in half. Wrap each half closely in heavy-duty aluminum foil and add to the hot coals in a pit.

2. Let the sausages cook about 10 minutes on one side. Turn them and cook about 10 minutes on the other side.

3. Open up the foil and cut the sausages into 1-inch lengths. Serve hot.

Yield: 12 to 16 cocktail servings.

Note: Portuguese sausages are available at the Portuguese American Delicatessen, 323 Bleecker Street.

As Costelas de Bife

(The beef ribs)

5 3-pound slabs of prime beef ribs (see note)
   Salt to taste
   Brine (see recipe)

1. Using a sharp boning knife, cut away most but not all of the fat from the tops and bottoms of the ribs. There will be pockets of fat between the ribs at the tips. Discard the fat.

2. Rub the ribs with salt and arrange the slabs of beef on 2 parallel skewers, threading them through the meaty portions between the ribs. For each 2 skewers, add 2 or 3 slabs, or whatever they can accommodate properly.

3. Place the ribs over the hot coals. Let cook without basting until nicely browned and seared on one side. Turn, repositioning the skewers, so that the ribs cook on the opposite side. Brush the seared side with brine. Continue cooking, turning as necessary and brushing with brine. The total cooking time is about 40 minutes, although the time will vary depending on the size of the meat and the proximity to the coals. To test for doneness, run a knife into the meat between 2 of the bones.

4. When ready, remove the skewers from the grill and wipe off the pointed ends. Remove the ribs and place on a flat surface. Slice between the individual ribs and serve.

Yield: 12 to 16 servings.

Note: These slabs of prime beef ribs consist of about 7 uncut ribs with the main part of the beef removed. There was no problem in ordering them a few days in advance from our local butcher. These are one of the best things about a churrasco. If they are not available, you can use trimmed fillets of beef in 1 piece or porterhouse or other steaks. Skewer the meat, either the fillets or the steaks, before cooking.

As Galinghas

(The chickens)

3 *chickens, each about 2½ pounds, split down the back for broiling and opened up but left whole*
1 *tablespoon salt*
¾ *cup olive oil*
3 *cloves garlic, crushed and peeled*
   Brine (see recipe)

1. Rub the chickens all over with salt and place in a deep pan. Add the oil and garlic and massage well with the fingers.

2. Cover and let stand 3 hours.

3. When ready to cook, use 2 skewers about 5 feet long. Run the skewers parallel through the birds, inserting them left and right through the bodies of the birds. Center the 3 birds on the skewers, bodies touching, neck to tail.

4. Place the chickens 12 to 16 inches above the hot coals. Let them cook without basting until nicely browned and seared on one side. Turn them, repositioning the skewers over the coals. Brush the seared side with brine. Continue cooking, turning as necessary and brushing occasionally with brine. The total cooking time for the chickens is about 1 hour, although the cooking time will vary depending on the size of the chickens and the proximity to the hot coals.

5. Remove the skewers from the grill and wipe off the pointed ends. Remove the chickens and place them on a flat surface. Cut, slice and chop the chickens as desired for serving.

Yield: 12 to 16 servings.

O Porco

(The pork)

1 *4½- to 5-pound loin of pork*
   Salt
   Brine (see recipe)

1. Bone the loin of pork or have it boned by the butcher. Have most but not all of the surface fat cut away from the meat.

2. Using a sharp knife, butterfly the large meaty portion of the loin. That is, slice almost but not quite through the meat, opening it up to lie flat. If there is a smaller tenderloin, use that but leave it intact. Rub the meat with salt to taste.

3. When ready to cook, use 2 skewers about 5 feet long. Run the skewers parallel through the butterflied loin. Skewer the tenderloin if there is one. The pork will not occupy all the cooking room on the skewers so other meats may be added as desired.

4. Place the meat over the hot coals, fat side down. Let cook without basting until nicely browned and

seared on one side. Turn, repositioning the skewers over the coals. Brush the seared side with brine. Continue cooking, turning as necessary and brushing with brine. The total cooking time is about 1½ hours, although the time will vary depending on the size of the meat and the proximity to the coals.

5. Remove the skewers from the grill and wipe off the pointed ends. Remove the meat and place on a flat surface. Cut and slice as desired for serving.

Yield: 12 to 16 small servings.

O Carneiro
(The lamb)

1   *2¾-pound loin of lamb*
    Salt to taste
    Brine (see recipe)

1. Bone the loin of lamb or have it boned. Have most but not all of the surface fat trimmed away. Rub the meat with salt to taste. Skewer the boned loin lengthwise on 1 skewer. If there is a small fillet of lamb, skewer that as well. The loin will occupy very little space on the skewer; therefore, other meats, such as the loin of pork, may be added to the skewer or skewers before placing over coals.

2. Place the meat over the hot coals, fat side down. Let cook without basting until nicely browned and seared on one side. Turn, repositioning the skewer over the coals. Brush the seared side with brine. Continue cooking, turning as necessary and brushing with brine. The total cooking time is about 1 hour, although the time will vary depending on the size

of the meat and the proximity to the coals.

3. Remove the skewers from the grill and wipe off the pointed ends. Remove the meat and place on a flat surface. Cut and slice as desired for serving.

Yield: 12 to 16 small servings.

A salmoura
(The brine)

8   *peeled cloves garlic*
2   *cups kosher salt*
13 *cups water*

1. Combine the garlic, ½ cup of salt and 1 cup of water in the container of a food processor or electric blender. Blend thoroughly.

2. Empty the brine into a large vessel and add the remaining salt and water. Stir to blend thoroughly. Use as a basting brine for barbecues.

Note: Any large traditional instrument for basting may be used to dip into this brine for brushing the meats. This includes barbecue mops and brushes. The best device for brushing the meats for a churrasco à gaucha is a bundle of sturdy twigs with leafy ends. Birch, as one example, is good.

Molho de cebola
(Onion sauce)

6   *cups finely chopped onion*
3   *whole cloves garlic, peeled*
2½ *cups olive oil*
1⅓ *cups red wine vinegar*
½   *cup finely chopped parsley*

⅓   cup finely chopped fresh
     coriander leaves, available in
     Chinese and Mexican markets
     where fresh vegetables are sold
     Salt to taste
3   cups cored tomatoes cut into
     ½-inch cubes

1. Put the onions in a mixing bowl. Use 3 skewers or toothpicks and skewer each clove of garlic. Add them to the bowl.

2. Add the oil, vinegar, parsley, coriander and salt. Blend well.

3. Shortly before serving, add the tomatoes. Remove the garlic cloves and serve at room temperature.

Yield: 12 to 16 servings.

Farofa

¾   pound butter
5   cups thinly sliced onions
10   to 12 sweet, firm, ripe bananas
4   cups manioc flour (see note)
     Salt to taste

1. Heat 6 tablespoons butter in a large skillet and add the onion. Cook, stirring, until wilted. Continue cooking, stirring often, until they start to turn golden.

2. Peel the bananas and cut them on the bias into ½-inch slices. Heat 10 tablespoons of butter in a saucepan and add the bananas. Cook, stirring gently on occasion, until they start to turn golden.

3. Add the manioc flour and stir gently to blend the bananas and flour. Add the onions and stir gently to blend. Cook, stirring occasionally,

about 10 minutes, or until manioc flour loses its raw taste.

4. Add remaining 8 tablespoons of butter and salt and stir gently until butter is blended.

Yield: 12 to 16 servings.

Note: Manioc flour is a staple in Brazilian cookery. It is made from the ground root of the manioc plant. It is available in New York at Portuguese American Delicatessen, 323 Bleecker Street.

Salada de Legumes

(Brazilian vegetable salad)

3   potatoes, about 1¼ pounds
      Salt to taste
1½   pounds broccoli
¾   pound green beans
¾   pound small zucchini
1   head cauliflower, about ¾
      pound
¾   pound carrots
3   pounds fresh peas in the pod,
      or use 2 10-ounce packages
      frozen peas
2   cans hearts of palm, drained
2   cups chopped celery
1½   cups chopped scallions
3   cups mayonnaise, preferably
      homemade

1. Put the potatoes in a saucepan and add cold water to cover and salt to taste. Bring to the boil. Let simmer, partly covered, about 20 minutes or until tender. Drain and let stand until cool enough to handle.

2. Meanwhile, prepare the remaining vegetables. Break or cut the broccoli head into small, bite-size "flowerettes." There should be about 3 cups.

3. Trim off the ends of the green beans. Cut the beans into ½-inch lengths. There should be about 3 cups.

4. Trim off the ends of the zucchini. Cut the zucchini into ½-inch slices. Cut the slices into ½-inch strips. Cut the strips into ½-inch cubes. There should be about 2½ cups.

5. Break off or cut the cauliflower into small, bite-size "flowerettes." There should be about 5 cups.

6. Trim the carrots. Cut them into ¼-inch or slightly larger cubes. There should be about 2 cups.

7. Shell the peas. There should be about 2 cups.

8. Put the broccoli, green beans, zucchini, cauliflower, carrots and peas into individual saucepans (the same saucepan may be used as each vegetable is cooked). Add cold water to cover and salt to taste. Bring to the boil and simmer until each vegetable is crisp-tender. The broccoli should require 8 to 10 minutes; the green beans and zucchini, 2 to 3 minutes each; the cauliflower, 8 to 10 minutes; the carrots, 1 to 2 minutes. As each vegetable is ready, empty it into a colander or sieve and run cold water over it to chill quickly. Drain each vegetable well and set aside.

9. Peel the potatoes. Cut into ½-inch-thick slices. Cut each slice into ½-inch strips. Cut each strip into ½-inch cubes.

10. Combine all the cooked, well-drained vegetables in a large mixing bowl.

11. Quarter the hearts of palm lengthwise. Cut the quarters into ½-inch lengths. Add to the bowl.

12. Add the celery and scallions. Add the mayonnaise and remaining ingredients and blend well. Taste the salad and add more seasonings as desired such as salt, Tabasco, lemon juice and so on.

Yield: 12 to 16 servings.

Work List for a Churrasco à Gaucha for from 12 to 16 People

  A pit measuring about 3 feet by 4 feet by 14 inches

6 *or 8 metal skewers, preferably flat rather than round, each measuring 4½ to 5 feet in length*

10 *to 12 fireplace logs*

40 *pounds charcoal (preferably pure charcoal, which is hard to find, or charcoal briquettes)*
  Brown paper to cover dining tables
  Forks, knives, napkins
  A cutting block or slab for preparing meats after they are cooked
  A basting "mop" made of leafy branches tied together, or a purchased basting utensil
  Sponges and clean cloths to wipe off the ends of skewers

Moussaka for the Masses

WITH PIERRE FRANEY

Although the goings-on in home kitchens are drastically different from those in a restaurant kitchen, there are certain dishes and techniques that the home cook might well borrow, particularly where cooking for crowds is concerned. The recipe on this page is a case in point.

The meat and eggplant dish known as moussaka is a well-known crowd-pleaser. One of the best moussakas we know is that made by Steve Johnides, chief cook and proprietor of the Old Stove Pub in our home town, East Hampton.

Although the dish is excellent if served shortly after it is taken out of the oven, it is improved if it is made at least one day in advance before serving. That way, the moussaka gets a chance to "set," and, therefore, is easier to cut into serving pieces. It is ideal when cut into squares and reheated the second time around in a light layer of milk. And dishwashing is simplified if it is reheated in disposable aluminum baking pans as it is at the Old Stove Pub. The moussaka also freezes well.

Although the length of this recipe makes it look difficult, it is actually quite easy to prepare.

The Old Stove Pub's Moussaka à la Grecque

(An eggplant and meat casserole)

6   tablespoons olive oil
3   cups finely chopped onion
3   cups rich, concentrated but not too salty beef broth
3   pounds lean ground chuck
    Salt and freshly ground pepper
2   cups tomato sauce, approximately (see recipe)

3   large eggplants, about 4 pounds total weight
3   cups water
¾   cup dry red wine
2   quarts béchamel sauce, approximately (see recipe)
¼   cup fine bread crumbs
4   cups freshly grated cheese, preferably a combination of Parmesan and pecorino, (use twice as much Parmesan as pecorino) or use all Parmesan
2   eggs, lightly beaten
    Milk

1. Preheat oven to 400 degrees.

2. Heat 4 tablespoons oil in a large kettle and add the onion. Cook, stirring, until wilted and add ½ cup beef broth. Cook, uncovered, until most of the liquid has evaporated.

3. Add the ground meat and stir briefly. Add the remaining broth and cook, breaking up any lumps with the side of a wooden spoon. Add very little salt. Remember that the meat will become saltier as the broth cooks down. Add pepper to taste. Cover closely and let simmer about 1½ hours.

4. As the meat cooks, prepare the tomato sauce and set aside.

5. Meanwhile, trim off the ends of the eggplant but do not peel the eggplant. Cut the eggplant lengthwise into slices about ⅛ inch thick. Save the outside, unpeeled slices of the eggplant along with the inside slices.

6. Select a baking pan, preferably an enameled pan measuring about 17-by-11½-by-2-inches. Arrange the unpeeled outside slices of eggplant against the inside of the pan, resting them upright, slices slightly overlapping.

7. Arrange more slices of eggplant, standing them upright and edges slightly overlapping. Arrange them in neat rows, one against the other, until all the slices are used. They probably won't fill the pan. Add 3 cups of water and cover closely with foil.

8. Bake 35 minutes and remove. Uncover and pour off most of the liquid from the pan. Let the eggplant slices stand until cool.

9. When the meat has cooked the specified time, select a small wire strainer and a small ladle. Dip the strainer into the meat, pressing down to allow the liquid to accumulate in the center of the strainer. Use the ladle to scoop out most of the liquid. Specifically, scoop out and discard all but about 1 cup of liquid.

10. Add the tomato sauce and red wine to the meat sauce and continue cooking about 1 hour, or until the meat sauce is quite thick. Remove from the heat and let cool slightly while proceeding to the béchamel sauce.

11. Rub a 17-by-11½-by-2-inch baking pan (you may use the same pan in which the eggplant slices were baked) with 2 tablespoons of oil. Sprinkle with bread crumbs and shake to coat the bottom and sides of the pan. Shake out the excess.

12. Discard the sliced, outside ends of the eggplant. Arrange about half the remaining slices of eggplant over the crumb-coated pan, edges slightly overlapping. Sprinkle with ¾ cup of cheese.

13. Beat the eggs with ¼ cup of grated cheese and stir it into the meat sauce. Bring to the boil, stirring.

14. Spoon the meat sauce over

the layer of eggplant, smoothing the top with a rubber spatula. Sprinkle the meat with another ¾ cup of cheese.

15. Arrange a second layer of eggplant over, edges slightly overlapping. There may be too many slices. Use for another purpose or discard. Sprinkle the second layer of eggplant with ¾ cup of grated cheese.

16. Spoon the béchamel sauce over the top and smooth it over with a spatula. Sprinkle with ¾ cup of cheese.

17. When ready to cook the moussaka, preheat the oven to 350 degrees.

18. Place the pan in the oven and bake 40 to 45 minutes, or until the topping is barely set in the center. Remove the moussaka from the oven and let cool 30 minutes or longer.

19. Although the moussaka could be served directly from the oven, it is infinitely preferable to refrigerate it overnight before serving. This will allow the moussaka layers to become firm prior to cutting into serving pieces.

20. After refrigeration, remove the moussaka and cut it into 12 to 20 pieces of more or less equal size.

21. When ready to serve, preheat the oven to 500 degrees.

22. Pour a thin layer of milk into the bottom of 1 or more baking pans. Disposable aluminum foil baking pans are good for this. Arrange 2 or more squares of moussaka in each pan and bake until piping hot throughout, about 15 minutes. The pieces should be almost but not quite touching. Transfer the squares to individual dishes, sprinkle with more cheese and serve immediately.

Yield: 12 to 20 pieces.

Tomato sauce
(For moussaka only)

2   *cups tomato purée*
     Salt and freshly ground pepper to taste
1   *tablespoon nutmeg*
½   *teaspoon ground cinnamon*
2   *tablespoons sugar*

Combine all the ingredients in a saucepan and cook, uncovered, about 30 minutes.

Yield: About 2 cups.

Béchamel sauce
(For moussaka only)

½   *pound butter*
¾   *cup flour*
½   *cup cornstarch*
7   *cups hot milk*
3   *eggs, lightly beaten*
¼   *teaspoon nutmeg*

1. Heat the butter in a 3-quart

saucepan. When melted, add the flour, stirring with a wire whisk. Add the cornstarch and stir to blend.

2. Add about ⅓ of the milk, stirring rapidly with the whisk. Quickly add another ⅓, stirring rapidly and constantly, covering all the bottom and sides of the saucepan. Add the last of the milk, stirring rapidly and constantly.

3. When thickened and smooth, remove from the heat. Beat the eggs and nutmeg and add to the saucepan, stirring with the whisk. Cook briefly, stirring constantly.

Yield: About 2 quarts.

Home-cooking,
Roman Villa Style

Legend has it that the finest food in all of Italy is not to be found in restaurants and trattorias but rather in private homes. And a visit to the country residence of the Angelo Bettojas—one and one-half hours drive from Rome in the province of Viterbo—is eloquent testimony to the fact. Here, in a home almost poetically surrounded by groves of hazelnuts and olive trees, is a corner of heaven for cooking buffs. And that includes the owner and his wife, the gamekeeper and his wife and assorted guests who come to call almost any weekend throughout the year.

Before we arrived we had been advised by a friend that there are always susurrations of cooking in the Bettoja kitchen.

"You take a nap in the afternoon to the sound of rolling pins stretching the dough for a pastry shell or dish of fine noodles. If you walk out to the gamekeeper's cottage, you'll find a fire going almost all day and night in the built-in brick oven, waiting for another loaf of bread or a roast of some sort or a kettle of beans or those marvelous homemade hazelnut cookies known as tozzetti."

Indeed. As we walked into the kitchen, Angelo, the head of the household, wiped his hands and greeted us. Before him were sprigs and branches of rosemary, sage and garlic ready to be chopped as seasoning for a roast of pork to be wrapped in pastry and baked in the oven. Jo, his wife, and a friend named Anna Maria Cornetto were shaping balls of fresh pasta to be deep fried and served with bolognese meat sauce.

Giovanni Grossi, the handsome young gamekeeper, was slicing his home-cured prosciutto and salami, serving the thin portions directly from the knife to anyone who paused in the kitchen. A chilled glass of Est! Est!! Est!!!, the well-known wine from the Montefiascone vineyards, about twenty-five kilometers away, was poured. The prosciutto was magnificent, slightly winey; the salami neatly flecked with bits of peppercorns; both of the aged meats good and perfectly matched by a somewhat coarse-textured bread fresh from the oven.

An hour or so later with the preliminaries of the evening out of the way— the herb-seasoned pork ready for an initial roasting, the yeast dough in the initial stages of rising—guests were escorted on a tour of the immediate grounds.

A trip to the brick oven to inspect the fire. That dwindling pyre smelled sweet and good from burning laurel and oak was in its last stage of rage. Giovanni pointed to the rear of the dwindling embers and explained that within half an hour the enclosure would be ready for working. "You can tell," he explained, "when the back bricks are white hot. Then the ashes are raked out, the floor scrubbed with a damp mop."

We walked along bridle paths bordered on either side with wild oregano, thyme and dill and our bodies brushed against laurel bushes. And there in a sizable enclosure, artichokes and mustard greens flourished alongside fennel, celery, fresh peas, zucchini, eggplant, scallions, basil, tarragon and a dozen other herbs and vegetables. Protecting this garden from the winds were great surrounding stands of cyprus, oak, pine and wild fig trees, beneath whose shade roamed pheasant, woodcock and wild hare. The latter sometimes appeared on the Bettoja table in one of Italy's most famous and tempting game dishes, pappardelle con la lepre, or homemade wide noodles with a delectable meat sauce made from the flesh of the hare.

We were fascinated by Jo Bettoja's scarcely disguised accent, indisputably that of the American south. She is a strikingly handsome woman and the Bettojas are the parents of three: Maurizio, 21; Roberto, 19; Georgia, 17.

"I was born in a small town named Millen, not far from Savannah," Mrs. Bettoja explained. "I had done some modeling in New York, but I came to Italy on a holiday with two friends." Someone told her that an American model in Italy would be a novelty, and she was offered a job. She did not add, although her visitors will willingly testify to it, that Jo Patterson was also considered one of the most beautiful women in her profession.

"Modeling, in those days, was a tremendous business," she said. "*Vogue* did their collections here and I modeled the fashions of Givenchy, Belenciaga, Dior and Simonetta, among numerous others. Then I met Angelo and we were married."

Angelo's family are relative newcomers to the Rome scene. They've only been there for 150 years. Before that the Bettojas were Piedmontese for several centuries. His family came to Rome in the early 1800s and became hotel keepers. Today they own the Hotel Mediterraneo and the Hotel Massimo d'Azeglio. They maintain a home in Rome and spend a few weeks each year in Greece.

Angelo stated that he learned to cook while courting the young women about town in Rome.

"I had worked in several hotels in Paris including the Grand, the Meurice and the Prince de Galles, but always in reception, management and so on and never in the kitchen. Of course, I've watched professional chefs and cooks in our hotels throughout my life, but it was in my bachelor days that I became fairly expert. At least the ladies thought I was a good cook."

Jo stated that although she grew up on fine southern cooking, she had never so much as cooked fried chicken until a few years ago. Her interest in food preparation began when her children were starting to approach adulthood.

Throughout that day we'd been much impressed with the cooking skills and

the dexterity of Anna Maria Cornetto, a contemporary of Jo's with whom she
had modeled during their early years in Rome. At the behest of Angelo, Jo and
Anna Maria returned to the kitchen where the host had assembled his splendid
roast of pork perfumed with sage and rosemary. He wrapped it in yeast dough,
let it rise briefly and carried it to the waiting brick oven. His timing was ideal.
He arrived just as Assunta, the gamekeeper's wife, removed from the heat several score of baked tozzetti, crunchy, rich sweet biscuits made with hazelnuts
buried in their depths, the nuts slightly toasted as they baked in their fiery cof-
fin. The tozzetti (which resemble the almond biscotti one finds in bake shops in
Manhattan's Little Italy) would be eaten later with a sweet dessert wine called
vino santo, or holy wine, from a region around Venice.

Despite the diversity of that meal, it was triumphant from stuffed cold veal
and filled crepes, through the deep-fried pasta with bolognese sauce and the
main dish, Angelo's pasta-baked pork, to the assorted desserts. Even a local
nightingale added to the proceedings. It sang loud and clear just as the first
stars came out.

Angelo Bettoja in villa kitchen

Caponata

(An Italian vegetable appetizer)

4 to 6 small or medium zucchini
4 cups onions cut into 1-inch cubes
4 cups sweet peppers, preferably a combination of green and red peppers, cored, seeded and cut into 1-inch cubes
1 medium eggplant, about ¾ pound, cut into 1-inch cubes
½ cup olive oil
4 cups tomatoes cored and cut into 1-inch cubes
2 cups potatoes peeled and cut into 1-inch cubes
2 cloves garlic, finely minced
2 teaspoons oregano
Salt and freshly ground pepper to taste

1. Preheat oven to 350 degrees.

2. Trim the ends of the zucchini. Split the zucchini lengthwise in half. Cut each half into 1-inch lengths.

3. Arrange the zucchini, onions, peppers and eggplant in one layer in a baking pan and place in the oven. Bake 15 minutes to let part of the moisture in each vegetable evaporate.

4. Heat the oil in a large casserole and add all the vegetables including the tomatoes and potatoes. Sprinkle with the garlic, oregano, salt and pepper. Cook briefly and stir. Transfer to the oven. Do not cover. Bake 40 minutes. Remove and cook over high heat until most of the liquid evaporates. Let cool. Refrigerate.

Yield: 8 or more servings.

Palle di Pasta

(Deep-fried fettucine balls)

3 tablespoons butter
3 tablespoons flour
1 cup milk
½ cup heavy cream
Salt and freshly ground pepper to taste
¼ teaspoon freshly grated nutmeg
¼ cup grated Parmesan cheese
6 ounces (½ package) fettucine, preferably imported (see note)
2 eggs, lightly beaten
2 tablespoons water
1½ cups bread crumbs
Oil for deep-frying
Ragu bolognese (see recipe)

1. Melt the butter in a saucepan and add the flour, stirring with a wire whisk. When blended, add the milk, stirring rapidly with the whisk. Add the cream and continue stirring until blended and smooth and simmering.

2. Add salt and pepper to taste and the nutmeg. Stir in the cheese. Let cool about ½ hour.

3. Drop the fettucine into boiling salted water and cook until tender. Take care not to overcook, however, or the pasta will become mushy. Drain the pasta well.

4. Fold the pasta into the cream sauce. Let cool. Chill overnight.

5. With the hands, scoop up equal amounts of the pasta mixture. Shape into balls rolling between the palms. There should be about 10 balls.

6. Beat the eggs with salt, pepper and water. Dredge the balls all over with the egg mixture, then in bread crumbs.

7. Heat the oil for deep-frying and, when quite hot, add the balls. Cook, turning often and controlling the heat as necessary so that the balls cook properly and are crisp and golden all over without becoming too dark. Total cooking time should be about 8 minutes. Serve with ragu bolognese and, if desired, additional Parmesan cheese.

Yield: 5 to 10 servings.

Note: Fresh noodles made with about 1 cup of flour may be used for this dish. If used, cook briefly, less than a minute, or until tender.

Ragu bolognese
(Bologna-style meat sauce)

½	*pound ground beef*
½	*pound ground pork*
¼	*pound rolled, salt pancetta (see note), or use lean salt pork*
4	*tablespoons butter*
1	*cup finely chopped onion*
⅓	*cup finely chopped celery*
½	*cup finely chopped carrot*
	Salt and freshly ground pepper to taste
½	*cup dry red wine, preferably Italian*
2	*cups fresh or canned beef broth*
2	*tablespoons tomato paste*
½	*cup milk*

1. Blend the beef and pork. Chop the pancetta until fine and add it.

2. Heat the butter in a large heavy skillet and add the meat mixture, stirring to break up any lumps. Cook briefly and add the onion, celery and carrots. Continue cooking, stirring often, until the meat is nicely browned. Add salt and pepper to taste.

3. Add the wine and cook, stirring occasionally, until wine is reduced.

4. Add ½ the broth and cook until most of the liquid disappears. Add the remaining broth and cook until that has cooked down and little liquid remains. Add the tomato paste and cook briefly.

5. Meanwhile, heat the milk almost but not quite to boiling. Add it to the meat and simmer until most of the milk is absorbed.

Yield: 4 to 6 servings.

Note: Pancetta is available in Italian pork stores, including Manganaro Foods, 488 Ninth Avenue, in New York.

Lombatine di Maiale al Panne
(Roast loin of pork baked in pastry)

The roast pork

1	*4½-pound loin of pork, boned (see note)*
	Salt and freshly ground pepper to taste
2	*tablespoons olive oil*
2	*sprigs fresh rosemary*
½	*cup dry white wine*

The pastry

3½	*cups flour*
1	*envelope yeast*
¾	*cup plus 5 tablespoons lukewarm water*
2	*teaspoons salt*
1½	*tablespoons olive oil*

The final preparation

1½	*teaspoons finely chopped rosemary*

1   *teaspoon finely chopped garlic*
1½   *teaspoons finely chopped sage*

1. Preheat oven to 425 degrees.

2. Sprinkle the boned pork loin all over with salt and pepper. Add the oil to a small roasting pan. Add the pork, chopped bones and rosemary sprigs. Cook briefly on top of the stove. Place uncovered in the oven and bake 20 minutes, turning the meat occasionally. Add the wine and continue baking 20 minutes, basting often. Remove from the oven. Discard the bones or use them for another purpose. They are tasty. Transfer the pork to a rack to cool. Turn off the oven heat until ready to complete the baking.

3. Pour off and reserve the basting liquid.

4. Meanwhile, as the pork cooks, prepare the pastry.

5. Put the flour in the bowl of an electric mixer outfitted with a dough hook. Or, if you are to knead by hand, put the flour in a heavy mixing bowl.

6. Put the yeast in a small bowl and add 3 tablespoons lukewarm water. Stir to dissolve. Let stand in warm place about 10 minutes.

7. Add the yeast mixture to the flour and start kneading with the dough hook or by hand.

8. Blend the remaining water with salt and oil and add it to the flour mixture, kneading constantly. Knead with the hook or by hand until the dough is smooth and satiny. Shape it into a ball and put it in a lightly oiled mixing bowl. Cover with a towel and let stand in a warm place until double in bulk, about 45 minutes.

9. Preheat oven to 375 degrees.

10. Lightly coat a marble or Formica surface with olive oil. Turn the dough out onto it and roll it into a rectangle. You may carefully stretch it by hand if desired. The dough should be large enough so that when the pork is added it will completely enclose the meat when folded over.

11. Sprinkle the center of the dough with half the chopped rosemary, garlic and sage. Add the meat and sprinkle it with the remaining herbs. Fold the upper flap of dough over the meat in toward you. Fold over the lower flap of dough. Fold over both ends of dough to totally envelop the meat.

12. Carefully place the dough, seam side down, on a baking sheet. Cover with a towel and let rise 15 or 20 minutes. Uncover and place in the oven. Bake 1 hour, turning the baking sheet as necessary so that the crust browns evenly. Let stand 15 minutes before serving. Serve sliced like beef Wellington. Before serving, reheat the reserved pan liquid. Skim off fat and serve as a sauce.

Yield: 8 or more servings.

Note: To prepare this dish, the pork loin must be boned. Do this yourself or have it done by the butcher. In any event, save the pork bones. Have the bones chopped between the ribs.

Zucchini alla Menta
(Zucchini with mint)

2   *pounds zucchini, the smaller the better*
     Salt
     Oil for deep frying

2   *to 4 sprigs fresh mint, depend-*
      ing on size
¼   *cup red wine vinegar*
1   *clove garlic*
     Freshly ground pepper to taste

1. Trim off and discard the ends of the zucchini. Using a knife, run the tip lengthwise down the side of the zucchini at ½-inch intervals. This is purely decorative. The incisions will show when the pieces are cut.

2. Cut the zucchini into ¼-inch rounds. Sprinkle all over with salt and arrange the rounds separately and in 1 layer on a baking sheet. If you have access to sunlight, let the zucchini stand in the sun until the pieces dry on one side. Turn and let dry on the other. A couple of hours to each side is sufficient. Otherwise, bake the zucchini in a slow oven (200 degrees) about ½ hour until they are no longer damp. Do not brown, however.

3. Heat oil for deep frying and cook half the zucchini until golden brown, 3 to 4 minutes. Drain. Add the remaining batch and cook until golden. Drain.

4. Arrange half the zucchini rounds in a baking dish and cover with pieces of mint. Add the remaining layer of zucchini.

5. Bring the vinegar and garlic to the boil. Pour over the zucchini. Spoon about 3 tablespoons of the oil in which the zucchini were fried over the zucchini. Add salt and pepper to taste. Let marinate for at least 2 hours, or preferably overnight. Stir gently on occasion so that the pieces marinate evenly.

Yield: 8 or more servings.

Tozzetti or Biscotti
(Hazelnut cookies)

2   *cups flour*
1⅓   *cups sugar*
2   *large eggs*
1   *tablespoon grated lemon rind*
¼   *cup anise-flavored liqueur*
     such as Sambuca
¼   *cup rum*
1½   *cups peeled, blanched hazel-*
     nuts, or whole or slivered
     almonds
2   *teaspoons baking powder*

1. Preheat oven to 350 degrees.

2. Lightly oil a large baking pan and dust with flour. Shake off excess flour.

3. Combine the flour, sugar, eggs, lemon rind, anise liqueur and rum in a mixing bowl and beat with a wooden spoon until thoroughly blended.

4. Beat in the hazelnuts and baking powder.

5. Using the hands, pick up half the dough and shape it into a long sausage shape. Arrange it on the prepared baking pan, off center and not too close to the edge of the pan. Arrange the other half alongside but not too close. Both masses will spread as they bake.

6. Place in the oven and bake 1 hour. Remove the pan and let cool about 20 minutes.

7. Carefully and gently run a spatula or pancake turner under the 2 pastries. Let stand until almost at room temperature. Using a serrated bread knife, cut each pastry into crosswise slices, each about 1-inch thick. Arrange these in one layer on a baking sheet and return to the oven to dry out, about 10 minutes. Let cool and store. These cookies are improved if a little anisette or other anise-flavored liqueur is poured or brushed over then in advance of serving.

Yield: About 36 cookies.

Mexican Magic

For some confounding reason known only to a few Aztec gods, the authentic flavor of the Mexican kitchen, like certain fine wines and certain exotic plants, with rare exceptions does not travel well. It transports poorly through some curious dilution of tastes, some diminution of savor, some evanescence of essences.

Once in a rare while, however, in the hands of an expert cook—it's primarily a matter of soul and feeling, of course—the tastes, the nuances of the Mexican table (and Mexican food is, after all, one of the great cuisines of the world) are recreated with such subtlety and sensitivity there's immediate and happy transition to the land of Yucatan and Guadalajara and Mexico City.

There is in Manhattan una maga, a lady blessed with the magic touch where Mexican cooking is concerned, and she is Margarita de Rosenzweig-Diaz, wife of Roberto de Rosenzweig-Diaz, the Mexican ambassador to the United Nations.

The family name, incidentally, dates back to the days of the Emperor Maximilian. The grandfather of Robert de Rosenzweig-Diaz was an Austrian named Fernando de Rosenzweig, who came to Mexico during Maximilian's reign. He was an engineer who designed Mexico City's well-known Avenida Reforma. He married a Diaz and joined the two names to give it a Mexican ring.

We dined in Mrs. de Rosenzweig-Diaz's home recently in a sort of pre-celebration of the Mexican National Day, which occurred on September 16.

It was indeed a festival of eating—cocktail tostadas with salsa picante; two beef casseroles, one in the savory green tomato sauce, the other in a spicy sauce made red with ancho chilies; the most extraordinary bread to ever pass these lips, a sweet corn bread made with masa harina, a fine ground corn meal found wherever Mexican and Spanish groceries are sold; a delectable dessert made with soursop, the fruit, in frozen form, sold locally, and fine-grained sweet butter cookies known as polvorones. The meal also embraced a seductive soup made with cuitlacoche, or huitlacoche, the prized corn fungus that is rarely sold in America. Mrs. de Rosenzweig-Diaz had the basic ingredient, in cans, shipped in from Mexico.

I took advantage of our friendship and arrived early at the Rosenzweig-Diaz apartment to watch preparations for the meal, and reflected that one of the most pleasurable sights on this earth is that of a highly skilled artisan at work, whether it be a professional chef chopping an onion or a virtuoso at the pianoforte. There was something awesome about watching the lady on that day kneading masa dough, rolling it into balls and shaping the corn mixture in her tortilla press. She went about it carrying on a conversation simultaneously.

First off, she explained that she had been infatuated with the kitchen since her earliest childhood, which was uncharacteristic of most women born in those days into well-to-do Mexican homes.

"I was taught to cook," she added, "by two unmarried aunts—my father's sisters." For them cooking had become a kind of mad passion, and they took delight in shaping the interests of one who showed interest in the likes of molcajetes and tejolotes, metates and manos.

Roberto de Rosenzweig-Diaz has been a career diplomat all his adult life and the couple have lived in numerous outposts and inposts (if there is such a thing) on this globe. Curiously, she stated, she has found that no matter where they have been stationed, she has been able to procure authentic ingredients for the Mexican cooking, although many times she has stretched hard to improvise. In some capitals some of the ingredients were tinned; in some, most of the ingredients had to be shipped from Mexico.

"In Cairo," she said, "I could substitute hot chilies from the Sudan. And we did a lot of pit barbecuing. We had a hole dug in the garden, the pit fired with wood and charcoal.

Traditionally, of course, in Mexico, we wrap the meat in leaves from the maguey plant, which protects the meat from burning and adds flavor. In Cairo, I used banana leaves. It worked well."

Mrs. Rosenzweig-Diaz considers New York one of the best metropolises for authentic ingredients. Much of it is purchased—both fresh and tinned—from the celebrated Spanish-Mexican store, Casa Moneo, at 210 West 14th Street. She also shops for chilies, cilantro (fresh coriander) and so on on Ninth Avanue as well at the marqueta at Park Avenue and 150th Street. One of the revolutions of this decade has been the widespread availability of fresh coriander.

"I find it in several shops in my neighborhood in the 90s," she said, "both on Lexington and Madison Avenue. So many people seem to be into cooking Mexican or Chinese or Vietnamese, and fresh coriander is essential.

Cocktail Tostadas

¼ cup peanut, vegetable or corn oil

30 cocktail tortillas (see recipe)

1½ cups refried beans, prepared according to recipe in any standard Mexican cookbook

½ head iceburg lettuce, finely shredded and chopped

1 avocado, cut into very small, short strips

1½ cups finely shredded mozzarella cheese

¾ cup sour cream

2 cups salsa picante (see recipe)

1. Heat the oil in a skillet and cook the tortillas until crisp and browned on both sides, turning as

necessary. Drain on absorbent toweling as they cook. Add more oil if necessary. Let cool.

2. Smear the tortillas on one side with beans. Sprinkle first with lettuce, then avocado and mozarella cheese. Add a dollop of sour cream and serve with salsa picante on the side to be added at will.

Yield: 30 tostadas.

Margarita de Rosenzweig-Dias

Tortilla dough

1   *cup masa harina, a fine-grained corn meal (see note)*
⅔   *cup warm water*

1. Place the masa harina in a mixing bowl and gradually add the water, working the dough with the fingers. It should hold together when pressed into a ball.

2. Shape the dough into round balls before pressing out in a tortilla press or by hand. The size of the dough balls will depend on the size of the tortillas desired. To use the tortilla press, add a sheet of clear plastic wrap to the bottom of the press. Add the ball of dough and cover with another sheet of clear plastic. Press down to make a very thin tortilla. Remove the pancake and place on a hot, ungreased griddle. Cook, turning, until done.

Yield: About 30 cocktail tortillas, or 1 dozen regular size tortillas.

Note: Masa harina is widely available where Mexican specialties are sold.

Salsa picante

1   *pound red, ripe tomatoes*
2   *or more hot green chilies, according to taste*
½   *cup water*
2   *large cloves garlic*
¼   *cup finely chopped fresh coriander (cilantro, culantro or Chinese parsley)*

1. Core the tomatoes. Do not peel. Cut the tomatoes into quarters. Place in a saucepan and add the green chilies. Add the water and bring to the boil. Simmer about 30 seconds and drain.

2. Blend the tomatoes, chilies and garlic to a fine purée. Spoon and scrape into a bowl. Add the coriander and let stand until ready to serve.

Yield: About 2 cups.

Carne en Salsa Verde

(Beef in green tomato sauce)

4   pounds chuck steak
¼   cup oil
2   15¼-ounce cans whole green Spanish tomatoes (see note)
1   large bunch, about ¼ pound, fresh coriander leaves (cilantro, culantro or Chinese parsley)
1   onion, about ¼ pound, peeled and cut into eighths
6   whole cloves garlic, peeled
    Salt to taste
6   to 8 medium size zucchini, about 2 pounds

1. Cut the meat or have the butcher cut the meat into 1½-inch cubes.

2. Heat the oil in a large, heavy skillet or casserole. Add the meat and cook, stirring occasionally, until it gives up its liquid. Continue cooking until most of the liquid evaporates, about 20 minutes.

3. Meanwhile, add the contents of the canned tomatoes to the container of a food processor or electric blender. Because of the volume of the ingredients, it will be necessary to do this entire step in 2 stages. Rinse and drain the coriander. Chop coarsely, discarding only very tough stems. There should be about 3 cups loosely packed. Blend the tomatoes, coriander, onion and garlic to a fine purée. There should be about 8 cups.

4. Add the puree to the meat and add salt. Cover and cook 30 minutes.

5. Add 2 cups of water and bring to the boil. Simmer 30 minutes.

6. Meanwhile, trim the zucchini. Cut each zucchini into thirds. Cut each section into 8 lengthwise pieces. Add the zucchini to the beef. Cook 1 hour longer.

Yield: 8 to 12 servings.

Note: Green spanish tomatoes, or tomatillo entere, are available at Casa Moneo, 210 West 14th Street, and other Spanish markets.

Carne en Salsa Roja

(Beef in red chili sauce)

4   pounds chuck steak
¼   pound dried chilies, a combination of about 12 chilies pasilla and 6 chilies anchos (see note)
5   cups water
1   onion, about ¼ pound, peeled and cut into eighths
6   whole cloves garlic, peeled
¼   cup peanut, vegetable or corn oil
    Salt to taste
3   cups potatoes cut into ¾-inch cubes

1. Cut the meat or have the butcher cut it into 1½-inch cubes. Set aside.

2. Pull off and discard the tough stems of the chilies. Split the chilies open. Remove and discard the seeds and veins.

3. Place the chilies in a saucepan and add the water. Bring to the boil and simmer about 10 minutes, stirring occasionally to redistribute the chilies. Remove from the heat and let cool.

4. Add the chilies with all their cooking liquid to the container of a food processor or electric blender. This may have to be done in 2 or more steps. Add the onion and garlic and

blend all the ingredients thoroughly. As they are blended, pour the mixture into a bowl. Set aside.

5. Heat the oil in a large, fairly deep, heavy skillet or casserole. Add the meat and cook until brown, stirring occasionally, about 10 minutes. Add the chili mixture and salt to taste. Bring to the boil. Cover and simmer 30 minutes.

6. Add the potatoes and cook 40 to 45 minutes, or until meat is tender and potatoes are cooked. When ready to serve, the sauce for this dish should be ample but not too liquid.

Yield: 8 to 12 servings.

Note: Chilies pasilla and chilies anchos are available at, among other sources, Casa Moneo, 210 West 14th Street.

Torta de Masa

(A fine-grained, sweet Mexican corn loaf bread)

1   *cup masa harina, a fine-grained corn meal (see note) Salt to taste*
1½   *teaspoons baking powder*
10   *tablespoons sugar*
10   *tablespoons butter, cut into small pieces*
¾   *cup plus 1 tablespoon water*
6   *eggs, separated*

1. Preheat the oven to 375 degrees. Butter a standard-size loaf pan measuring 9½-by-5¼-by-2-inches.

2. Sift together the masa harina, salt, baking powder and sugar into a mixing bowl.

3. Add the butter, blending with the fingers or a pastry blender until the mixture looks like coarse corn meal. Scrape the mixture into the bowl of an electric mixer.

4. Add the water, beating on low speed. Add the yolks, beating on medium speed until well blended.

5. Beat the whites until stiff and fold them in. Pour and scrape the mixture into the loaf pan. Place it in the oven and bake about 45 minutes. Unmold the bread while it is still hot. Slice and serve hot or lukewarm.

Yield: 1 loaf.

Note: Masa harina is available at, among other sources, Casa Moneo, 210 West 14th Street.

Polvorones

(Mexican butter cookies)

½   *pound butter at room temperature*
⅓   *cup confectioners' sugar*
1   *egg yolk*
1   *tablespoon liqueur such as cognac, rum, kirsch, mirabelle*
2   *cups flour*
1   *cup granulated (not superfine) sugar*
3   *tablespoons cinnamon*

1. Preheat oven to 325 degrees.

2. Place the butter in the container of an electric mixer. Add the sugar and start beating. Add the egg yolk and continue creaming with the beater. Add the liqueur and beat in the flour.

3. Shape the dough into 52 balls, each about 1 inch in diameter. Arrange the balls on an ungreased baking sheet and bake 25 minutes, or until firm.

4. Let cool briefly and roll each ball in a blend of sugar and cinnamon.

Yield: 52 cookies.

How Long Island
Got the Duck

There are scores of foods on this earth that are irrevocably, reflexively linked to the names of regions and villages. Bresse chickens, Kobe beef, Galway oysters, Maine lobsters, Dublin Bay prawns, the oranges of Seville, the foie gras of Strasbourg, the truffles of Perigord, and so on. These associations came about primarily because of some natural liaison between nature and the inventiveness, curiosity and taming instinct of man.

There are three places on this globe that are, more than any others, unfailingly identified with the cultivation of ducks. They are Peking in China, Rouen in France and that forked, hundred-odd mile stretch of land east of Manhattan called Long Island.

There are numerous families on Long Island whose histories for three-quarters of a century or more have been closely associated with the raising of ducks, but there is none more intimately tied into duck culture than the Corwins of this small community.

The Corwins have lived in Aquebogue for more than two hundred years, more than a century before ducks were even introduced into America. They got into the duck business back in the days when the land values in these parts were generally conceded to be worthless. When one Henry Corwin told his father that someday he would earn his living out of that sandy loam, his father replied: "It can't be done! A happy toad would die crossing that land."

The Crescent Duck Farm here, founded by that Henry Corwin, is said to be the fourth largest duck farm in America. They produce three-quarters of a million ducks a year, which are shipped throughout the United States, including Hawaii (one of the best markets for ducks) and the Caribbean. Ironically, the other three leading duck farms are not on Long Island. There is one in Wisconsin, another in Indiana and the third in Virginia.

In a recent visit to Lloyd Corwin, the affable 43-year-old present owner of the farm, I learned that ducks arrived on Long Island in what was, indeed, a circuitous fashion. As with most hundred-year-old legends, it is difficult to separate duck fact from fiction.

Corwin family history has it, nonetheless, that the Long Island duck industry began more than one hundred years ago when a British major named Ashley, then stationed in Peking, cultivated a few white native ducks of uncommon size for his private consumption. In the year 1873, an American clipper ship, based in Stonington, Connecticut, entered the port of Peking and among the passengers was a Yankee trader named James Palmer.

Palmer was introduced to Ashley, and it turned out to be, as far as ducks are concerned, one of those historic meetings like Lewis and Clark, Currier and Ives and Moët and Chandon. Palmer persuaded Ashley to allow him to carry with him on his return to America a small flock of those unusual specimens. Several of the prized creatures were lost during a storm at sea while the boat was en route home. Palmer arrived at the port of New York on March 13, 1873, with one drake and three ducks still encaged, enough to start a fledgling enterprise on the island of Manhattan. Thus, the hegira began. The offspring of the original ducks were transferred to Connecticut, and shortly thereafter to the tidewater streams of eastern Long Island. Within a very short while there were more than one hundred twenty-five small duck farms on the island.

One of those tidewater streams was known as Meeting House Creek, located in or near the farming community of Aquebogue, a named derived from an Indian tribe named Occabauk, which wintered there. Although the Corwins owned a good deal of property in the region, the men were mostly farmers and carpenters. It was not until 1909 that Henry Corwin started pairing off ducks that would someday become Crescent.

Because of the community's proximity to New York and because of the railroad that passed through the village, which facilitated shipping, the duck farm flourished. Oddly, Lloyd Corwin attributes that success not to the sophisticated tastes of New Yorkers as a whole, but rather to the immigrants who lived in the city.

In those days, he says, the average citizen from Maine to California knew little about ducks and less about how to cook them. But the immigrant population, those who had come from Czechoslovakia, Poland, Hungary and Germany, had an appetite for ducks, an appetite that had naturally developed in their homelands. Ducks were popular in French restaurants, but home-cooked ducks were rarely considered.

The earliest ducks shipped to the city were what were known as "New York dressed." That was back in the days before refrigeration, before mechanical pluckers and machines that eviscerated fowl were even dreamed of. Instead, the ducks were plucked by hand, quickly cooled and packed thirty to a barrel for shipping. All the duck pickers were women, and the most skilled of them could pick from sixty to a hundred ducks a day.

Today, the Crescent duck farm is equipped with the most modern duck-processing equipment. The ducks are waxed, plucked, eviscerated, plastic wrapped, frozen and shipped throughout the country to reach their destination in a matter of hours.

That ducks were so little used for home consumption in the early days seems odd. Ducks are, if you simply want a plain roast bird, one of the easiest of birds to cook. The elaborate preparations such as duck à l'orange are a bit more tedious, but the results are well worth the effort.

But, as Lloyd Corwin says, "My wife cooks a fantastic duck. She puts it on a rack in the oven and lets it cook plain. All you have to do is pour off the fat and carve it."

Here is a fairly broad scope of plain-roasted and more elaborate preparations of duck.

Canard Roti à Plat

(A basic recipe for roasting a duck)

1   4- to 5-pound duckling
     Salt and freshly ground pepper to taste
1   large clove garlic
¼   cup dry white wine
½   cup fresh or canned chicken broth
2   tablespoons butter, optional

1. Preheat oven to 375 degrees.

2. Truss the duck with string and sprinkle it inside and out with salt and pepper. Chop the neck into 1- or 2-inch lengths. Cut away the tough outer membrane of the gizzard. Sprinkle the pieces of neck and gizzard with salt and pepper.

3. Place the duck on its back in a roasting pan. Surround it with the neck and gizzard. Place in the oven and bake 30 minutes.

4. Remove the pan and pour or spoon off the accumulated fat. Turn the duck on its side and return to the oven. Roast 30 minutes.

5. Remove the pan and spoon or pour off the fat. Take care not to pour off the nonfat liquid in the pan.

6. Increase oven heat to 400 degrees. Turn the duck breast side down and return to the oven. Bake 30 minutes.

7. Turn the duck on its other side and bake 30 minutes.

8. Remove the pan. Remove and discard the trussing string from the duck. Transfer the duck, back side down, to another roasting pan. If desired, rub the skin all over with the garlic. Return to the oven for 10 minutes. As it roasts, rub it once more all over with garlic.

9. Meanwhile, place the original roasting pan on top of the stove and add the wine, stirring with a wooden spoon to dissolve the brown particles that cling to the bottom and sides. Cook until reduced by half and add the chicken broth. Bring to the boil and strain the sauce. Reheat.

10. Traditionally, this sauce is enriched before serving by adding browned butter to it. This is optional, however. To make the butter, place it in a skillet and swirl it around and around over high heat until it foams up and then becomes hazelnut brown. Do not burn. Quickly add this to the sauce.

11. Cut the duck into quarters or carve it as desired. Serve with the hot sauce.

Yield: 4 servings.

Canard à l'Orange

(Roast duck with oranges)

4   whole seedless oranges
1   4- to 5-pound duckling

   Salt and freshly ground pep-
   per to taste
¾   *cup fresh or canned chicken*
   broth
¼   *cup sugar*
¼   *cup red wine vinegar*
1   *teaspoon cornstarch*
1   *tablespoon water*
2   *tablespoons Grand Marnier*

1. Preheat oven to 375 degrees.

2. Using a swivel-bladed vegetable peeler, peel off and reserve the extreme outer yellow surface of 1 orange. Discard any of the white pulp that may cling to this "zest." Cut the zest, or yellow strips, into very fine shreds (julienne). Drop the shreds into boiling water and let simmer about 30 seconds. Drain and set aside.

3. Completely peel all the oranges and carefully section them, cutting between the membranous intersections around each section. There should be about 1½ cups of sections. Set these aside.

4. Truss the duck with string and sprinkle it inside and out with salt and pepper. Chop the neck into 1- or 2-inch lengths. Cut away the tough outer membrane of the gizzard. Sprinkle the pieces of neck and gizzard with salt and pepper.

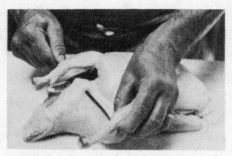

Let the needle push through left flap at the cavity opening, then the right or opposite flap

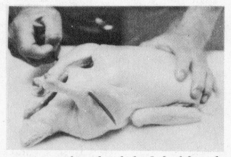

Continue pushing though the flesh of the right leg, inserting needle directly above the leg bone

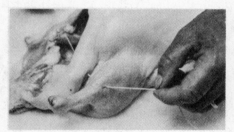

Pull the string through the bird

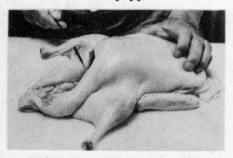

To truss duck, thread a trussing needle with string. Place duck on its back. Push the needle into flesh of left leg, inserting it directly above leg bone.

5. Place the duck on its back in a roasting pan. Surround it with the neck and gizzard. Place in the oven and bake 30 minutes.

6. Remove the pan and pour or spoon off the accumulated fat. Turn the duck on its side and return to the oven. Roast 30 minutes.

7. Remove the pan and spoon or pour off the fat. Take care not to pour off the nonfat liquid in the pan.

8. Increase oven heat to 400 degrees. Turn the duck breast side down and return to the oven. Bake 30 minutes.

9. Turn the duck on its other side and bake 30 minutes.

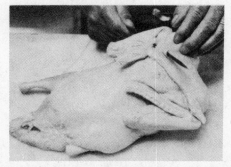

Turn duck over on its breast. Insert needle through middle of right second joint then right wing tip. Pull up neck flap to enclose neck opening.

10. Remove the pan. Remove and discard the trussing string from the duck. Transfer the duck, backside down, to another roasting pan. Return to the oven for 10 minutes.

11. Meanwhile, place the original roasting pan on top of the stove and add the chicken broth, stirring and scraping with a wooden spoon to dissolve the brown particles that cling to the bottom and sides of the pan.

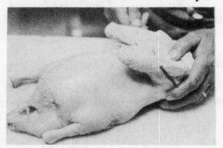

Run the needle through neck into the neckbone and through the neck flap. Push the needle through the left small wing bone, then the left second joint and pull the thread through. Tie the loose end of the string and the string attached to the needle. Cut off the two string ends.

Bring to the boil. Strain into a saucepan.

12. Blend the sugar and vinegar in a very small saucepan and cook, watching carefully, until large bubbles form on the surface. Continue cooking until the syrup is thickened and slightly caramelized. This is called a gastrique. Add the sauce from the roasting pan. Bring to the boil.

13. Blend the cornstarch and water and stir it into the sauce.

14. Just before serving, add the zest and Grand Marnier to the sauce. Drain the orange sections and add them. Cook, stirring gently just until sections are thoroughly hot. Do not break them in stirring and do not overcook or they will become mushy.

15. Serve the duck cut into quarters or carved. Pour a little of the sauce over the duck and serve the remainder separately.

Yield: 4 servings.

Canard Vasco da Gama

(Roast duck with green peppercorns)

1 *4- to 5-pound duckling*
  Salt and freshly ground pepper to taste
¼ *cup Calvados, apple jack or cognac*
½ *cup water*
1 *cup rich chicken broth, fresh or canned*
1 *tablespoon green peppercorns (or more if you like it hot)*
2 *tablespoons butter*

1. Preheat oven to 375 degrees.

2. Sprinkle the duck inside and out with salt and pepper and truss with string. Chop the neck into 1- or 2-inch lengths. Cut away the tough outer membrane of the gizzard. Sprinkle the pieces of neck and gizzard with salt and pepper.

3. Place the duck on its back in a roasting pan. Surround it with the neck and gizzard. Place in the oven and bake 30 minutes.

4. Remove the pan from the oven and pour or spoon off the accumulated fat. Turn the duck on its side and return to the oven. Roast 30 minutes.

5. Again, remove the pan from the oven and spoon or pour off the accumulated fat, being careful to guard the nonfat liquid in the pan.

6. Increase oven heat to 400 degrees. Turn the duck breast side down and return to the oven. Bake 30 minutes.

7. Turn the duck on its other side and bake 30 minutes more.

8. Remove the pan from the oven. Remove and discard the trussing string from the duck. Transfer the duck, back-side down, to another roasting pan. Return to the oven for 10 minutes.

9. Pour or spoon off all the fat from the roasting pan. Add the Calvados and flame it. Add the water and broth and stir with a wooden spoon, scraping to dissolve the brown particles that cling to the bottom and sides of the pan. Strain the sauce into a saucepan and add salt and pepper to taste and the green peppercorns. Bring to the boil. Skim off any fat. There will be very little.

10. Carve the duck into serving pieces.

11. Swirl the butter into the sauce and serve it with the carved duck.

Yield: 4 servings.

Canard au Citron

(Roast duck with lemon)

1	4- to 5-pound duckling
	Salt and freshly ground pepper to taste
½	cup coarsely chopped carrots
⅔	cup coarsely chopped celery
¾	cup coarsely chopped onion
3	cups chicken broth
3	sprigs fresh parsley
3	sprigs fresh thyme, or ½ teaspoon dried
1	bay leaf
4	peppercorns
1	lemon
¼	cup sugar
¼	cup wine vinegar
½	cup sweet sherry or madeira wine
1	tablespoon cornstarch
1	tablespoon water
¼	cup Grand Marnier

1. Preheat oven to 375 degrees.

2. Sprinkle the duck inside and out with salt and pepper. Truss the duck with string and arrange breast side up in a roasting pan. Place in the oven and bake 30 minutes.

3. Remove the pan from the oven and pour or spoon off the accumulated fat. Turn the duck on its side and return to the oven. Roast 30 minutes.

4. Again, remove the pan from the oven and spoon or pour off the accumulated fat, being careful to guard the nonfat liquid in the pan.

5. Increase oven heat to 400 degrees. Turn the duck breast-side down and return to the oven for another 30 minutes. Turn the duck on its other side and bake 30 minutes more.

6. Meanwhile, cut or chop the duck neck and wing tips into 1-inch lengths. Cut the gizzard into quarters. Place these in a heavy saucepan without additional fat and cook, stirring frequently, until nicely browned, about 10 minutes. Sprinkle with salt and pepper. Add the carrots, celery and onion to the saucepan and continue cooking, stirring frequently, about 10 minutes.

7. Add the chicken broth, parsley, thyme, bay leaf, peppercorns, salt and pepper. Cook, skimming the surface as necessary to remove foam and scum, about 45 minutes. Strain and reserve. There should be a bit less than 2 cups.

8. Carefully peel 1 lemon, removing only the yellow outer skin. Cut the skin into very thin strips (julienne). Use the peeled lemon for juice to be added later.

9. Drop this skin into a small saucepan of boiling water. Boil about 1 minute and drain. Set aside.

10. Blend the sugar and vinegar in a wide-mouth saucepan and cook over high heat, watching carefully, until the mixture is dark amber and large bubbles form on the surface. Take care that it does not burn or it will be bitter. This is called a gastrique.

Canard au Citron

11. Remove the duck from the oven. Remove and discard the trussing string from the duck. Transfer the duck, back side down, to another roasting pan. Return to the oven for 10 minutes.

12. Pour off the fat from the original roasting pan. Place the pan on the stove and add the sherry, stirring with a wooden spoon to dissolve the brown particles that cling to the bottom and sides of the pan. Strain into the gastrique.

13. Blend the cornstarch and water and stir this into the sauce. Cook 5 minutes and add the juice of 1 lemon. Cook 1 minute and add salt and pepper to taste.

14. Add the julienne strips of lemon and bring to the boil. Add the Grand Marnier.

15. Serve the duck cut into quarters or carved. Pour the sauce over the duck.

Yield: 4 servings.

October

I FIRST HEARD of Mollie Chappelet from Danny Kaye, the protean comedian, maestro, Chinese cook and friend. "Mollie Chappelet," he told me, "is one of the most inventive cooks in the whole Napa Valley. Until you have dined with her, seated beneath those spreading trees, eating the vegetables direct from the garden that are served with local olive oil, the family's homemade bread, vinegar and wine straight from their own caves, you haven't really dined."

Danny's enthusiasm was by no means misplaced. It was, however, one of the most difficult meals I've ever had to write about. What kind of recipes can you give for the gratification of dining with friends when you go to the garden, harvest your own cucumbers, tomatoes, lettuces, radishes and carrots and, after these are trimmed and washed, sit down to concoct your own vegetarian meal? It was different and delectable. Mollie had brought in two ingredients not of their own growing—fresh mushroom caps and avocados. The homemade breads were superb as was a gossamer, snow-white meringue dessert that had sat in the oven all night and then been smeared with whipped cream fresh from the farm.

It was, in fact, a month of vegetables. There was re-created in my kitchen what may be the most talked about spaghetti dish in America today. That is spaghetti primavera, a marvelous mélange of assorted crisp-tender vegetables tossed with spaghetti, butter and cheese, an outstanding creation of Le Cirque, one of the grandest luxury restaurants in Manhattan. It was owned by Sirio Maccioni, the handsome maître d'hôtel-owner, and Jean Vergnes, the ebullient chef-owner, both old friends of ours.

We have never over the years concentrated on the cooking of England, but there is one dish that to our palates is absolutely irresistible. This is chicken pot pie, a succulent, savory, pastry-covered entree that is to some few epicures preferable to the much touted rare roast beef with Yorkshire pudding. The pie contains a myriad of flavors and is cooked with the meat of the chicken left on the bone.

Spaghetti with a French Accent

WITH PIERRE FRANEY

By far the most talked-about dish in Manhattan today is a creation of Italian origin that flourishes in one of the most popular of the city's luxury French restaurants, Le Cirque. It is an inspired blend of pasta and crisp-tender vegetables such as zucchini, mushrooms, broccoli and green beans plus cream and cheese and toasted pine nuts. These are tossed hot and crowned with a mound of delicate fresh tomato sauce. Although the dish is called spaghetti primavera— spaghetti with a springtime air—it is served all year long at Le Cirque and can be reproduced easily in the home.

The dish as served in the restaurant is the collaboration of Jean Vergnes, the French owner-chef, and Sirio Maccioni, his elegant Italian co-owner and major domo of the dining room. They are two of our long-time friends and came to our kitchen in East Hampton to demonstrate the makings of the dish tailored to one pound of spaghetti.

Le Cirque's Spaghetti Primavera

1   bunch broccoli
2   small zucchini
4   asparagus spears, each about
     5 inches long
1½   cups green beans, trimmed
     and cut into 1-inch lengths
     Salt
½   cup fresh or frozen green peas
¾   cup fresh or frozen pea pods,
     optional
1   tablespoon peanut, vegetable
     or corn oil
2   cups thinly sliced mushrooms
     Freshly ground pepper

1   teaspoon finely chopped hot,
     fresh, red or green chilies, or
     about ½ teaspoon dried red
     pepper flakes
¼   cup finely chopped parsley
6   tablespoons olive oil
1   teaspoon finely chopped garlic
3   cups red, ripe tomatoes cut
     into 1-inch cubes
6   fresh basil leaves, chopped,
     about ¼ cup, or about 1 tea-
     spoon dried basil
1   pound spaghetti or spaghettini
4   tablespoons butter
2   tablespoons fresh or canned
     chicken broth
½   cup heavy cream, approxi-
     mately
⅔   cup grated Parmesan cheese
⅓   cup pine nuts

1. Trim the broccoli and break it into bite-size "flowerettes." Set aside.

2. Trim off and discard the ends of the zucchini. Do not peel the zucchini. Cut the zucchini into quarters. Cut each quarter into 1-inch or slightly longer lengths. There should be about 1½ cups, no more. Set aside.

3. Cut each asparagus spear into thirds. Set aside.

4. Cook each of the green vegetables separately in boiling salted water to cover. The essential thing is to cook each vegetable so that it remains crisp but tender. Cook the broccoli, zucchini, green beans and asparagus about 5 minutes. Drain well, run under cold water to chill and drain thoroughly. Combine them in a mixing bowl.

5. Cook the peas and pea pods about 1 minute if fresh, or 30 seconds if frozen. Drain, chill and drain again. Combine all the vegetables in the mixing bowl.

6. Heat the peanut oil in a skillet and add the mushrooms. Add salt and pepper to taste, shaking the skillet and stirring. Cook about 2 minutes. Add the mushrooms to the vegetables. Add the chopped chilies and parsley.

7. Heat 3 tablespoons olive oil in a saucepan and add half the garlic, the tomatoes, salt and pepper to taste. Cook about 4 minutes, stirring gently so as not to break up the tomatoes more than is essential. Add the basil, stir and set aside.

8. Heat the remaining 3 tablespoons olive oil in a large skillet and add the remaining garlic and the vegetable mixture. Cook, stirring gently, just to heat through.

9. Drop the spaghetti into boiling salted water. Cook until almost but not quite tender. That is to say, al dente. The spaghetti when ready must retain just a slight resilience in the center. Drain well. Return the spaghetti to the kettle.

10. Select a utensil large enough to hold the drained spaghetti and vegetables. To this, add the butter. When it melts, add the chicken broth, ½ cup cream and cheese, stirring constantly. Cook gently on and off the heat until smooth. Add the spaghetti and toss quickly to blend. Add half the vegetables and pour in the liquid from the tomatoes, tossing and stirring over very low heat.

11. Add the remaining vegetables and, if the sauce seems too dry, add about ¼ cup more cream. The sauce should not be soupy. Add the pine nuts and give the mixture one final tossing.

12. Serve equal portions of the spaghetti mixture in 4 to 8 hot soup or spaghetti bowls. Spoon equal amounts of the tomatoes over each serving. Serve immediately. Four portions will serve as a main course; 6 to 8 as an appetizer.

Yield: 4 to 8 servings.

English Pie
par Excellence

WITH PIERRE FRANEY

Although French is generally accepted in the Western world as the language of classic menus, there are some dishes so typically un-French the names are rarely translated from the country of origin. One of these is chicken pot pie, which can be one of the great dishes of the world. We do not speak of the basic and hearty pie of New England and Pennsylvania Dutch territory made with boiled birds. No offense intended, but that is wine from a lesser bottle. What we do speak of is the elegant, when perfectly made, chicken pot pie of England.

Chicken Pot Pie

The pastry

2   cups flour
8   tablespoons butter
4   tablespoons lard
    Salt
2   to 3 tablespoons cold water

The filling

5   tablespoons butter
2   2½-pound chickens, cut into
    serving pieces
    Salt and freshly ground pepper
½   cup coarsely chopped carrots
½   cup coarsely chopped celery
1   cup small white onions, peeled
½   pound mushrooms, thinly
    sliced
3   sprigs fresh parsley
2   whole cloves

3   sprigs fresh thyme, or ½ teaspoon dried
4   tablespoons flour
1   cup dry white wine
4   cups chicken broth
    A few drops Tabasco sauce
5   strips bacon
3   hard-cooked eggs, peeled
1   cup heavy cream
1   teaspoon Worcestershire sauce
1   egg, beaten

1. For the pastry, put the flour in a mixing bowl and add the 8 tablespoons of butter, lard and salt to taste. Using a pastry blender, work the mixture until it looks like coarse corn meal. Add the water a little at a time, working the dough lightly with the fingers. Add just enough water to have it hold together. Shape into a ball and wrap in wax paper. Refrigerate at least ½ hour.

2. To make the filling, melt 3 tablespoons butter in a skillet and add the chicken, skin-side down. Sprinkle with salt and pepper. Cook over low heat without browning about 5 minutes, turning once. Scatter the carrots, celery and white onions over.

3. Heat the remaining 2 tablespoons of butter in another skillet and add the mushrooms. Cook, stirring, until they give up their liquid. Continue cooking until most of the liquid evaporates. Add the mushrooms to the chicken.

4. Tie together in a cheesecloth square the parsley, cloves and thyme. Add it to the chicken. Cook, stirring frequently, about 10 minutes. Do not burn.

5. Sprinkle with the flour, stirring to distribute it evenly. Add the wine and broth. Add the Tabasco sauce and cover. Simmer ½ hour.

6. Preheat oven to 400 degrees.

7. Meanwhile, cut the bacon into 2-inch lengths. Cook the pieces until crisp and brown. Drain.

8. Strain the chicken and pour the cooking liquid into a saucepan. Discard the cheesecloth bag. Arrange the chicken and vegetables in a baking dish (we used a 16-by-10½-by-2-inch oval dish). Cut the eggs into sixths and arrange them over the chicken and vegetables. Scatter the bacon bits over the chicken and vegetables.

9. Skim off and discard the fat from the cooking liquid. Bring the liquid to the boil and add the heavy cream. Bring the sauce to the boil. Simmer about 20 minutes. Add the Worcestershire sauce, salt and pepper to taste.

10. Pour the sauce over the chicken mixture.

11. Roll out the pastry. Cut a round or oval just large enough to fit the baking dish. Arrange it over the chicken mixture and cut out a small hole in the center to allow steam to escape. Brush with beaten egg. Bake 30 minutes.

Yield: 6 to 8 servings.

Good Things from a California Garden

Beneath a pair of black oak trees, under a cloudless sky, we dined on a most unlikely late-autumn feast. It was shortly afternoon and all around there were immaculately tended rows of vines of the Chappellet vineyards, heavy with October grapes, the green grape known as chenin blanc and on the lower slopes, the succulent, dark purple cabernet sauvignon.

It was an uncommon meal, for the most part meatless, and as gratifying and convivial as it was novel.

The hosts' table was a groaning board of good things from the garden, which, despite the lateness of the season, flourished. Spread before the guests were those things that would serve as the main course of the meal: lettuces like barbe-de-capucin (monk's beard), limestone and bronzeleaf; more substantial edibles like cherry tomatoes, long yellow Hungarian sweet peppers, squash and zucchini, carrots, avocados, cucumbers; assorted aromatics like basil and chives, scallions and tarragon sprigs, fresh coriander leaves, oregano and parsley. Plus locally made, pure and unadulterated Napa Valley olive oil and, of course, wines from the family vineyard. There were California cheeses and sweet, freshly churned butter, a good neighbor's gift.

It is Molly Chappellet's concept that most of her family (the Chappellets have six children, all of whom came down to dine between harvesting grapes) and guests are frustrated cooks. To help them fulfill this fantasy she has contrived the notion of compose-your-own, sit-down luncheon.

On this particular day the meal began with a hot, insidiously good consommé made with a blend of homemade chicken and clam broths topped with whipped cream and a slight grating of nutmeg. The main segment of the meal was the garden produce, "scattered" symmetrically, wheel-spoke fashion before each place. Place settings consisted of flat knives and swivel-bladed gadgets for paring and slicing.

"A meal like this is basically selfish," Mrs. Chappellet told us. "I'm more of a gardener than cook. Most of the time I let guests go out in the garden and pluck their own." Actually, Molly Chappellet is celebrated as a California cook. She and Dinah Shore swap recipes. Danny Kaye had flown in for the meal.

We admired enormously a homemade, basil-flavored egg bread that Lygia, her 23-year-old daughter, had contributed to the occasion and were told that it is a family tradition that all the Chappellet offspring at an early age learn to fend for themselves in the kitchen. That includes Dominic, 9, who, Danny Kaye informed us, has the fastest skillet in the West where elegant scrambled eggs are concerned.

Danny, in the midst of anointing the cavity of his avocado with that local, chartreuse-colored olive oil, declared that it was "the finest olive oil made in this country. All the other olive oils made here are pasteurized, refined and filtered." He added a few drops of wine vinegar and told us that it is the fabrication of the host, Donn Chappellet, who has owned his highly regarded vineyards and tended his vines for a little more than ten years.

"To make a fine vinegar," Mr. Chappellet stated, "it helps to start with a fine wine." He added that he did not use a "mother" to convert his wine into vinegar, but simply renewed a master batch of wine that came into his possession some years ago.

"I started with a gallon of vinegar from Swan's Oyster Depot," he said, referring to a well-respected seafood restaurant in San Francisco.

"Someone gave me a quart, which I added to a barrel. I added pure wine from my vineyard and in three months it was ready to use. As the vinegar develops, I keep adding wine. I use about 25 percent red wine and 75 percent white wine when I replenish the casks. And let it stand ninety days."

The salads were composed at each place with great enthusiasm and panache (one of the guests fluted his mushroom) and in addition to the basil bread, great loaves of a nut-and-seed bread (the contribution of Alexa, "going on 16").

After the broths and salads and cheese and breads were duly devoured, Mrs. Chappellet served her "forget-it" meringue torte, an irresistible confection made by adding a batch of meringue to an angel food cake pan, shoving it into a hot oven, turning off the heat and "forgetting" it overnight. The meringue is unmolded, smeared with whipped cream and served with sweetened fresh fruit or berries. Delectable!

Molly Chappellet's Clam and Chicken Consommé

1   roast chicken carcass (see rec-
    ipe)
    The apple cavity fillings from
    the roast chicken (see recipe)
10 cups water
    Salt and freshly ground pep-
    per to taste
3   cups fresh or bottled clam
    broth
⅛   teaspoon cinnamon
8   to 16 tablespoons whipped
    cream
    Nutmeg

Danny Kaye admires Donn Chappellet's wine vinegar

1. Combine the remains of the chicken carcass and the quartered apples from the cavity filling in a kettle. Add the water, salt and pepper and bring to the boil. Simmer about 1 hour. Strain through a fine sieve lined with cheesecloth.

2. Combine the chicken broth and clam broth and cinnamon. Bring just to the simmer. Serve piping hot in hot bowls with 1 tablespoon whipped cream and a sprinkling of nutmeg on each serving.

Yield: 8 to 16 servings.

1. Preheat the oven to 450 degrees.

2. Sprinkle the chicken inside and out with salt and pepper.

3. To the cavity add the quartered apples and oranges. Rub the chicken with the butter and dust all over with paprika. Place the chicken in a clay pot. Add the orange juice, cover and bake 1 hour.

Yield: 4 servings.

Alexa Chappellet's Nut and Seed Bread

Roast chicken

1   3- to 4-pound chicken
    Salt and freshly ground pep-
    per to taste
2   apples, quartered
2   oranges, quartered
1   tablespoon butter
1   teaspoon paprika
2   tablespoons orange juice

1   cup quick-cooking oatmeal
2¾   cups cold water
1   tablespoon salt
½   cup molasses
4   tablespoons melted butter
2   packages active dry yeast
½   cup lukewarm water

⅛ teaspoon sugar
1 cup rye flour
1 cup whole wheat flour
½ cup wheat germ
⅓ cup bran flakes
1 cup plus 2 tablespoons broken
walnuts or other nuts, or a
combination of nuts and edible
seeds such as hulled sunflower
seeds, sesame seeds, pumpkin
seeds
4 to 5 cups unbleached white
flour

1. Combine the oatmeal and 2 cups of the cold water in a saucepan and bring to the boil. Remove from the heat.

2. Place the salt, molasses and butter in the bowl of an electric mixer and add the oatmeal mixture. Blend and let cool to lukewarm.

3. Blend the yeast with the ½ cup of lukewarm water and sugar and stir until dissolved. Let stand in a warm place until foamy. Add this mixture plus the remaining ¾ cup cold water to the dough, beating until smooth.

4. Stir on low speed and add the rye flour, whole wheat flour, wheat germ and bran flakes. Beat until smooth. Add the nuts and/or seeds and gradually add enough unbleached white flour to make a workable, soft dough. Turn the dough out onto a lightly floured board and knead about 10 minutes.

5. Shape the dough into a ball and put it in a lightly greased bowl. Cover with a damp cloth and let stand until double in bulk, 45 minutes to 1 hour.

6. Preheat the oven to 375 degrees.

7. Punch the dough down. Divide it in two and shape each half into an oval. Put each oval in a lightly buttered standard-size loaf pan. Cover and let rise.

8. Place the pans in the oven and bake 35 to 40 minutes. Turn out onto a rack to cool.

Yield: 2 loaves.

Lygia Chappellet's Too-Good Herb Bread

1 cup milk
3 tablespoons sugar or honey
3 tablespoons butter
1 teaspoon salt
1½ packages active dry yeast
2 eggs
3½ cups flour, plus more flour as
necessary for kneading
1 tablespoon chopped fresh
basil, or 2 teaspoons dried

1. Combine the milk, sugar, butter and salt in a saucepan. Heat just until the butter melts. Let cool to lukewarm and stir in the yeast.

2. Spoon the flour into the container of a food processor (see note). Add the eggs.

3. Start beating the flour and eggs and add the yeast mixture. Process the dough until a ball forms and the dough pulls away from the sides of the container. It may be necessary to add another spoonful or so of flour to the dough to prevent it from sticking to the sides of the container.

4. Turn the dough out onto a lightly floured board and knead briefly, kneading in a little more flour if necessary but use as little flour as possible.

5. Shape the dough into a ball and put it in a lightly greased bowl. Cover with a damp towel and let stand until double in bulk, 45 minutes to 1 hour.

6. Punch the dough down. Knead briefly and shape it into an oval. Put this in a lightly buttered standard-size loaf pan. Cover and let rise 45 minutes or longer.

7. Preheat the oven to 375 degrees.

8. Place the pan in the oven and bake. Check the bread after about 10 minutes and, if it is getting too brown, cover loosely with a sheet of aluminum foil. Reduce oven heat to 350 degrees and continue baking until done. Total baking time is 35 to 40 minutes. Turn out onto a rack to cool.

Yield: 1 loaf.

Note: This dough may, of course, be made in an electric mixer, in which case, add the milk and yeast mixture to the mixer bowl. Add the eggs and beat them to blend. Gradually add the flour, adding only enough so that the dough can be shaped into a ball without feeling sticky.

"Forget-it" Meringue Torte

   Butter
9 to 11 egg whites
¼ teaspoon cream of tartar
2½ cups sugar

1 teaspoon pure vanilla extract
½ teaspoon almond extract
1 cup heavy cream, whipped
   and sweetened to taste
   Sliced sweetened fruit such as
   peaches, or berries such as
   strawberries or raspberries

1. Preheat oven to 450 degrees.

2. Butter the bottom and sides of an angel food cake pan with removable bottom.

3. Use enough egg whites to make 1½ cups. Empty them into the container of an electric mixer. Beat them until they become frothy and add the cream of tartar. Gradually add the sugar, beating constantly. After all the sugar has been added, beat in the vanilla and almond extracts. Continue beating until the meringue is quite stiff and has a high, glossy sheen.

4. Spoon the meringue into the prepared pan. Smooth over the top.

5. Place the pan in the oven and immediately turn off the oven heat. Do not open the oven door for several hours, preferably overnight.

6. Remove the meringue from the oven. Remember that the meringue will have a ragged look at this point. A crisp, browned crust may have formed that clings to the rim of the pan. Do not bother. Break it off and discard, or crumble it for decoration. In any event, remove the center section of the pan. Using a spatula or pancake turner, loosen the bottom of the meringue. Unmold the meringue ring onto a round plate.

7. Garnish the bottom and sides of the meringue ring with sweetened whipped cream and decorate with the crumbled meringue topping and the sliced sweetened fruit or berries. A good sauce is 3 packages of frozen raspberries, defrosted, sweetened with ½ cup of sugar and framboise or kirsch liqueur to taste.

Yield: 12 or more servings.

The Chappellet family returns from vineyards

Variation on a Miracle

WITH PIERRE FRANEY

Although most of the dining public looks on a well-made soufflé as a minor miracle, it is equally possible to view them with greater wonder because of the flavor variations possible. Take a basic cheese soufflé. It is delicious in itself provided the cheese is of good flavor and the eggs fresh. It takes on added interest, however, if there is a "surprise" element at its base, a shrimp with tarragon sauce, for example. There can be a dozen variations on this theme, creamed chicken, for example, creamed fish such as salmon or tuna, or curried lobster. One of the most unusual of soufflés is.the one in which raw eggs are broken into the center of the soufflé before it is baked. When the soufflé is cooked, the egg yolks remain soft and runny, creating a nice contrast in textures when the soufflé is eaten.

Soufflé au Fromage

(Cheese soufflé)

¼   *pound gruyère or Swiss cheese, cut into ¼-inch slices*
8   *large eggs*
6   *tablespoons butter*
5   *tablespoons flour*
2   *cups milk*
    Salt and freshly ground pepper
⅛   *teaspoon grated nutmeg*
    Pinch of cayenne pepper
2   *tablespoons cornstarch*
3   *tablespoons water*
¼   *cup grated Parmesan cheese*
2   *tablespoons grated gruyère or Swiss cheese*

1. Preheat oven to 400 degrees.
2. Stack the cheese slices on a flat surface. Using a sharp knife, cut into ¼-inch strips. Cut the strips into ¼-inch cubes. There should be about 1 cup. Set aside.

3. Separate the eggs, placing the yolks in one bowl and the whites in another.

4. Use 2 tablespoons of butter and butter all around the inside rim and bottom of a 2-quart soufflé dish. Place the dish in the freezer until ready to use.

5. Melt the remaining butter in a saucepan and add the flour, stirring with a wire whisk. When blended, add the milk, stirring rapidly with the whisk. Add salt and pepper to taste, nutmeg and cayenne. Cook 30 seconds, stirring.

6. Blend the cornstarch and water and add this to the bubbling sauce, stirring. Cook about 2 minutes. Add yolks, stirring vigorously. Cook, stirring, about 1 minute.

7. Spoon and scrape the mixture into a large mixing bowl. Add the cubed gruyère or Swiss cheese and the Parmesan cheese. Blend well.

8. Beat the egg whites until stiff. Add half the whites to the soufflé mixture and beat them thoroughly. Add the remaining whites and fold them in quickly but gently with a rubber spatula.

9. Spoon and scrape the mixture into the soufflé dish. Sprinkle with the grated gruyère and place in the oven.

10. Bake 15 minutes. Reduce the oven heat to 375 degrees and bake 15 minutes longer.

Yield: 4 to 6 servings.

Soufflé aux Oeufs

(Eggs baked in a soufflé)

1   *recipe for cheese soufflé (see recipe)*
4   *small eggs*
    Salt and freshly ground pepper

1. Preheat oven to 400 degrees.

2. Prepare the soufflé dish as indicated in the recipe. Prepare the basic mixture for the soufflé up to and including folding in the egg whites.

3. Spoon half the soufflé mixture into the soufflé dish. Using a spoon, make 4 indentations spaced about halfway between the rim and the center of the soufflé.

4. Break 1 egg over each indentation. The yolks should fall into the indentations. The whites may run to the center or rim. Don't be unnerved.

5. Sprinkle the eggs with salt and pepper to taste.

6. Spoon and scrape in the remaining soufflé mixture.

7. Sprinkle the soufflé with grated gruyère cheese and place in the oven. Bake 15 minutes. Reduce the oven heat to 375 degrees and bake 15 minutes longer.

Yield: 4 servings.

Soufflé aux Crevettes à l'Estragon

(Soufflé with shrimp and tarragon)

1   *recipe for cheese soufflé (see recipe)*
1   *recipe for shrimp with tarragon sauce (see recipe)*

1. Preheat oven to 400 degrees.

2. Prepare the soufflé dish as indicated in the recipe. Prepare the basic mixture for the soufflé up to and including folding in the egg whites.

3. Add the shrimp with tarragon sauce to the bottom of the prepared soufflé dish. Spoon and scrape the soufflé mixture on top of the shrimp and, as indicated, sprinkle with the grated gruyère cheese.

4. Place in the oven and bake 30 minutes. Serve, scooping deeply into the soufflé. Serve a large spoonful of the puffed soufflé mixture on a hot dish and scoop deeper to serve the shrimp in sauce next to it.

Yield: 4 to 6 servings.

Crevettes á l'estragon
(Shrimp with tarragon sauce)

4   *tablespoons butter*
2   *tablespoons finely chopped onion*

1   *tablespoon finely chopped
    shallots*
1   *teaspoon finely minced garlic*
2   *cups chopped fresh or canned
    peeled tomatoes
    Salt and freshly ground pep-
    per*
1   *tablespoon chopped fresh tar-
    ragon, or half the amount
    dried*
1   *tablespoon chopped parsley*
⅓   *cup dry white wine*
1   *pound shrimp, peeled and
    deveined*
1   *hot, dried red pepper, optional*
2   *tablespoons cognac*

1. Melt half the butter in a skillet and add the onion, shallots and garlic.

Cook briefly, stirring, until wilted. Add the tomatoes, salt and pepper to taste, tarragon and parsley and cook about 5 minutes.

2. Add the wine and simmer about 15 minutes.

3. Heat the remaining butter in a skillet large enough to hold the shrimp in one layer. Add the hot pepper, shrimp, salt and pepper to taste. Cook about 45 seconds, turning the shrimp until they turn pink. Add the cognac.

4. Add the tomato sauce, salt and pepper to taste and remove from the heat. Use as a base for a shrimp soufflé or serve hot with rice.

Yield: 2 to 4 servings.

November

ONE OF THE NICEST BITS of serendipity to which Pierre Franey and I were exposed in the waning months of the year occurred on a visit to Portland, Oregon. We had traveled to that city to give a cooking demonstration for the town's splendid arts and crafts society. While there, we were entertained at a buffet in a private home and the food was cooked by a Taiwanese named Jeri Sipe. It was impressive in all respects, from the sesame chicken wing appetizers and the Chinese-style barbecued pork to the lemon chicken and spicy kung pao shrimp. We asked for an interview the next day and the story that Jeri told was something that a Chinese Charles Dickens would be hard put to contrive. A victim of child abuse, Jeri emerged as an extraordinary human being and woman of great talent.

On an infinitely less dramatic plane, we had spent a good deal of time in late summer concocting various formulas for mincemeat, that sweet savory filling almost imperative to year-end dining. In all modesty, we arrived at our own formula for mincemeat that I sincerely believe to be the best we've found anywhere.

Those year-end holidays encompassed, of course, turkey stuffing, as this column has for lo these past twenty and more years. Once more, we were grateful to the West Coast for an unusual contribution. It was offered by James Nassikas, the director of that splendid hostelry, the Stanford Court in San Francisco. Jim is Greek by origin and the recipe is a traditional family stuffing made with ground meat and pine nuts.

One of the pleasures of the Thanksgiving table is an elaboration of another sort—things to do with leftover turkey. It is my opinion that the chief benefit of roasting a turkey in the first place is how good it can be the next day, thinly sliced and made into a sandwich.

Oriental Cooking in the Far West

"When I was 19 years old," Kui Yun Sipe was saying, "my master had two wives. The first wife always wanted me to cook the food longer and softer. The second wife always wanted me to cook the food quickly and make it crunchy on the outside."

Precisely what effect such training had on the cooking abilities of Jeri Sipe, as she is known in America, can never be measured. But she is one of the finest Chinese cooks west of the Mississippi River.

The saga of Jeri Sipe is novelesque.

She was born in Taiwan and given to foster parents when she was forty days old because of her natural family's poverty. She tells tales of an atrocious, unloved childhood. She was forced to cook for the family from her ninth year. On the wall of her home hung a bamboo whip. She was disciplined daily and when the whip did not suffice she was sent to the yard for sticks better suited to sterner punishment.

At 12, she was "farmed out" to the home of aunts who paid the family $2 a day for her services.

Most such miseries ended when she was 16 years old.

"My parents lived in fields where rice and vegetables were grown. When I was 16, I ran away from home because on that day I had been beaten six times. July is what we call Ghost Month in Taiwan. I ran and ran and changed clothes in the vegetable field. Then I saw my mother running after me in the night. All night I walked through rice paddies, sugar cane fields and cemeteries. I was so certain I heard ghosts around me, laughing and talking. I felt them chasing me. I ran and walked for hours. I finally found my sister's house and hid in the attic for five days."

It was then that her sister got her a job with the master with two wives. The master's family numbered thirteen.

In the years that followed she cooked for many people, a couple from Shanghai, a family from Peking, one family that was Japanese, another that was French. And she borrowed as much learning as she could from each.

The great turning point in her life arrived in 1964 when she met her husband, James Sipe of Bellingham, Washington. She alludes to him as a kind of

American Pygmalion. When they met, he was an electronics engineer with the United States Government. She was a waitress in an officer's club.

When they married, he bought her school books designed for third, fourth and fifth-grade students. He taught her multiplication and division. Because of him, she studied English for two years. And, she says, in a voice that is not without tenderness, "he taught me not to speak so loud."

In all her life, she says, she has never lost her enthusiasm for cooking. And farm life, apparently. The Sipes, who are the parents of three children, ages 10 through 17, live on two acres outside Portland. There she tends a varying number of animals, but now numbering one hundred chickens, four pigs, two cows and an uncounted number of turkeys and ducks. She arises at six o'clock and before to attend their needs.

In their early years in America, in Seattle, her friends told her that with the scale on which the couple entertained, her house resembled a train station or hotel. They stated often she should open a restaurant.

Her husband suggested that cooking classes would be less work. She first taught cooking in a Japanese grocery store and the owner, a Mr. O-Mori-Ya, paid to have her recipes typed.

I first met Jeri Sipe at an elaborate buffet dinner where she had prepared all the Chinese foods. She cooks for from two to two hundred people, never makes a shopping list and only on a rare occasion uses more than one helper in the kitchen. She teaches cooking at one of the finest pot and pan shops in America, the Kitchen/Kaboodle in Portland. She plans, eventually, to publish a cookbook.

I have never watched Jeri cook in depth—only a dish or two here, a dish or two there. One remarkable thing, however. She offered me several of the recipes that she had composed for her cooking classes. These recipes were brought back to New York and tested in my own kitchen. She has an uncanny ability to compose recipes with clarity.

Of her recipes she says: "I don't type. I don't read or write much. I learned everything when I came to this country with my husband in 1966. A recipe takes me hours to put together. After I finish writing I read it through myself. If it does not sound too good, then I change it over and over. I type with the two-finger method. Each recipe takes me one and one-half hours to type. If the recipe is longer, it takes me two hours, sometimes more."

I can vouch for the fact that her recipes work. Admirably.

Sesame Chicken Wing Appetizers

12   chicken wings
1   tablespoon salted black beans
1   tablespoon water
1   tablespoon peanut, vegetable or corn oil
2   cloves garlic, crushed
2   slices fresh ginger root cut into very fine shreds
3   tablespoons dark soy sauce
1½   tablespoons dry sherry or shao hsing wine
½   teaspoon monosodium glutamate, optional
2   teaspoons Maggi seasoning, optional
¼   teaspoon ground black pepper
1   tablespoon toasted sesame seeds
2   tablespoons chopped green onions, green part and all

1. Cut off and discard the small wing tips. Cut between and reserve the main wing bones and the second wing joint.

2. Crush the beans and add 1 tablespoon of water. Let stand.

3. Heat the oil in a wok or skillet and add the garlic and ginger. Stir briefly and add the chicken wings. Cook, stirring, until lightly browned, about 3 minutes. Add the soy sauce and wine and cook, stirring, about 30 seconds longer. Add the soaked black beans.

4. Cover closely and let simmer 8 to 10 minutes. Uncover, turn the heat to high and continue cooking, stirring, until liquid is almost evaporated and chicken pieces are glazed with sauce.

5. Remove from the heat and add the monosodium glutamate, Maggi seasoning and pepper. Toss. Just before serving, toss in the sesame seeds and onion. This dish can be made in advance and reheated.

Yield: 8 or more appetizer servings.

Jeri Sipe's Lemon Chicken

The chicken

2   *skinned, boned chicken breasts, about 1¼ pounds*
2   *tablespoons soy sauce*
2   *teaspoons dry sherry or shao hsing wine*
½   *cup plus 1 tablespoon cornstarch*
¼   *teaspoon sugar*
1   *egg yolk*
4   *cups plus 1 tablespoon peanut, vegetable or corn oil*
   Salt and freshly ground pepper to taste
¼   *cup flour*

The lemon sauce

1½   *tablespoons salted black beans*
1   *tablespoon water*
3   *tablespoons fresh lemon juice*
½   *cup fresh or canned chicken broth*
3   *tablespoons sugar*
½   *teaspoon sesame oil*
2   *teaspoons cornstarch*
   Salt to taste
   Drops yellow food coloring
2   *tablespoons peanut, vegetable or corn oil*
2   *cloves garlic, finely minced*
¼   *teaspoon crushed red pepper flakes*

1. Place the chicken breasts on a flat surface and cut into thin (¼-inch thick) slices about 2 inches wide and 1½ inches long. Put them in a mixing bowl. Add the soy sauce, wine, 1 tablespoon of cornstarch, sugar, egg yolk, 1 tablespoon of oil, salt and pepper to taste. Let stand 10 minutes or longer.

2. Blend remaining ½ cup of cornstarch with the flour. Coat each piece of chicken in this mixture.

3. Heat remaining 4 cups of oil for deep frying (400 degrees). Add the chicken, stirring to separate the pieces. Cook about 30 seconds, or until chicken is golden brown. Drain well and transfer to a platter. Keep warm until the sauce is made.

4. Crush the black beans and add 1 tablespoon of water. Let stand until ready to use.

5. Blend the lemon juice, chicken broth, sugar, sesame oil, cornstarch, salt and food coloring in a small bowl. Heat 1 tablespoon of oil in a saucepan and add the garlic. Stir in the lemon sauce. Bring to the boil, stirring, and add the black beans and red pepper flakes. When clear and thickened, sprinkle with the remaining 1 tablespoon of oil. Pour this over the chicken and serve hot.

Yield: 6 servings.

Sesame Chicken with Garlic Sauce

The chicken

6   *chicken thighs, about 1¾ pounds*
1   *egg yolk*
1   *tablespoon soy sauce*
1   *clove garlic, finely minced*

The batter

1   *cup plus 2 tablespoons flour*
3   *tablespoons cornstarch*
1¼   *teaspoons baking powder*
¾   *cup cold water*
2   *eggs, lightly beaten*

2 teaspoons peanut, vegetable or corn oil
1 tablespoon sesame seeds

The garlic sauce

1 tablespoon peanut, vegetable or corn oil
4 cloves garlic, finely minced
1 teaspoon finely chopped fresh ginger
½ cup fresh or canned chicken broth
1½ teaspoons sugar
2 tablespoons dark soy sauce
¼ teaspoon ground black pepper
¼ teaspoon monosodium glutamate, optional
¾ cup chopped green onions, green part and all
1 tablespoon sesame seeds
4 cups peanut, vegetable or corn oil

1. Bone the thighs or have them boned. Slice the thighs into 4 or 6 squares of approximately the same size. Place the pieces in a bowl and add the egg yolk, 1 tablespoon soy sauce and minced garlic. Let stand.

2. Sift the flour, cornstarch and baking powder into a bowl. Stir in the water, eggs, 2 teaspoons oil and sesame seeds.

3. To prepare the sauce, heat 1 tablespoon of oil and add the garlic and ginger. Cook briefly and add the chicken broth, sugar, soy sauce, ground pepper and monosodium glutamate. Simmer about 5 minutes.

4. Add the chicken to the batter.

5. Heat 4 cups of oil in a wok or skillet and add the batter-coated chicken pieces, one at a time. Do not add all the chicken pieces at once. Cook, stirring to separate the pieces, about 1 minute, or until golden brown. Drain each batch as they cook.

Pour out the oil after cooking the chicken pieces. Return the chicken pieces to the wok.

6. Add the garlic sauce and blend well. Stir in the chopped green onions and one tablespoon of sesame seeds and heat through.

Yield: 4 servings.

Kung Pao Shrimp with Cashew Nuts

The marinated shrimp

¾ pound shrimp
½ teaspoon chopped fresh ginger
1 teaspoon chopped garlic
1½ tablespoons cornstarch
¼ teaspoon baking soda
Salt and freshly ground pepper to taste
¼ teaspoon sugar

The thickening sauce

¼ cup fresh or canned chicken broth
1½ teaspoons cornstarch
½ teaspoon monosodium glutamate, optional
1 teaspoon chili paste with garlic
1 teaspoon bean paste, optional
1 teaspoon sesame oil
1 tablespoon dry sherry or shao hsing wine

The cooking procedure

¼ cup peanut, vegetable or corn oil
¾ cup chopped onion
1 cup zucchini cut into ½-inch cubes
½ cup sweet red pepper cut into ½-inch cubes
½ cup salted cashew nuts

1. Shell and devein the shrimp. Cut them into ½-inch pieces. Place them in a bowl and add the remaining ingredients for marinated shrimp. Let stand at least 20 minutes.

2. Blend the ingredients for the thickening sauce.

3. Heat 3 tablespoons of oil in a wok or skillet and add the shrimp. Cook, stirring, over high heat about 20 seconds or just until shrimp change color. Transfer to a platter.

4. To the same wok or skillet add the remaining tablespoon of oil and add the onion. Cook quickly and add the zucchini and red pepper. Cook about 45 seconds.

5. Stir the sauce mixture and add it. Cook, stirring, until the sauce is slightly thickened. Add the shrimp and nuts and toss quickly to heat through.

Yield: 6 servings.

Hot Spicy Cucumber Salad

2	large cucumbers
1½	teaspoons salt
3	tablespoons soy sauce
2	teaspoons Maggi seasoning, or ½ teaspoon monosodium glutamate
½	teaspoon crushed red pepper, or ¼ teaspoon cayenne
1	teaspoon sesame oil
1	tablespoon vinegar

1. Wash the cucumbers and pat dry. Pound the cucumbers lightly all over with a cleaver.

2. Trim off the ends. Peel the cucumbers and cut them lengthwise into quarters. Cut or scrape away and discard the seeds.

3. Cut each cucumber strip into 1½-inch lengths. Trim the corners of each piece to make them neater. Put the pieces in a bowl and add a teaspoon of salt. Let stand 10 minutes.

4. Drain the cucumbers well and add the remining ingredients. Chill and serve.

Yield: 4 servings.

Chinese-style Barbecued Pork

2	pounds boneless pork loin in one piece
1	green onion, green part and all, chopped
3	thin slices ginger, finely chopped
2	tablespoons plus 2 teaspoons soy sauce
2½	tablespoons hoisin sauce
2	tablespoons dry sherry or shao hsing wine
8	drops red food coloring
1	teaspoon sesame oil
¼	cup hot water
1	tablespoon honey

1. Cut the pork into thin slices. Cut the slices into thin strips. Place the strips of pork in a bowl and add the chopped green onion, ginger, 2 tablespoons soy sauce, hoisin sauce, wine, food coloring and sesame oil. Blend well and let stand at least 2 hours, or overnight.

2. Preheat the oven to 375 degrees.

3. Fit a rack in a shallow roasting pan and arrange the strips of meat on it. Place in the oven and bake for 30 minutes.

4. Turn the strips and continue baking 30 minutes.

5. Blend the hot water, honey and remaining 2 teaspoons of soy sauce. Brush the strips of pork on all sides with this sauce. Return the meat to the oven and bake 10 minutes longer. Let cool at least 15 minutes before serving. Serve hot or cold with hot mustard (see method for making), barbecue sauce (see method for making) and/or soy sauce.

Yield: 12 appetizer or buffet servings.

Hot mustard

2　*tablespoons or more dry mustard*
1½　*tablespoons cold water*

Blend the mustard with water to make a smooth paste. Let stand at least 20 minutes to develop flavor and strength. Thin with a little more water if desired.

Yield: About 3 tablespoons.

Barbecue sauce

3　*tablespoons tomato ketchup*
1　*teaspoon Worcestershire sauce, or to taste*
　Few drops Tabasco sauce

Blend all the ingredients and add more seasonings to taste if desired.

Yield: About ¼ cup.

Vive Vinaigre!

WITH PIERRE FRANEY

When meats, poultry, fish and the like are sautéed in a skillet or other utensil, they often leave a brown, savory, caramel-looking deposit on the bottom and sides of the pan. In French kitchens, when a liquid such as wine or water or cider is added to the pan, it is known as a déglacage.

We have remarked earlier that one of the hallmarks of what is widely touted as la nouvelle cuisine is the use of vinegar to deglaze a pan; in other words, to make this déglacage. Vinegar has many other uses in cooking, in such diverse dishes as mussels vinaigrette, sautéed veal chops and a dish much prized in an earlier epoch, eggs au beurre noir, or eggs with black butter sauce with capers.

Moules Vinaigrette

(Mussels with oil and vinegar sauce)

- 7 quarts fresh mussels, well scrubbed
  Salt and freshly ground pepper
- 1 cup dry white wine
- ¾ cup finely chopped parsley
- 1 cup finely chopped red onion
- 1 teaspoon finely minced garlic
- 6 tablespoons red wine vinegar, more or less to taste
- ¾ cup olive oil
- 2 tablespoons finely chopped chives
  Salt and freshly ground pepper

1. Place the mussels, salt and pepper to taste and wine in a deep kettle and cover. Bring to the boil and cook 5 to 10 minutes, or until mussels are opened.

2. Drain the mussels. If desired, strain the broth and use it for cream of mussel soup or as a base for fish soup. Place the mussels in a large bowl.

3. Combine all the remaining ingredients for the vinaigrette sauce and stir to blend thoroughly. Pour the sauce over the lukewarm mussels and toss with the hands until they are thoroughly blended with the sauce. Serve lukewarm or at room temperature with French bread.

Yield: 20 to 30 servings.

Gras-Double Lyonnaise

(Tripe lyonnaise)

- 1½ pounds honeycomb tripe (see note)
- 4 cups water
  Salt

1   bay leaf
1   small onion, stuck with 3
    whole cloves
10 peppercorns
1   carrot, scraped and cut into 2-
    inch lengths
3   sprigs fresh parsley
1   rib celery, cut into quarters
2   sprigs fresh thyme, or ½ tea-
    spoon dried
1   hot red pepper
2   tablespoons butter
1   large or 2 medium-size onions,
    peeled and sliced as thinly as
    possible, about 2 cups sliced
1   small clove garlic, peeled but
    left whole
2   teaspoons red wine vinegar, or
    more to taste
    Chopped parsley for garnish
    Assorted mustards

1. Put the tripe in a kettle and add the water, salt to taste, bay leaf, onion stuck with cloves, peppercorns, carrot, parsley sprigs, celery, thyme and red pepper. Cover and cook about 5 hours. Let cool.

2. Drain the tripe and cut it into thin, bite-size strips (there should be about 2 cups).

3. Heat the butter in a skillet and add the tripe. Cook, stirring briefly, and add the sliced onions. Cook over moderately high heat until the onions start to brown, stirring gently and shaking the skillet. Add the garlic, turn the heat to low and cook, stirring frequently, about 10 minutes longer. Remove garlic.

4. Add the vinegar and serve sprinkled with chopped parsley. Serve mustard on the side, letting guests help themselves.

Yield: 4 to 6 servings.

Note: There are numerous kinds of tripe available in France, each with its own texture depending on what part of the animal's stomach is used. In the United States, only honeycomb tripe is generally used because of some government regulations (what they are I've never discovered). When the French cook tripe in the style of Lyon, the kind of tripe used is gras-double, or double-fat tripe. We are using the traditional name for the recipe even though honeycomb tripe is specified.

Maquereaux au Vin Blanc Provencale

(Mackerel with white wine and tomatoes)

2   tablespoons olive oil
1   cup thinly sliced onion
¼   cup thin carrot rounds
2   cloves garlic, finely minced
    Salt and freshly ground pep-
    per
2   tablespoons white vinegar
2   cups dry white wine
3   whole cloves
1   bay leaf
1   cup fresh or canned peeled
    tomatoes
5   pounds cleaned whole mack-
    erel (see note)
10 thin lemon slices
3   tablespoons lemon juice

1. Preheat oven to 400 degrees.

2. In a saucepan heat 1 tablespoon oil and add the onion. Cook, stirring, until wilted. Add the carrot rounds, garlic, salt and pepper to taste, vinegar, white wine, cloves, bay leaf and tomatoes. Cook 20 minutes and let cool.

3. Select a baking dish large enough to hold the mackerel in one layer. Rub the bottom of the dish with the remaining 1 tablespoon oil and sprinkle with salt and pepper. Arrange the mackerel in the dish. Arrange the lemon slices over the fish and sprinkle with lemon juice. Sprinkle with salt and pepper to taste.

4. Spoon the tomato and wine sauce over the fish and cover with a piece of buttered wax paper cut to fit the baking dish. Bake 15 to 20 minutes, just until the fish flakes easily when tested with a fork. Baking time will depend on the size of the fish.

Yield: 10 or more servings.

Note: Mackerel fillets may be used in this recipe and the cooking time will have to be adjusted accordingly.

Côtes de Veau Pavillon

(Sautéed veal chops with vinegar glaze)

4 *loin veal chops, about ½ pound each*
Salt and freshly ground pepper
2 *tablespoons butter*
4 *whole cloves garlic, peeled*
2 *bay leaves*
4 *sprigs fresh thyme, or ½ teaspoon dried*
1 *tablespoon red wine vinegar*
½ *cup chicken broth*

1. Sprinkle the chops on both sides with salt and pepper to taste.

2. Heat 2 tablespoons butter in a skillet and add the chops. Brown on both sides, turning once. They should cook about 5 minutes to a side.

3. Add the garlic, bay leaves and thyme and cook about 3 minutes.

4. Pour the vinegar around the chops and turn the heat to high. Add the broth, cover closely and cook about 20 minutes.

Yield: 4 servings.

Les Oeufs au Beurre Noir

(Eggs with black butter and capers)

1½ *tablespoons plus ½ teaspoon butter*
2 *eggs*
Salt and freshly ground pepper
1 *tablespoon drained capers*
½ *teaspoon red wine vinegar*
1 *teaspoon finely chopped parsley*

1. Melt the ½ teaspoon butter in a small, heavy skillet. Add the eggs and salt and pepper to taste and cook gently until set to the desired degree of doneness, 1 or 2 minutes.

2. Empty the eggs carefully onto a plate.

3. To the skillet add the remaining butter and cook, swirling it around until it is darker than nut brown. Do not burn it, however. Remove from the heat and add the capers. Cook, swirling, briefly. Add the vinegar and pour this over the eggs.

4. Sprinkle with chopped parsley and serve.

Yield: 1 serving.

Turkey Sidebars

It is one man's considered opinion that there are two things better than the Thanksgiving turkey. The first is a well-made stuffing; the other is the turkey, second time around, turned into a cold sandwich with freshly made mayonnaise.

In that America is a polyglot, melting-pot nation, it is small wonder that the character of turkey stuffings in this country (and in the homes of Americans abroad) frequently take on fascinating "foreign" flavors.

One of the best turkey stuffings I've ever sampled is, oddly enough, Greek. Or rather of Greek inspiration. It is that of James Nassikas, the proprietor of the Stanford Court Hotel in San Francisco. That stuffing is a "specialty of the house" in the Stanford Court's restaurant called Fournou's Oven.

"This recipe," Mr. Nassikas wrote recently when he dispatched a copy of the stuffing, "is my mother's and we've had it every Thanksgiving of my life. My mother can't recall the origin of the dish and I've never known." Actually, the stuffing is made with hamburger meat and pine nuts, flavored with such à la grecque seasonings as cinnamon and cloves.

Since earliest childhood I have been able to salivate reflexively while dining on the thinly sliced meat of a golden brown turkey fresh from the oven. My friends aver I salivate for all the wrong reasons. Those gastric juices are not triggered by that bird on the table there, delicious though it may be. The gastro-fluvial action comes from the thought of the cold turkey sandwiches that will follow on the morrow—sandwiches made of thin slices of breast, nestled between thin slices of good sandwich bread (preferably homemade), neatly smeared with homemade mayonnaise.

A turkey sandwich has been one of the ultimate creations of this earth since the fourth Earl of Sandwich lost (or won) at the gaming tables of England.

Christine Cotsibos' Hamburger and Nut Stuffing à la Grecque

½	cup uncooked rice
1½	cups water
	Salt to taste

¼	pound butter
2	cups finely chopped onion
1	cup seedless raisins
¾	pound peeled, blanched chestnuts (see method for peeling)
½	cup pine nuts
1½	pounds ground top-quality beef
1	teaspoon ground cloves

2 *teaspoons ground cinnamon*
Salt and freshly ground pepper to taste

1. Pour the rice into a saucepan and add water and salt to taste. Bring to the boil and simmer 6 minutes, no longer. Drain.

2. Melt the butter in a large skillet and add the onion. Cook, stirring, until wilted. Add the rice, raisins, nuts and ground meat. Stir frequently, using the side of a heavy metal kitchen spoon to break up lumps in the meat. Add the cloves and cinnamon and salt and pepper and remove from the heat. Let cool.

3. Use the stuffing to fill the cavity of a 12- to 16-pound turkey. If there is leftover stuffing, set it aside.

4. Roast the bird in the usual fashion. Skim off most of the fat from the roasting pan. Spoon and scrape the stuffing from inside the turkey into the pan drippings. Add any reserved stuffing. Mix well and bake 30 minutes longer at the same temperature used for the roasting.

Yield: 8 cups of stuffing.

How to prepare fresh chestnuts for peeling

Using a sharp paring knife, make an incision around the perimeter of each chestnut, starting and ending on either side of the "topknot," or stem end. Place the chestnuts in one layer in a baking dish just large enough to hold them. Place them in a preheated 450-degree oven and bake about 10 minutes, or until they open. Let the chestnuts cool just until they can be handled. Peel them while they are hot.

The Plain Turkey Sandwich

Thinly slice the best sandwich bread you can find, preferably your own. Smear one side of each slice with homemade mayonnaise. Arrange the slices of turkey over one slice and sprinkle the meat with salt and pepper to taste. Cover with the other slice. Neatly trim off the crusts of the sandwich. Slice the sandwich in half. Serve with good pickles, radishes and cherry tomatoes.

Turkey sandwich with cucumbers

To the plain turkey sandwich add one layer of thinly sliced firm cucumber, preferably the so-called "gourmet" or "burpless" type.

Turkey club sandwich

Toast 3 slices of bread that has been trimmed of crusts. Place the slices on a flat surface and smear them liberally with mayonnaise or, preferably, Russian dressing (see recipe). Arrange crisp lettuce leaves on one of the smeared pieces of toast. Add 2 strips of crisp bacon, each cut in half to fit. Place a second slice of toast on this, smeared side up. Arrange thin slices of turkey on top, sprinkle with salt and pepper. Cover with the third slice of toast, smeared side down. Cut in half and serve with green and black (imported) olives, pickles and—if you want to be American—traditional potato chips.

Russian dressing

½   cup mayonnaise
1   tablespoon chili sauce or
    tomato ketchup
1   teaspoon finely grated or
    chopped onion
½   teaspoon horseradish
¼   teaspoon Worcestershire sauce

1   tablespoon finely chopped
    parsley
1   tablespoon black or red caviar,
    optional

Combine all the ingredients in a mixing bowl. Blend well.

Yield: About ½ cup.

Mincemeat Now,
Pies Later

It is a curious fact that the most coveted character of some of the world's foods came about not as ends in themselves, but as a matter of food preservation. The list is long and would include scores of smoked foods such as ham and sausages; salted foods such as cod, and other fish such as salmon and sturgeon. And to a lesser but by no means less delectable extent, food preserved in alcohol including cherries and the multiple fruits in tutti frutti.

This came to mind while delving into the origins of mincemeat and, if you wish to know, the season for making—if not eating—mincemeat is here. The best mincemeat should ripen for several weeks before it is turned into Christmas pies.

Mincemeat, according to food histories, originally came about as a matter of preserving various meats, including games such as venison and rabbit. Both alcohol and spices were added to retard spoilage. Around the middle of the seventeenth century these meats were made more sophisticated and palatable through the addition of various preserved fruits and spices. According to Dorothy Gladys Spicer in her almost twenty-year-old volume, *From an English Oven*, (The Women's Press, 1948) the predecessor of today's English mince tarts was a gigantic affair, "weighing over a hundred weight and bursting with neats' tongues, chicken, eggs, raisins, orange and lemon peel" plus other ingredients including large quantities of sugar and spices. (Neat, in case you didn't know it, is an old English term for ox.)

There is an entry in Samuel Pepys' diary dated January 6, 1662, which notes that he had dined at Sir W. Pen's, who celebrated his wedding anniversary with "eighteen mince pies in a dish, the number of years that he had been married."

Presumably he dined on the newer, sophisticated version of mincemeat.

There are probably as many recipes for mincemeat both in England and this country as there are for Welsh rabbit or Yorkshire buck.

Many recipes call for the addition of both beef and beef tongue, while others eliminate these entirely and consist solely of preserved fruits, apples, spices, a bit of brandy and so on.

To show the various and varying natures of mincemeat, we offer here a composite of mincemeat recipes to make and let ripen. The first is a personal creation. Another is the late Paula Peck's "wonderful mincemeat," adapted from her book *The Art of Fine Baking* (Simon and Schuster, 1961). To illustrate a meatless mincemeat we have adapted Margaret Costa's recipe from the *Four Seasons Cookery Book* (The Cookery Book Club, London, 1970). Margaret is a good friend and food editor of the London *Times*.

Mincemeat

½	pound cooked beef
½	pound cooked beef tongue
1	pound black currants
1½	pound black raisins
2	ounces chopped candied lemon peel
2	ounces chopped candied orange peel
½	cup chopped diced candied citron
½	cup chopped glacéed cherries
½	cup chopped glacéed pineapple
¾	pound finely chopped or ground suet
2	cups brown sugar
2	cups peeled, cored, finely diced apple
	Grated rind of 1 lemon
	Grated rind of 1 orange
¼	cup lemon juice
1	teaspoon ground nutmeg
½	teaspoon ground cloves
½	teaspoon ground allspice
1	teaspoon ground cinnamon
2	cups cognac or other brandy
½	cup dry sherry
½	teaspoon salt, or to taste

1. The texture of mincemeat is a question of personal taste. Some like it fine, some medium and some coarse. If you want it coarse, the various fruits and meats should be chopped or cubed by hand. If you want it medium or fine, use a food processor or, more tediously, an electric blender and process or blend to the desired texture. Some sources recommend grinding the mince meat; others recommend grinding half the ingredients and chopping the rest. Take your choice.

2. Cube or chop the beef, tongue, currants, raisins, lemon peel, orange peel, candied citron, cherries, pineapple and suet. Pour this mixture into a bowl.

3. Add the remaining ingredients and mix well with the hands. There should be about 12 cups. Spoon the mixture into fruit jars and seal tightly. This mincemeat is not destined to be cooked until it is made into pies. Let it age for at least 3 weeks, and preferably a month, before using. Store in a cool place to age. Use 3 to 4 cups for 1 pie.

Yield: 12 cups.

Paula Peck's Wonderful Mincemeat

2	pounds lean uncooked beef
2	pounds uncooked fresh tongue
	Salt
1	pound beef suet, chopped
4	cups seedless raisins
4	cups seeded raisins
2	cups currants

periods as moisture is absorbed. This mincemeat will keep indefinitely.

6. When ready to use, add 1 cup of chopped tart apples for each 1¼ cups of mincemeat. Drain the mincemeat before blending with the chopped apples.

Yield: About 3 quarts.

Margaret Costa's Christmas Mincemeat

1 cup diced citron
1 cup diced orange peel
½ cup diced lemon peel
1 cup chopped figs
2½ cups sugar
2 teaspoons ground nutmeg
2 teaspoons ground cinnamon
2 teaspoons ground allspice
1 teaspoon ground cloves
5 cups cognac, approximately
4 cups dry sherry, approximately
Chopped tart apples

1. Cook the beef and tongue in salted water to cover until tender. Let cool in the cooking liquid.

2. Grind the beef, tongue and suet together.

3. Add the raisins, currants, citron, orange peel, lemon peel, figs, sugar, 2 teaspoons salt and spices. Add enough cognac to make a thick, soupy mixture.

4. Place the mixture in a crock and let stand in a cool place at least 1 month. Refrigeration is unnecessary.

5. Check the mincemeat after 1 week. If most of the liquid is absorbed and it seems a bit dry, add enough sherry to moisten. Check each week and add cognac and sherry at alternate

⅔ cup blanched almonds
2 cups chopped candied orange or lemon peel
1 cup chopped glacé cherries
½ cup crystallized ginger
½ cup chopped crystallized pineapple
2 tart apples, peeled, cored and chopped
1 pound seedless black raisins
1 pound golden seedless raisins
1 pound currants
1 pound shredded suet
¾ pound soft brown sugar
Salt to taste
½ teaspoon ground nutmeg
½ teaspoon ground cinnamon
½ teaspoon ground allspice
½ teaspoon ground cloves
Grated rind of 1 orange
Juice of 1 orange
Grated rind of 1 lemon
Juice of 1 lemon
½ cup brandy, rum or whiskey

1. Chop the nuts and blend with the candied orange peel, cherries, crystallized ginger, pineapple and apples.

2. Set aside about ¼ of this mixture. Set aside also about ¼ of the raisins and currants.

3. Grind the suet plus the remaining candied fruit mixture, raisins and currants, using the coarse blade.

4. Blend all the ingredients, including the reserved mixture and brandy. Pack into jars and seal. Let stand 3 weeks or longer in a cool place to ripen.

Yield: About 12 cups.

December

SOMEONE ONCE SAID in a jocular sense that we are like some vast vacuum crawling over the world sucking up recipes from no matter what source. "As long as it tastes good, you'll print it." In a sense that is true. We have frequently found that because of lack of space or some equally valid reason, we may delay a recipe that has fallen into our possession for weeks, months and years. But eventually, if the recipe is good enough, it will surface. We thought of this in that one Christmas holiday season we were invited into the home of the Countess Ulla Wachtmeister, the wife of the Swedish Ambassador to the United States. The meal had not really been related to the year-end holidays, but one of the dishes, a cured goose, seemed infinitely appropriate for a Yuletide buffet. Happily, we remembered the Countess' offering and listed it in December alongside roast stuffed goose and other dishes for a Christmas feast.

All of the items that December were related to the holidays. One that pleased us most was the opportunity to garner and publish some of the recipes of good friends and great cooks—their proposals of foods that might be prepared in their home kitchens suitable for gift-giving. Among them was a neighbor's baked nut cake, one of the finest pastries ever to come out of a home oven.

As we have observed, it is difficult to detail precisely why one food or another seems so inherently associative with year-end revelry. Oysters are, simply because they are. In a somewhat lesser sense, so are pecans, whether offered in an assortment of other holiday nuts in the shell, or cooked and served as appetizers, in stuffings and desserts.

Good Enough to Give

Christmas came early to my kitchen this year.

Weeks ago I asked numerous acquaintances, all of them known as first-rate cooks, to "lend" me their favorite recipes, either those that they would make to give to friends during the Yuletide season or their favorite recipes that could be used as gifts. The response was magnanimous. A wealth of recipes came this way ranging from some embarrassingly rich cakes and cookies to curiously appealing, very-low-calorie bottled celery sticks to be served as an appetizer.

One of the donors was Eleanor Hempstead, a neighbor at whose table we have dined sumptuously and well for almost fifteen years. She contributed a veritable cornucopia of good things, including whisky balls, candied grapefruit peel, her admirable homemade tarragon-flavored mustard called "J. A.'s mustard." In addition she gave us a tangy pepper and pear relish and "thin mint" cookies.

Rita Alexander, that tall, handsome cordon bleu who lives a mile or so down the road, came up with the most insidiously good and rich date and nut bread we could ever hope to uncover. Trouble is, it is supposed to be cooled before wrapping and giving as a gift. It is intensely devourable and the first loaf at least will probably not make it out of the kitchen.

Her pine nut cookies are guaranteed to gladden the spirit and appetite of anyone fortunate enough to be on her giving list. They both crunch and melt in the mouth—a brief moment of ecstasy.

Of the celery sticks, she says: "In spite of being totally dietetic, these are delicious and none is ever leftover from cocktail parties."

Months ago we had the rare good fortune to be aboard Bob and Ann Bolderson's good ship, the *Nymph Errant II,* down Florida way and she volunteered her recipe for an excellent mango chutney.

The recipe for hazelnut crescents came from Miki Benhof's highly reputable kitchen in the town of East Hampton.

Yours, to be wrapped in a ribbon and tied in a bow.

An Incredible Date-Nut Cake

(From Rita Alexander)

8   tablespoons (1 stick) butter
    plus butter for greasing the
    pan
    Flour
1   cup pitted diced dates
¾   cup dark seedless raisins
¼   cup golden seedless raisins
1   teaspoon baking soda
1   cup boiling water
1   cup sugar
1   teaspoon vanilla
1   egg
1⅓ cups sifted flour
¾   cup walnuts broken into small
    pieces

1. Preheat the oven to 350 degrees.

2. Butter a standard loaf pan (9½-by-5½-by-2¾-inches). Line the bottom with a rectangle of wax paper. Butter this rectangle and sprinkle with flour. Shake out the excess flour.

3. Put the dates and raisins into a mixing bowl.

4. Dissolve the baking soda with the boiling water and pour it over the date mixture.

5. Cream together the sugar and remaining 8 tablespoons butter. Beat in the vanilla and egg. Add the flour and mix well. Add the date mixture, including the liquid. Add the walnuts. Please note that this will be a quite liquid batter.

6. Pour the mixture into the prepared pan and smooth over the top. Place in the oven and bake from 1 hour to 1 hour and 10 minutes, or until the top of the cake is dark brown and a knife inserted in the center comes out clean.

7. Let cool about 5 minutes. Unmold onto a rack. Remove the paper.

Yield: 1 loaf.

Pine Nut Cookies

(From Rita Alexander)

¼   pound sweet butter
½   cup granulated sugar
1   egg yolk
1   teaspoon vanilla
1   cup sifted flour
½   cup toasted pine nuts

1. Preheat the oven to 300 degrees.

2. Cream together the butter and sugar.

3. Beat in the egg yolk, vanilla and flour. Mix in the nuts.

4. Drop the batter, a teaspoon or so at a time, onto a buttered, floured cooky sheet. Bake 20 to 25 minutes, or until pale golden. While still hot, remove with a spatula to a rack and let cool.

Yield: About 30 cookies.

Cocktail Celeries

(From Rita Alexander)

1   unblemished bunch of celery
     including outside ribs
1½   cups water
     Juice of 1 lemon
2   tablespoons white vinegar
2   to 3 cloves garlic, finely
     minced

½ teaspoon rosemary
½ teaspoon sage
1 small branch of fresh fennel,
   or 1 teaspoon ground fennel
   seeds
1 teaspoon dried thyme
½ bay leaf
¾ teaspoon ground coriander
8 peppercorns, crushed
1 teaspoon salt
½ teaspoon celery salt
2 tomatoes, peeled and chopped, about ½ pound

1. Separate the ribs from the bunch of celery. Using a swivel-bladed vegetable peeler, peel the ribs. Depending on size, split the ribs lengthwise. Cut the lengths of celery into cocktail sticks, each 3 or 4 inches long, to fit comfortably upright in ½-pint canning glasses.

2. Combine the remaining ingredients in a large saucepan. Bring to a boil.

3. Add the celery sticks. When the mixture returns to the boil, cover the saucepan and cook 5 minutes.

4. Remove the celery sticks with tongs. Strain the cooking liquid, pressing the solids with the back of a kitchen spoon to release their juices. Pack the celery sticks neatly and compactly into ½-pint jars, adding liquid to fill. Seal. Keep chilled until ready to use. They will remain fresh up to 3 weeks under proper refrigeration.

Yield: 1 dozen or more ½-pint jars.

J. A.'s Mustard
(From Eleanor Hempstead)

1 4-ounce can dry mustard
1 cup tarragon vinegar
6 eggs
¾ cup sugar
¼ pound butter
1 teaspoon salt

1. Put the mustard in a mixing bowl and pour the vinegar over it but do not mix. Cover and let stand overnight or at least 3 hours.

2. Put the mustard mixture in the top of a double boiler and mix with a wire whisk over hot water. Add the eggs, one at a time, whisking all the while until thoroughly mixed.

3. Add the sugar, butter and salt and cook over hot water 5 minutes. Do not overcook or the eggs will curdle. Put in individual jars and refrigerate. This will keep for months and is delicious with all meats, fish and in sandwiches.

Yield: 4 cups.

Pepper-Pear Relish

(From Eleanor Hempstead)

3 pounds ripe pears (about 9),
  unpeeled, cored and chopped
2 large green peppers and 2 red
  peppers, seeded and chopped
1 large onion, chopped
1½ cups cider vinegar
1½ cups sage honey
1 teaspoon soy sauce
2 canned, whole, green chili
  peppers, rinsed, partly seeded
  and chopped
½ teaspoon ground ginger
½ teaspoon salt

Put all the ingredients into a large kettle. Bring to a boil and simmer, uncovered, about 1 hour. Stir often as mixture thickens. Pour into sterilized jars and seal with paraffin.

Yield: About 6 cups.

Note: Use with cream cheese on crackers as an hors d'oeuvre or with cold meats.

Mint Surprise Cookies

(From Eleanor Hempstead)

½ cup butter
½ cup granulated sugar
¼ cup firmly packed brown sugar
1 egg
1½ teaspoons water
½ teaspoon vanilla
1½ cups flour
½ teaspoon baking soda
½ teaspoon salt
24 thin, chocolate-covered mints,
  approximately
24 walnut halves, approximately

1. All of the ingredients should be at room temperature. Cream the butter and gradually add the granulated sugar, then the brown sugar. Beat in the egg, water and vanilla.

2. Sift together the flour, baking soda and salt. Blend into the butter mixture. Wrap in wax paper and chill for at least 2 hours.

3. Preheat the oven to 375 degrees.

4. Enclose each thin mint with about 1 tablespoon of the dough. The mints may be cut in half for a smaller cooky. Place on a cooky sheet lined with parchment paper or greased. Top each cooky with a walnut half. Bake in the oven 10 to 12 minutes, until lightly browned. Let stand a minute or so, then remove and cool on a cake rack.

Yield: About 24 cookies.

Whisky Balls

(From Eleanor Hempstead)

3 cups vanilla wafer crumbs
½ cup finely chopped pecans
½ cup powdered cocoa
2 cups confectioners' sugar
½ cup whisky (see note)
3 tablespoons light corn syrup
  Salt

1. Make 3 cups of vanilla wafer crumbs in a blender at high speed, adding a few wafers at a time.

2. Chop the nuts in a food processor or blender. Blend together the crumbs, nuts, cocoa, 1 cup confectioners' sugar, whisky, corn syrup and a dash of salt. Form into small balls, about walnut size.

3. Roll each ball in the remaining cup of confectioners' sugar and place on a cooky sheet. Chill in the refrigerator for several hours or overnight.

Yield: About 3 dozen.

Note: It is traditional in the South to use bourbon, but rye may also be used.

Candied Grapefruit Peel

(From Eleanor Hempstead)

Choose 8 large grapefruits free of blemishes. Using a potato peeler, shave the rind off the fruit very thin, in pieces as large as possible. Then cut the peel into thin strips. Cover with water, bring to the boil and drain. Repeat this 3 times. The fourth time cook the peel, after it comes to the boil, for 15 minutes. Drain thoroughly.

Combine 1½ cups sugar and 1½ cups water. Add the peel and cook over low heat about 45 minutes, until syrup has almost evaporated. Keep an eye out while syrup cooks so peel doesn't stick to the pan and scorch.

Sprinkle a large tray with lots of granulated sugar. Add the drained peel and mix until every piece is thickly coated with sugar. Dry on a wire rack. This will take a day (in dry weather).

Yield: About 1½ cups.

Note: This recipe can be made using 12 large lemons or 8 large navel oranges, using the same instructions.

Hazelnut Crescents

(From Miki Denhof)

1¾	cups flour
12	tablespoons butter
½	cup sugar
½	cup ground hazelnuts, or walnuts
⅛	teaspoon salt
	Grated rind of 1 lemon
1	egg yolk
½	teaspoon pure vanilla extract
¼	cup confectioners' sugar

1. Preheat oven to 350 degrees.

2. Combine the flour and all the remaining ingredients except the confectioners' sugar in a mixing bowl. Blend and knead until the mass is cohesive. Shape into approximately 50 balls, using about 1 teaspoon of dough for each. Flatten the balls and shape them into crescents. As they are shaped arrange them on an ungreased baking sheet.

3. Place the crescents in the oven and bake 10 to 12 minutes. Sprinkle with confectioners' sugar and let cool.

Yield: 50 crescents.

Mango Chutney

(From Ann Bolderson)

4	cloves garlic, crushed
10	cups cubed mangoes or apples
2	cups chopped onions
2	pounds brown sugar
3	cups vinegar
1	cup lime juice
2	lemons, chopped, peel and all
	Peel of 2 oranges
	Peel of 1 grapefruit
1	pound raisins

10   *slices pineapple, drained*
1   *tablespoon ground nutmeg*
1   *tablespoon cinnamon*
1   *tablespoon ground ginger*
1   *tablespoon cloves*
1   *tablespoon salt*
1   *teaspoon freshly ground pepper*
1   *drop Tabasco sauce*
1   *cup pitted prunes or dates*

Put the garlic, mangoes, onions, sugar, vinegar and lime juice in a saucepan and simmer 10 minutes. Add the remaining ingredients and cook until the fruit is soft, about 20 minutes. The chutney can be kept in the refrigerator about 6 months without sterilization.

Yield: 8 pints.

Nutty About Pecans

"I have six packs stashed all over this apartment," Dorothy Guth was saying. "That closet is full and every inch of the refrigerator is taken."

It isn't exactly the sort of confession you'd expect to wring out of a stylish Smith College graduate who has just finished, among other things, editing *The Letters of E. B. White.*

What she was discussing had nothing to do with Anheuser Busch or other bubbly forms of hops and malt, but rather Georgia pecans, sealed in plastic and packaged six to a carton.

Mrs. Guth, a freelance editor, is much involved these holidays in disposing of nearly eight thousand pounds of pecans. The sale of the nuts will benefit a scholarship fund of the Smith College Club of New York.

"When I'm not testing recipes here," she said as the fine odor of pecan pralines wafted out of her Park Avenue kitchen, "I deliver pecans with my colleagues—singly or in pairs—all over the city. I spent the better part of yesterday delivering exactly four hundred thirty-two pounds around Manhattan."

The husbands of the women are much amused in a chauvinistic sort of way. "No man's college," one of them snorted recently, when he learned that his wife had been pushing a furniture dolly stacked with six cases of pecans past Brooks Brothers last week, "would ever get involved in a project like this."

The project, Mrs. Guth said, is not without its small headaches.

"The moving company that was transporting almost nine tons of pecans from Georgia called at 5 A.M. to tell us to have someone standing by for delivery. They didn't show up for forty-eight hours.

"One of the biggest problems has been finding storage space for the pecans. We have them all over town. There are sixteen boxes in a building across the way—a friend had an empty bedroom. There are several cases in the Time-Life Building; others at Avon products. There are twenty cases in a wine cellar on Ninety-first Street." The wine cellar is in the former residence of Basil Rathbone.

Giving credit where it is due, Mrs. Guth added that the idea of "pecans for scholarships" started in 1951, the idea of the Westchester County Smith College Club. "They sell a lot more pecans than we do," she said with some envy, "but this is only our second year."

Here are some of Mrs. Guth's pecan recipes, which she has accumulated from family and friends over the years.

Dixie Pecan Pie

Pastry for an 8- or 9-inch pie
3   large eggs
2   tablespoons flour
2   tablespoons sugar
2   cups dark Karo syrup
1   teaspoon pure vanilla extract
¼   teaspoon salt
1   cup pecan halves

1. Preheat the oven to 425 degrees.

2. Line an 8- or 9-inch pie plate with pastry. Refrigerate.

3. Beat the eggs until light. Blend the flour and sugar and add this to the eggs. Beat well. Add the remaining ingredients.

4. Pour the mixture into the pie shell. Bake 10 minutes.

5. Reduce the oven heat to 325 degrees and continue baking about 45 minutes.

Yield: 8 or more servings.

Creole Pralines

2   cups white sugar
1   cup dark brown sugar
¼   pound butter
1   cup milk
2   tablespoons corn syrup
4   cups pecan halves

1. Combine all the ingredients except the pecans in a heavy 3-quart saucepan. Cook 20 minutes, stirring constantly, after the boil is reached.

2. Add the pecans and continue cooking until the mixture forms a soft ball when dropped into cold water.

3. Arrange several sheets of wax paper over layers of newspapers.

4. Stir the praline mixture well. Drop it by tablespoons onto the sheets of wax paper. Let cool. When cool, stack the pralines in an airtight container with wax paper between the layers.

Yield: 2 dozen.

"Best Ever" Pecan Pie

Pastry for an 8-inch pie
2   eggs
1   cup sugar
1   teaspoon cinnamon
¼   teaspoon ground cloves
1   cup whole or broken pecan
    pieces
½   cup seedless raisins
4   tablespoons melted butter
2   tablespoons vinegar
    Unsweetened whipped cream
    for garnish

1. Preheat the oven to 400 degrees.

2. Line an 8-inch pie plate with pastry and refrigerate it.

3. Separate the eggs.

4. Put the yolks in the bowl of an electric mixer and beat until light and fluffy. Sift together the sugar, cinnamon and cloves. Gradually beat this into the egg yolks. Add the pecans, raisins and melted butter, beating on low speed. Stop beating.

5. Beat the whites until stiff. Using a rubber spatula, fold the whites into the nut batter, adding

them alternately with the vinegar. Pour this mixture into the prepared pie shell and bake 10 minutes.

6. Reduce oven heat to 350 degrees and bake 20 minutes longer. Let cool. Serve with unsweetened whipped cream.

Yield: 8 or more servings.

Bourbon-Pecan Cake

8	tablespoons butter at room temperature
½	cup dark brown sugar
2	large eggs
2½	teaspoons baking powder
2	cups flour
	Salt to taste
½	cup maple syrup
½	cup bourbon, rum or cognac
1½	cups coarsely chopped pecans
	Confectioners' sugar for garnish

1. Preheat oven to 350 degrees.

2. Put the butter into the bowl of an electric mixer. Start beating and gradually add the sugar, beating on high. Add the eggs, one at a time, beating well after each addition.

3. Sift together the baking powder, flour and salt. Beat the flour mixture, maple syrup and bourbon into the creamed butter, adding the ingredients alternately. Stop beating. Stir in the pecans.

4. Butter a small tube pan (one that measures 9½ inches in diameter, 6 cups is suitable), loaf or Bundt pan and spoon in the mixture, smoothing it over on top.

5. Bake 45 to 50 minutes. Let cool 10 minutes. Remove from the pan and let cool. Serve sprinkled with confectioners' sugar.

Yield: 8 or more servings.

A Christmas Cornucopia

Who knows how many decades ago I was obliged to compose what must have been my first—but doubtless not very original—essay on food and dining? And it had to do with the holidays.

In that long-distant age, a course in "writing" was an integral—and often painful—part of growing up. It was a time when you gazed for an extended period of time at a blank sheet of paper and thought such thoughts as "If I write with very large penmanship, perhaps the teacher won't know how short this essay really is."

As I recall it, that particular assignment had to be turned in before the year-end school holidays began. And the subject was, "What makes a dish a holiday food?" It is a thought that intrigued me then. And it intrigues me now. The answer is not easily obtained.

Cost is certainly not the answer. Caviar and foie gras and truffle-spiked terrines are most assuredly appropriate. But these are the trifles of the well-heeled.

As for breast of guinea hen under glass, I've heard of that dish all my life but have never met anyone who could honestly say he'd dined on it.

To say that a dish that demands hours and hours and much labor in its preparation makes it more festive is far short of the mark.

One of the grandest fruitcakes I've ever eaten requires less than half an hour in its preparation. Matter of fact, you can make a dessert that smacks of Christmas with no more effort than sprinkling first-quality store-bought ice cream with a fresh grating of nutmeg and a light lacing of bourbon or rum. Instant eggnog.

As much as anything, it is the seasonal nature of certain dishes and sheer tradition of the ages that are important to holiday foods. Charles Dickens in *A Christmas Carol*, doubtless without the least intention of doing so, made roast goose almost synonymous with the Christmas feast.

To my mind, if there ever was a time when all the rules and regulations, when all the things that are and are not proscribed for dining should be sent up the chimney, it is now. So you want to start the feast with an elegant cream of celery soup and accompany the holiday bird with a few creamed vegetables here and there, why not? And proceed to a marvelous, gossamer mousse made of chestnut cream. After all, it's celebration time.

The accompanying recipes are not a menu, but a cornucopia of holiday-oriented foods for both Christmas and the New Year. There is, for example, a delicious Swedish recipe for cured goose. It is a recipe from the Washington household of the Count and Countess Wilhelm Wachtmeister, the Swedish ambassador to the United States. A splendid buffet item given to me by the chef, Gunter Kraftner.

And if cold cured goose with mustard sauce does not appeal, a recipe for roast goose with chestnut stuffing is volunteered. It is presumed, of course, that the world is sufficiently endowed with formulas for roast turkey. And if you don't plan to stuff your goose or any other bird with chesnuts, there are two holiday desserts with chestnuts, one a mousse, the other a mont blanc.

One of the most unusual offerings in this collection is a no-bake fruitcake, a recipe received some weeks ago from a reader, Rita Rosner of Saugerties, New York. Talk about hasty cooking.

Happy holidays.

Cream of Celery Soup

4 tablespoons butter
1 clove garlic, finely minced
1 cup coarsely chopped onion
¼ cup flour
4 cups cubed root or knob celery, about 1¼ pounds
8 cups rib celery, trimmed and cut into 1-inch lengths
4 cups chicken broth
4 cups water
 Salt
½ cup heavy cream
 Freshly ground pepper to taste

1. Heat half the butter in a kettle or large saucepan and add the garlic and onion. Cook until wilted. Sprinkle with flour and stir to blend. Add the knob celery, rib celery, chicken broth, water and salt. Bring to the boil and simmer about 45 minutes.

2. Purée the mixture in a food processor or electric blender and return it to kettle or saucepan. Add the cream, salt and pepper to taste. Swirl

in remaining 2 tablespoons of butter and serve.

Yield: 9 to 10 cups.

Cured Goose Swedish-style

15 quarts water
6 pounds salt
2 tablespoons saltpeter, available in drug stores
¾ cup sugar
1 bay leaf
12 allspice
1 12- to 14-pound goose
 Quick aspic (see recipe)
 Mustard sauce (see recipe)

1. Combine the water, salt, saltpeter, sugar, bay leaf and allspice. Bring to the boil, stirring occasionally. Let cool.

2. Place the goose in a deep bowl

and add the curing liquid. Let stand in a cool place or in the refrigerator for 3 days.

3. Drain the goose and place it in a kettle. Add cold water to cover. Do not add salt. Cook about 2 hours, or until tender. (Cooking time will depend on size and age of the goose.)

4. Remove the goose but reserve the cooking liquid. Strain all the fat from the surface of the cooking liquid. Return the goose to the kettle and let stand overnight.

5. Remove the goose and chill it. Place it on a rack, breast side up. Spoon cool but still liquid aspic all over the exposed portions of the goose. Chill. Spoon more aspic over and continue until the goose has a nice glaze and all the aspic is used.

If desired, garnish the aspic with cutouts of truffles, black olives, scallions, egg white and so on. Dip the cutouts in aspic before applying. Serve sliced with mustard sauce.

Yield: 24 to 36 appetizer servings.

Quick Aspic

3 *cups chicken broth*
1 *cup tomato juice*
4 *envelopes unflavored gelatin*
   Salt and freshly ground pepper
1 *teaspoon sugar*
2 *egg shells, crushed*
2 *egg whites, lightly beaten*
2 *tablespoons cognac*

1. In a saucepan combine the chicken broth with the tomato juice,

gelatin, salt, pepper, sugar, egg shells and egg whites and heat slowly, stirring constantly, until the mixture boils up in the pan.

2. Remove the pan from the heat and stir in the cognac.

3. Strain the mixture through a sieve lined with a flannel cloth that has been rinsed in cold water and wrung out. If the aspic starts to set or becomes too firm, it may be reheated, then brought to any desired temperature.

Yield: About 1 quart.

Countess Wachtmeister's mustard sauce

3 *egg yolks*
1 *teaspoon Swedish, Dijon or Düsseldorf mustard*
2 *teaspoons white vinegar*
2 *cups peanut, vegetable or corn oil*
2 *tablespoons madeira wine*
1 *tablespoon soy sauce*
   Salt to taste

Place the yolks in a mixing bowl and add the mustard and vinegar. Using a wire whisk or electric beater, start beating and gradually add the oil. Beat briskly until a mayonnaise is formed. Beat in the madeira wine and soy sauce. Add salt to taste.

Yield: About 2½ cups.

Roast Stuffed Goose

1 *12- to 14-pound oven-ready goose*
1 *pound chestnuts in the shell*
   Salt to taste

2   *cups chicken broth*
3   *pounds boneless pork shoulder, fat and lean*
⅓   *cup finely chopped onion*
1⅛   *teaspoons chopped garlic*
½   *cup dry white wine*
1   *tablespoon chopped sage*
   Freshly ground pepper to taste
   Peanut, vegetable or corn oil

1. Preheat the oven to 400 degrees.

2. Remove the liver, neck, gizzard and heart from the goose if they are in the cavity. Set aside.

3. Use a sharp paring knife and insert the tip to one side of the thick, oval "crown" of a chestnut. Bring the tip around the chestnut, circular fashion, to the other side of the crown. Continue until all the chestnuts are thus carved. Put the chestnuts in a skillet with water to cover and salt to taste. Bring to the boil and simmer 15 to 20 minutes or until the shells can easily be removed with the fingers. Drain. When cool enough to handle, peel the chestnuts. Remove both the outer shell and the inner peel.

4. Place the peeled chestnuts in a saucepan and add chicken broth to cover. Simmer until tender. Drain.

5. When the chestnuts are cool enough to handle, crush or break them into pieces and put them in a large mixing bowl.

6. Grind the pork and add it to the chestnuts.

7. Chop the goose liver finely and add it to the pork. Add the onion, garlic, wine and sage. Stuff and truss the goose and sprinkle it with salt and pepper. Rub the goose all over with a little oil.

8. Place the goose breast side up on a baking dish. Arrange the neck, gizzard and heart around the goose. Bake 3 hours. If necessary, cover the goose lightly with a sheet of aluminum foil to prevent burning.

9. When the goose is done, remove it to a serving platter. Untruss it.

10. Pour off the fat from the baking dish and add 2 cups of water. Stir to dissolve the brown particles that cling to the bottom and sides of the dish. Strain the sauce.

Yield: 8 to 10 servings.

Red Cabbage Alsatian-style

2   *pounds red cabbage*
3   *tablespoons peanut, vegetable or corn oil*
2   *whole cloves, crushed*
1   *tablespoon red wine vinegar*
2   *tablespoons brown sugar*
   Salt and freshly ground pepper to taste
3   *tablespoons butter*

1. Pull off and discard any tough

or wilted outer leaves from the cabbage. Trim away and discard the core from the cabbage.

2. Shred the cabbage finely. There should be about 10 cups.

3. Heat the oil in a heavy skillet and add the cabbage. Cook, stirring, to wilt. Add the cloves, vinegar, sugar, salt and pepper. Cook 10 or 15 minutes, stirring often. Stir in the butter and serve.

Yield: 10 or more servings.

Creamed Fennel

1¾ *pounds tender, unblemished fennel bulbs with stems*
     Salt and freshly ground pepper to taste
3   *tablespoons heavy cream*
2   *tablespoons butter*

1. Trim and quarter the fennel but save the tender stems. Place the pieces in a saucepan and add cold water to cover. Add salt to taste. Bring to the boil and simmer about 20 minutes, or until tender. Drain.

2. Purée the fennel in a food processor or blender and empty it into a saucepan. Bring to the boil and add the remaining ingredients. Serve piping hot.

Yield: About 2 cups.

Acorn Squash with Green Peas

6   *unblemished acorn squash*
4   *tablespoons butter at room temperature*

Salt and freshly ground pepper to taste
4   *tablespoons light brown sugar*
3   *cups buttered, cooked fresh peas or use 2 packages frozen peas, cooked*

1. Preheat oven to 450 degrees.

2. Split the squash in half lengthwise. Scoop out and discard the seeds. Cut off and discard a small slice from the bottom of each squash half so they will sit flat in a baking dish.

3. Arrange the squash halves in a large dish. Brush the cavities and tops with butter. Sprinkle with salt and pepper.

4. Sprinkle 2 teaspoons of brown sugar around the inside of each squash. Bake 45 minutes to 1 hour. Spoon equal amounts of peas into each cavity and serve hot.

Yield: 12 servings.

Carrot Purée

2   *pounds carrots, trimmed and scraped*
     Salt to taste
2   *tablespoons butter*
½   *cup heavy cream*
     Freshly ground pepper to taste
⅛   *teaspoon grated nutmeg*

1. Cut the carrots into ¾-inch lengths. There should be about 6 cups.

2. Place the carrots in a saucepan and add cold water to cover and salt to taste. Bring to the boil and simmer 20 to 25 minutes, or until the pieces are tender without being mushy.

3. Put the carrots through a food

mill, food ricer or food processor to make a fine, smooth purée. Return them to a saucepan.

4. Place over very low heat while beating in butter, cream, salt, pepper and nutmeg.

Yield: 8 or more servings.

Baked Rutabagas à la Crème

7   *pounds rutabagas (yellow tur-nips)*
2   *pounds potatoes*
     Salt to taste
4   *tablespoons butter*
1   *cup heavy cream*

1. Preheat oven to 400 degrees.

2. Peel the rutabagas and pota-toes. Cut the rutabagas into 2½-inch cubes. Slice the potatoes into approxi-mately the same size.

3. Place the vegetables in a kettle and add cold water to cover and salt to taste. Bring to the boil and cook 25 to 30 minutes, or until tender. Drain and put through a food mill.

4. Return the vegetables to the kettle and add the butter. Beat it in over low heat. Bring the cream to the boil and beat it in with a whisk. Spoon the mixture into a baking dish.

5. Bake about 20 minutes, or until bubbling hot throughout. Brown briefly under the broiler.

Yield: 12 or more servings.

Cranberry, Ginger and Grapefruit Relish

1   *pound fresh cranberries*
2   *cups sugar*
¼   *to ½ cup chopped candied ginger*
     Grated rind of one grapefruit
¼   *cup grapefruit juice*
½   *cup blanched, slivered almonds*

1. Combine the cranberries, sugar, ginger, grapefruit rind and grapefruit juice in a saucepan. Cover and bring to the boil. Cook over low heat until cranberries pop open, about 10 minutes.

2. Stir in the almonds and let cool. Serve cold.

Yield: About 12 servings.

Mousse de Marrons
(Mousse of brandied chestnuts)

2   *10-ounce jars imported bran-died chestnuts in syrup*
3   *cups cold milk*
2   *envelopes gelatin*
2   *tablespoons cornstarch*
2   *tablespoons cognac*
4   *eggs, separated*
½   *cup sugar*
1   *cup heavy cream*

1. Remove and reserve 2 of the whole chestnuts to use later as gar-nish.

2. Put the remaining contents of the chestnuts and their syrup in the container of a food processor or electric blender. Blend to a purée.

3. Spoon and scrape the purée into a mixing bowl. Add the milk and gelatin and stir until well blended. Spoon and scrape this into a saucepan and bring slowly to the boil, stirring constantly.

4. Blend the cornstarch with the cognac and add it to the mixture, stirring. When thickened, add the yolks, stirring rapidly. Remove from the heat. Let cool.

5. Beat the whites and, when they stand in soft peaks, beat in half the sugar. Fold the whites into the chestnut mixture.

6. Whip the cream, gradually beating in the remaining sugar. Fold this into the mousse.

7. Pour the mixture into a crystal bowl. If desired, reserve a bit of the mixture to pipe on top as a garnish. To do this, let the mixture set only slightly. Using a star tube, pipe rosettes around the rim of the mousse and chill until set, preferably overnight.

8. As an added garnish, split the 2 reserved whole chestnuts in half. Arrange them symmetrically, cut side down, on top of the mousse. Serve cold.

Yield: 8 to 12 servings.

Mont Blanc

(A classic chestnut dessert)

The meringue

⅔   cup egg whites
14   tablespoons superfine granulated sugar

The chestnuts

2   pounds chestnuts, peeled (see instructions)
3   cups water
3   cups sugar
1   vanilla bean, or 2 teaspoons pure vanilla extract

The garnish

1½   cups heavy cream
2   tablespoons superfine granulated sugar
1   teaspoon pure vanilla extract
¼   cup confectioners' sugar

1. Preheat oven to 150 degrees.

2. Put the egg whites into the bowl of an electric mixer and start beating on low speed. Gradually increase the speed to high while adding 7 tablespoons of sugar, 1 tablespoon at a time. Remove the bowl and, using a plastic spatula, fold in the remaining 7 tablespoons of sugar.

3. Butter a baking sheet and sprinkle with flour. Shake it around to coat the surface evenly. Shake off excess flour. Using a round 9-inch cake tin or false bottom and a pointed knife, outline a perfect circle over the flour-coated baking sheet.

4. Outfit a pastry bag with a No. 4 star pastry tube. Add the meringue to the bag and squeeze out the meringue in a neat spiral to completely fill the circle. Cover this layer with another layer of meringue, squeezing out the meringue in the same pattern.

5. Transfer the point of the pastry tube to the center and make a small, piled up beehive pattern, circling around and around with the tip while pushing out the meringue. The "beehive" should measure about 3½ inches wide and 2½ inches high.

6. Place the baking sheet in the oven and bake about 2 hours, turning the sheet in the oven so that the meringue bakes evenly. When ready, the meringue should be dried out and crisp. Remove and let cool.

7. Meanwhile, as the meringue bakes, peel the chestnuts.

8. Combine the chestnuts, water, sugar and vanilla bean, if used. If not used, add the vanilla extract later. Bring to the boil and simmer about 2 hours, or until the chestnuts are thoroughly tender. Do not drain. If the vanilla extract is used, add it. Cool.

9. Put the chestnuts through a food mill, and blend well with a spoon. Refrigerate until the mixture is quite cold.

10. Outfit a meat grinder with a large blade. Hold a six-cup ring mold under the blade where the chestnut purée will come out. Add the chestnut purée to the grinder and grind, turning the mold gradually to catch the strands of chestnuts as they emerge. It should look like strands of macaroni.

11. Carefully invert the meringue over the mold, fitting the center of the meringue into the center of the mold. Invert both, letting the chestnut ring fall onto the meringue border.

12. Whip the cream and flavor it with the sugar and vanilla extract. Pipe it onto the center of the meringue, using a pastry bag outfitted with a star tube. Sprinkle with confectioners' sugar through a sieve onto the chestnut ring and serve cold.

Yield: 12 servings.

How to peel chestnuts

Use a sharp paring knife and insert the tip to one side of the thick, oval "crown" of a chestnut. Bring the tip around the chestnut, circular fashion, to the other side of the crown. Continue until all the chestnuts are thus carved.

Put the chestnuts in a skillet with water to cover and salt to taste. Bring to the boil and simmer 15 to 20 minutes, or until the shells can easily be removed with the fingers. Drain. When cool enough to handle, peel the chestnuts. Remove both the outer shell and the inner peel.

Rita Rosner's No-Bake Fruitcake

1   *pound seedless raisins*
1   *pound pitted dates*
1   *pound dried figs or figlets*
1   *pound shredded coconut, available in cans*
1   *pound shelled walnuts (other nuts may be substituted for all or part of this weight, such as hazelnuts, almonds and so on, but walnuts are best)*
¼   *teaspoon salt*
1   *teaspoon vanilla extract*
¼   *cup rum or cognac, optional (this is not in the original recipe)*

1. Put the raisins, dates, figs, coconut and walnuts through a food chopper, using the medium knife. Or chop coarsely, using a food processor. Do not overblend, however.

2. Empty the mixture into a large mixing bowl and add the salt and vanilla and, if desired, the rum or cognac. Blend well.

3. Spoon and pack the mixture into a mold or molds. Two 6-cup loaf pans are suitable. Cover and place a weight on top. Refrigerate 3 days or keep in a cold place to "age." Serve thinly sliced.

Yield: 5 pounds.

Oysters and New Year's: A Natural Pairing

Despite the elegance of oysters and the connoisseurs' utter delight in dining on oysters on the half shell, it is generally conceded that the man who swallowed the first oyster must have been of fearless spirit, redoubtable self-assurance, or, conceivably, fainting from hunger. Jonathan Swift put it succinctly: "He was a bold man that first eat an oyster."

And as John Gay, the poet who lived at the same time as Swift, expressed it:

> "The man had a sure palate . . . (who)
>   on the rocky shore
> First broke the cozy oyster's pearly coat
> And risked the living morsel down his throat."

In the ages since that first oyster was downed, however, a lust for them has continued unabated. According to the late epicure, André Simon, a marshal in Napoleon's army consumed one hundred oysters as a light prelude to breakfast. In the days of Louis XI of France, according to Simon, "the learned professors of the Sorbonne ate oysters lest their scholarship should become deficient."

It may well be that the oyster has been written about by serious essayists more than any other article of food. In *The Oysters of Locqmariaquer* (Pantheon Books, 1964), Eleanor Clark informs us that Nero claimed the ability of pinpointing the origin of his oysters by taste. Pliny called oysters "The palm and pleasure of the table." And Montaigne, speaking of the oysters of Bordeaux, exulted that "they are so agreeable, and of so high an order of taste that it is like smelling violets to eat them; moreover, they are so healthy, a valet gobbled up more than a hundred without any disturbance."

The reasons may defy analysis—many food associations do—but oysters and a New Year's feast are as natural a pairing as Moët and Chandon, Currier and Ives, ying and yang, death and taxes.

That consideration led to a perusal of Escoffier's book of menus, *Le Livre des Menus* (Flammarion, 1912), to uncover his recommendations for year-end feasts, particularly those for midnight reveillons. Just as we supposed, three of those holidays menus included oysters as a first course. One suggests caviar and "royal natives"—English oysters from native beds. Another suggests the green

Marennes oysters from France. One of the menus suggests the classic combination of raw oysters garnished with a spoonful of caviar, and the great chef seemed partial to the use of freshly grated horseradish as a garnish for oysters on the half shell.

One of the best places in America to learn about oyster culture is about one hour's drive from Manhattan. It is the Long Island Oyster Farm in Northport, an enterprise dedicated to the commercial replenishment of oyster beds on the East Coast to compensate for the severe depletion of oysters that has occurred within the past century.

There is a small museum there that offers a fascinating account of oyster consumption in this country even before Diamond Jim Brady.

One of the displays there notes that the first oyster "farmers" on Long Island were, of course, Indians. "When the early settlers arrived in the seventeenth century, they found oysters in natural abundance. Some oysters were as large as a foot long.

"Oysters were an important food for the early settlers, from Colonial days and into the mid-nineteenth century. In 1859, for example, the people of New York City spent more money on oysters than for meat. Some seven million bushels of oysters were consumed each year in those times—about ten bushels per person per year!"

Exclamation point, indeed!

Lament regarding over-use of this nation's natural resources is not all that new. There is an article in *Harper's Weekly*, dated August 18, 1883, that states that in 1860 ten million bushels of oysters were annually taken from the Chesapeake Bay alone. Twenty-three years later "probably thirty million bushels are withdrawn from the same beds. No natural increase can keep pace with such an exhaustive demand."

Before World War I, Diamond Jim Brady did his share in depleting America's oyster resources. According to one biographer, his evening meal frequently began with six dozen Lynnhaven oysters, followed by a saddle of mutton, half a dozen venison chops, roast chicken with caper sauce, a game dish and a twelve-egg soufflé.

The present relative scarcity of oysters is not due, of course, to overconsumption, but rather to pollution, diminished coastal places for harvests, and so on. Although the Long Island Oyster Farm is making heartening strides in cultivating oysters—production has increased ten-fold in the past decade—the company's year-round demands at present far outweigh its ability to supply.

We recently had a nice chat with George Vanderborgh, a vice president of the oyster farm, which was begun by his ancestors more than a hundred years ago.

He told us that thirty years and more ago Europe was the farm's largest customer and that the *Lusitania* had a large shipment of Long Island oysters aboard when it sank.

To breed oysters they are first collected by digging, dredging or tongs. And when they are bred it is best to have a "mix," that is, oysters from different areas, which produces a stronger strain.

Within twenty-four hours of dredging or whatever, the eggs are fertilized and swimming. After ten days or two weeks, an oyster stops swimming forever and, as Cole Porter once phrased it, becomes "sadder and moister" as he grows and grows. The word "he" is used ill-advisedly in this case. An oyster can change sex throughout its life span.

After the oyster becomes immobile, it is thereafter moved only by hand, by tide, by dredge or some other outside force.

An oyster drinks one hundred gallons of water a day and fattens on the algae it sucks out of the water. According to Mr. Vanderborgh, algae is to oysters what grass is to cattle.

At the farm, once the oysters are six weeks old, they are transferred to the temperature-controlled waters of a nearby lagoon until they grow to be three-quarters of an inch in diameter. Then they are uprooted and planted in bay bottoms such as Northport and Huntington Bay, New Haven, Oyster Bay, Gardiner's Bay, until maturity. An oyster, from spawning to table, requires about three years. The best time for oysters is late fall, winter and early summer. The worst months are August, September and October.

An unopened oyster will keep quite well under normal home refrigeration for at least a month. "If they don't have an odor," Mr. Vanderborgh says, "they are good to eat."

The best way to serve oysters for New Year's Eve or New Year's day:

1. Serve them chilled, raw and on the half shell. Serve with a small spoonful of caviar on top—red caviar will do—lemon wedges and buttered black bread or toast.

2. Serve on the half shell with fresh, finely shredded horseradish, lemon and buttered black bread or toast.

3. Serve on the half shell with very hot, freshly broiled or baked small sausages. Serve with buttered black bread or toast.

4. Serve with mignonette sauce, see recipe.

We also offer an assortment of recipes to serve whenever oysters are available.

Oyster Stew

3   cups milk
1   bay leaf
1   rib celery with leaves
1   small onion, peeled and quartered
2   sprigs fresh thyme, or ½ teaspoon dried
12   to 24 oysters, 1 to 2 cups, depending on size and whether you want several or few oysters in each serving
     Salt to taste
¾   cup heavy cream
1   egg yolk
     Tabasco sauce to taste
½   teaspoon celery salt
     Freshly ground pepper to taste
2   tablespoons butter
½   teaspoon Worcestershire sauce, optional

1. Combine the milk, bay leaf, celery, onion and thyme in a saucepan. Bring just to the boil but do not boil.

2. Pour the oysters into a deep skillet large enough to hold the stew. Sprinkle with salt and bring to the boil. Cook just until the oysters curl. Strain the milk over the oysters and stir. Discard the solids. Do not boil.

3. Beat the cream with the egg yolk and add Tabasco, celery salt, salt and pepper to taste. Add this to the stew. Bring just to the boil and swirl in the butter. Add the Worcestershire and serve piping hot with buttered toast or oyster crackers.

Yield: 4 servings.

Oysters Bienville

Rock salt
3 tablespoons butter
3 tablespoons flour
¾ cup milk
½ cup heavy cream
Salt and freshly ground pepper to taste
2 teaspoons finely chopped shallots (in Louisiana, chopped scallions are used in place of shallots)
1 clove garlic, finely minced
¼ pound mushrooms, finely chopped, about 1½ cups
¼ pound raw shrimp, shelled and deveined and finely chopped
2 tablespoons dry sherry wine
1 egg yolk
¼ teaspoon nutmeg
Pinch of cayenne
1 tablespoon finely chopped parsley
24 to 36 oysters on the half shell

1. Preheat oven to 500 degrees.

2. Pour rock salt into 4 or 6 (the number will depend on the size and number of oysters) rimmed, heat-proof dishes large enough to hold the oysters in one layer. Place the dishes in the oven to heat the salt at least 5 minutes.

3. Melt 2 tablespoons of butter in a saucepan and add the flour, stirring with a wire whisk. When blended, add the milk and cream, stirring rapidly with the whisk.

4. Add the salt and pepper to taste.

5. Heat the remaining 1 tablespoon of butter in a saucepan and add the shallots. Cook briefly and add the garlic and mushrooms. Cook briefly. Add the shrimp and cook, stirring, about 40 seconds. Add salt and pepper. Add the sherry, egg yolk, nutmeg, cayenne and parsley. Add the mixture to the cream sauce and blend well.

6. Top each oyster with equal amounts of the sauce mixture. Arrange the oysters on the rock salt and bake 10 minutes.

Yield: 4 to 6 servings.

Oysters Casino

Rock salt
8 tablespoons butter
½ cup chopped green or red sweet pepper
Salt and freshly ground pepper to taste
1 tablespoon finely chopped parsley
1 tablespoon finely chopped chives

Juice of ½ lemon
Grated rind of 1 lemon
12   oysters on the half shell
4   strips bacon
6   teaspoons bread crumbs

1. Preheat oven to 500 degrees.

2. Pour rock salt into 2 rimmed, heat-proof dishes large enough to hold 6 oysters on the half shell in one layer. Place the dishes in the oven to heat the salt at least 5 minutes.

3. Blend the butter and green peppers, salt and pepper. Add the parsley, chives, lemon juice, lemon rind and blend well. Spoon equal parts of this mixture onto each of the 12 oysters.

4. Cut the bacon strips into rectangles, each large enough to cover 1 oyster. Cover the butter topping with bacon and sprinkle each serving with half a teaspoon of bread crumbs.

Hold the oyster shell securely with the flat shell on top

5. Arrange the oysters on the rock salt and place in the oven. Bake 10 minutes, or until bacon is crisp and oysters are heated through.

Yield: 2 servings.

Deep-fried Oysters, Southern-style

For each 18 oysters, season 1 cup of yellow corn meal with salt and pepper to taste. Drain the oysters and dredge them, one at a time, in the corn meal. Heat 4 cups of peanut, vegetable or corn oil in a skillet or deep fat fryer. Add the oysters and cook until nicely browned, about 1 minute. Serve if desired with ketchup or tartar sauce.

Place the thumb a half inch below the tip of the oyster knife.

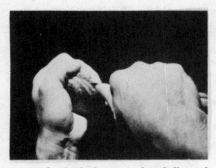

Insert the knife between the shells and work back and forth with a slight motion of the wrist until the shell opens

Mignonette Sauce for Oysters on the Half Shell

½ cup white vinegar
3 tablespoons finely chopped shallots
1 tablespoon white peppercorns, freshly and finely crushed
   Salt to taste
1 tablespoon chopped fresh tarragon, or ½ teaspoon dried, crushed

Combine all the ingredients and serve.

Yield: About ½ cup.

Open the shell about the width of the blade

Advance the blade into the shell along the bottom of the top flat shell to cut the top muscle and free the top shell

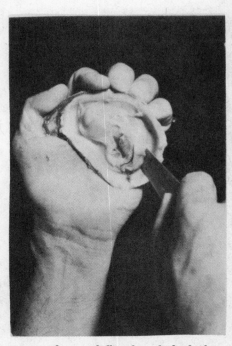

Remove the top shell and work the knife carefully around and under the oyster to cut the bottom muscle

Index